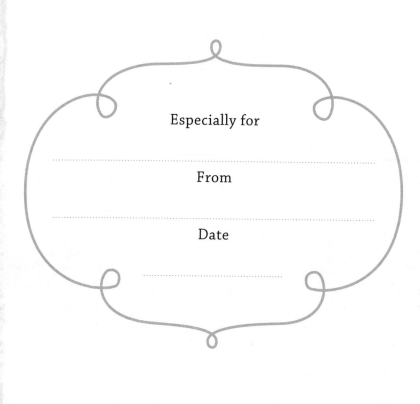

Especially for

From

Date

Daily Wisdom *for* Women

2019 Devotional Collection

BARBOUR BOOKS
An Imprint of Barbour Publishing, Inc.

Published by Barbour Books, an imprint of Barbour Publishing, Inc., 1810 Barbour Drive, Uhrichsville, Ohio 44683, www.barbourbooks.com

Our mission is to inspire the world with the life-changing message of the Bible.

Member of the
Evangelical Christian
Publishers Association

Printed in China.

INTRODUCTION

Amazing assurance can be found in Proverbs 3:5-6 (NLT): "Trust in the LORD with all your heart; do not depend on your own understanding. Seek his will in all you do, and he will show you which path to take." Yet you might wonder, *What does it mean to trust? And how do I build up a wholehearted trust?*

To help you find the answers to those questions, eight different women have combined their talents and voices in the *Daily Wisdom for Women 2019 Devotional Collection*. Here you'll find 365 scripture-based readings about trust to help you rely on God's character, live in the knowledge and power of His name, stand on His solid promises, take strength from His Word, have a confident expectation in His plan, take courage from His wisdom, and much more.

The Word of God makes it clear that trust is the essence of faith, for trust is faith in action. We pray these readings will help you see that God, Christ, and the Spirit are more trustworthy than anyone or anything you can touch, see, feel, or imagine.

Every devotion corresponds to a particular day's reading based on the "Read Thru the Bible in a Year" plan found at the back of this book. As you read each devotion and focus verse, allow them to shed light on the importance of your relying on God for everything. And, as your trust in God builds, may you discover the rewards of a woman ready to act in faith.

WITH US

All this took place to fulfill what the Lord had said through the prophet: "The virgin will conceive and give birth to a son, and they will call him Immanuel" (which means "God with us").

MATTHEW 1:22-23 NIV

Since before the beginning of time, God has had us in mind. He created a world designed just for us. He placed us in it, and walked with us. And even though we disobeyed, He had a plan for that too. He never wanted to leave us. He has written a story that from beginning to end, and all the parts in the middle, points to one conclusion: "God with us."

Mary didn't know what part in this story she was playing. She didn't know God had been planning for this moment from the time He said, "Let there be light" (Genesis 1:3). She didn't know this baby she was about to carry would be called the Light of the world.

But Mary believed. She believed the words of the angel, as did Joseph, a son from the line of the king of God's people. Mary and Joseph believed and obeyed. And that's how they became part of the story.

What part does God have for you to play? Believe what He says to you. Obey. And He will be with you every step of the way.

Lord, thank You for being with me as I begin this new year.

GETTING TO HOME

But the LORD God called to
the man, "Where are you?"

GENESIS 3:9 NIV

When was the last time you played hide-and-seek? How long did it take for someone to find you? Or better yet, how long did it take for you to get tired of hiding? Most people who play this game want to be found. It's no fun to hide forever by yourself. The reward comes when you try to make it "home" before getting caught.

Adam and Eve didn't want to stay hidden alone either. They wanted to be found. And they must have known God would find them. He had been with them in the garden before. So, why hide in the first place?

Shame. Shame causes us to feel bad about who we are. And it makes us forget what we know. But God calls out to us, reminding us. We are His. And the reward comes when we make it home—home with Him.

As you begin this new year, remember who you are. Remember *whose* you are. Leave behind whatever shame you're hiding behind and just come home.

Lord, I don't want to be afraid to face You. Help me make
the choices I need to make to stay on the right path.
Help me make it home—to You. Amen.

SURROUNDED

I lay down and slept,
yet I woke up in safety,
for the LORD was watching over me.
I am not afraid of ten thousand enemies
who surround me on every side.

PSALM 3:5-6 NLT

There was a time when the average person would never have known what it was like to have thousands of enemies. To achieve those numbers, one might have to be a celebrity—perhaps a hated villain in a movie, or the quarterback who choked in the championship game, or a radio host who opened his big mouth one too many times.

But in this age of social media, one wrong post can earn you millions of followers in seconds. Yet those millions might not like your message. In fact, they may well hate you for it. And they also might just tell you about it. A lot.

But our mighty God knows what it's like to be surrounded by enemy voices. He knows what it's like to have insults hurled at Him. He knows what it's like to have crowds shouting out His name—not in support, but in rage.

The One who faced such hatred is watching over you. He is surrounding you too—but with His love and strength. Wake up in safety and don't be afraid.

Lord, I know You can silence these voices that sometimes bring fear into my heart. Thank You for watching over me.

REMEMBERED

Whenever the rainbow appears in the clouds, I will see it and remember the everlasting covenant between God and all living creatures of every kind on the earth.

GENESIS 9:16 NIV

Early in the new year, many people, taking the opportunity to get their lives in order, make lists of resolutions. Sometimes those lists start looking like complaint logs: "Here's all the people I won't bother talking to this year." "These are the activities I'm not going to waste time on—AGAIN." "Things I need to get out of my life. . ."

Surely none of us has "spending months cooped up with large amounts of smelly, crabby animals" on our list of things not to do in the new year—unless maybe we've been summer camp counselors. But Noah could have had this on *his* list. Thankfully, he didn't have to think about sailing on the ark again, and neither do we. God made a promise to Noah, his family, and all of us living here on earth: never again would God destroy the earth with a flood.

God put His rainbow in the sky as a sign of this special promise. And several times in scripture, God said He would remember this covenant.

What an amazing thing to be remembered by the Creator of the universe! Perhaps you can add this to your resolution list: "Remember that I am remembered."

Lord, I will remember You. Thank You for remembering me. Amen.

BLESSED

Blessed are those who mourn,
for they will be comforted.

As we look to the year in front of us, we can't help but think of those loved ones who won't be with us. Many people must face entering a new year while still carrying a heavy burden of grief—the loss of a family member, a relationship, or a job. We attempt to make plans and take steps forward, even though the sorrow, loneliness, or feelings of failure drag us down.

But we have this promise: we will be comforted. There will be days that are hard and exhausting, but there will be days of hope and peace too. We may receive comfort from good friends who take care of us in practical ways—bringing us meals, taking us out, just talking, or even sitting in silence. We may receive comfort from reading God's Word and through prayer. Or we may receive relief through serving others.

The point is, we *will* be comforted. And through that comfort, we will become closer to the Comforter. And that is where the blessing comes. If we refuse to be isolated, if we let others help us, if we let God speak to us, and if we reach out to others, we will no longer be alone in our grief.

My Comforter, I give my burdens to You. Amen.

COUNTING STARS

*"Look now toward heaven, and count the stars
if you are able to number them." And He said
to him, "So shall your descendants be."*

GENESIS 15:5 NKJV

One, two, three, four, five. . . The night sky is filled with tiny dots of light. How many must there be? Millions? Billions? It's like a glitter explosion on a black tablecloth. Picking up each bit of glitter would be just as impossible as counting the stars.

God knew Abraham could never count the stars. But He wanted to give the man a picture to hold on to—a glimmer of the greatness God was going to display through him. And maybe that's exactly what Abraham needed so he could believe—an image he could understand.

God speaks to us in so many ways. He speaks to us through His written Word. He speaks to us through amazing natural glory. He speaks to us through music. He speaks to us through artistry. He speaks to us through hands of service. He speaks to us through hugs.

As many as the stars in the sky—that's how many ways God has of showing us His plan. All we have to do is keep our eyes and ears open, and look and listen for Him.

Six, seven, eight, nine. . . Keep counting on God.

Lord God, help me keep my eyes on You. Amen.

GOOD AND ANGRY

God is a just judge, and God is angry
with the wicked every day.

PSALM 7:11 NKJV

Think of a mother standing up for her child. Picture a loyal guard dog defending his territory. Imagine a police officer determined to capture an offender.

In the right hands and with the right circumstances, anger can be a useful emotional response. It is comforting to know that our God can be an angry God. When we look around our world, we can see so many disturbing things. Poor people being crushed by dictators. Refugees dying as they wait for food or medical care. Parents who harm their own children. It is a relief to know that our God is angry with the same wickedness that angers us.

It is also good to remember that our God is just. We may get angry quickly, without stopping to see all the sides of a situation or to consider all the circumstances. But God sees all and knows all. When He is angry, you can be sure it is righteous anger.

As we get to know Him better, we can trust God to show us what is worth getting angry about, and what isn't. We learn what we should overlook and what we should fight against. And we learn how not to make God angry!

Lord God, I'm so thankful You are a just judge.
Help me to know when it is good to be angry. Amen.

NO WORRIES

*So don't worry about tomorrow, for tomorrow will bring its
own worries. Today's trouble is enough for today.*

MATTHEW 6:34 NLT

In this part (Matthew 6) of the Sermon on the Mount, Jesus is
teaching about basic practices Christians everywhere try to follow:
giving, prayer, fasting. Much of what He teaches is about letting
go—letting go of our pride, our grudges, and our need for attention.

Then He challenges us even more—to let go of our worries. Maybe
you don't consider yourself a worrier. But imagine every possession
you have right now was suddenly taken away, and you had no way to
provide for yourself. Could you trust God to take care of you then?

Where do you spend most of your best time? Do you spend it
on the people you love? Or do you spend it trying to make more
money so you can buy more things? How much time do you spend
with God? Do you put Him first in your day, or does He come last?

It's natural to want to provide for yourself and for the ones
you love. There's nothing wrong with working hard. But becoming
worried or anxious over things is a red flag that your life might be a
little out of balance. Remember that the God who takes care of the
birds in the barns will not forget you.

Lord, help me trust You more with my tomorrows. Amen.

JUST ASK

"Ask and it will be given to you; seek and you will find;
knock and the door will be opened to you."

MATTHEW 7:7 NIV

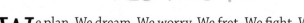

We plan. We dream. We worry. We fret. We fight. We strive. We try. We work. We struggle. We aim. We miss.

But the one thing we often forget to do is the simplest action we could take.

We could just ask.

God longs to be a part of our lives. He wants to help us. He wants to involve us in His work. He wants us to fully participate in His kingdom. He wants us to know Him. He wants us to love Him. He wants us to come to Him with every desire—even the ones we don't think He will like. (Remember, He knows what's in your heart before you ask it!)

What keeps us from asking Him for what we need or want? Maybe we don't feel worthy. Maybe we don't know if it's appropriate to do. Or maybe, just maybe, we don't really believe what He says. Or maybe we're afraid of the answer.

But friends, what have we got to lose? Just ask.

Lord, I know You will give only what is good for me. Remind me to come to You first with everything I need. Amen.

NOT FORGOTTEN

God will never forget the needy;
the hope of the afflicted will never perish.

PSALM 9:18 NIV

They are children hanging on to scraps of blankets in a shelter where there is no privacy.

They are young women, fleeing from danger to a land they don't know, leaving family far behind.

They are men with guns, driven to desperate acts with false promises for glory.

They are prisoners, beaten for their beliefs.

They are sick, they are cold, they are lost.

They feel all alone. But they are not alone.

Sometimes it's easy to look around our world and feel despair. It seems there are too many people hurting—how could we ever help them all? But we must not give up hope because we must not give up on God. And God promises that He will not forget every single person who is in need. He will bring them hope. And we may be just the people to help Him do that.

What can you do today to remember someone in need? You might be able to donate to a food pantry or serve in a soup kitchen. You might be able to lead a child in Bible study or visit a patient. And you can always pray.

Don't waste time worrying about all that you cannot do on your own. Just imagine what you can do with God!

God, in all my busyness, let me never forget
people who are struggling every day. Amen.

BECAUSE

Because you believed, it has happened.

MATTHEW 8:13 NLT

Quick: If you could have anything you wanted to happen right now, what would you ask for?

What came to your mind? Maybe you'd want healing for a loved one, or for yourself. Maybe you'd want one more day with someone who is gone. Maybe you'd ask for freedom from debt. Maybe you'd want a new job. Maybe you'd like a trip to an amusement park.

The centurion was a man with great responsibility and great courage. These officers in the Roman army would lead their men into battle—not hanging back and barking orders, but going first into the fighting, risking their lives to motivate their men to risk theirs.

The centurion risked his reputation to seek out Jesus and ask the Rabbi for help. Not that he thought he was too good to be seen with Jesus. On the contrary, he didn't think himself worthy for Jesus even to come to his house.

But the man was confident about two things—Jesus' ability to heal and his own authority to give orders. And because he showed this faith to Jesus, the man's servant was healed.

What kind of faith do you have? What are you confident about? Have you shown this to Jesus? Seek Him out. Talk to Him. You never know what might happen, just because you believe.

Lord Jesus, I come to You today to ask for _____.
I believe in You. Amen.

RUN TO JESUS

*Then he got up and rebuked the winds
and the waves, and it was completely calm.*

MATTHEW 8:26 NIV

Sailing on a large sea can be a little scary, even in the best weather. Sailing in the midst of a furious storm can be terrifying.

But for a storm to frighten the disciples of Jesus—some of whom were experienced fishermen—it must have been severe. The story from Matthew 8 tells us that the storm came up suddenly, and waves swept over the sides of the boat. The disciples ran to wake up Jesus, who was calmly sleeping through the event.

Before we go further, realize this: they ran to Jesus. Jesus wondered why they would come to Him, and yet be so panicked. But at least they came to Him. They knew He would be able to help.

What kind of crisis are you in right now? Perhaps you are not riding the waves in a little boat, being tossed about by angry waters—but maybe you are in a situation that feels just as stressful and overwhelming.

Run to Jesus. He's in charge. Even the wind and waves know they've done wrong when Jesus comes to yell at them.

*Lord, I honor You as the boss of my life.
Give me orders and I will follow. Amen.*

HE RULES

"The foundations of law and order have collapsed.
What can the righteous do?"

PSALM 11:3 NLT

Somehow the psalmist from thousands of years ago has voiced the thoughts of many who live today—many who see the shootings and murders and abuse and wars humans perpetrate on one another, and wonder, *Why is this happening? What can we do to stop it?*

Humans will always be humans. We are flawed creatures—products of the Fall—living in a broken world. We will always find ways to hurt each other, and justifications to do it. But even when it seems law and order has been abandoned, and peace is far away, the righteous can do one thing. They can trust God. Because no matter what, "the LORD is in his holy Temple; the LORD still rules from heaven" (Psalm 11:4 NLT).

We won't always be able to figure out how God will take control. We won't always be the instruments to bring about peace. But we can trust that the God who sees the hearts of men and women will be able to find a way to communicate with us. And because we trust Him, we can be confident that His way is the best one to follow—the only way that will lead to eternal life and eternal peace.

Lord, I know I don't have the answers to my own questions.
Help me to live in a way that shows my trust in You. Amen.

SILENCE

*May the LORD silence all flattering
lips and every boastful tongue.*

PSALM 12:3 NIV

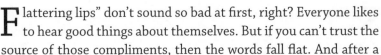

"Flattering lips" don't sound so bad at first, right? Everyone likes to hear good things about themselves. But if you can't trust the source of those compliments, then the words fall flat. And after a while, you begin to wonder what the motive is behind all this sweet talk. What is the person hiding?

The person who boasts creates a similar problem. Besides the fact that hearing about someone else's achievements all the time can get boring, the real problem is that it becomes difficult to tell when the person is telling the truth and when she is exaggerating. And if you can't trust what she says about herself, what can you trust? Has she really achieved all she says she has, or is she actually failing? And if she is failing, why can't she just trust you enough to confide in you? Why does she have to lie?

Lying, in whatever form it comes, causes barriers to rise up between people. It's hard to get close to someone whose words can't be trusted. It's hard to love people if you—or they—are hiding behind false words.

*God, silence my tongue when I am tempted to
say things that aren't true. Help me create honest
connections with people, even when it's hard. Amen.*

LIKE SHEEP

I am sending you out like sheep among wolves.
Therefore be as shrewd as snakes and as innocent as doves.

MATTHEW 10:16 NIV

Think about it. Sheep among wolves don't have much of a chance on their own. Sheep don't tend to work that well as a team. They don't have great tools for defense. They are fluffy and a little bit stupid. They are driven by food, not fierceness. They like to follow, not lead.

So why would Jesus send His disciples out like that? Why not send them out as something strong, like lions? Why not at least send them out as sheepdogs?

But Jesus, as always, speaks the truth. The disciples go out as sheep because they already have the good, the very best, Shepherd to follow. They go out as sheep because it's sheep they wish to know. They go out as sheep because sheep attract the wolves, and Jesus wants to win the wolves too.

But that doesn't mean the disciples go out weak. Christians should never leave their brains behind—they need all their wits about them to live and love in this world. So, Jesus gives them the advice to be both shrewd and innocent. Shrewd in their knowledge of the ways of the world and their ability to find their way among their enemies. Yet innocent in their hearts and pure in their motives.

Lord, help me take Your Gospel out in the
world with thoughtfulness and clarity. Amen.

ARE YOU THE ONE?

"Are you the Messiah we've been expecting,
or should we keep looking for someone else?"

MATTHEW 11:3 NLT

Sometimes it's a blessing to get to hear a little of what was going on in the heads of the people of the Bible—the people who walked with God, the men and women who knew and saw and lived with Jesus.

And sometimes it's good to know they are just like us. Here in Matthew 11, we meet John the Baptist in a low place. He's been put in prison—which isn't fun for anyone, but for a man who believes his whole purpose for living is to proclaim the coming of the Lord and to baptize people into the Spirit, being locked away from contact with others must be the worst form of punishment.

He hears what his relative, Jesus, the man he baptized with his own hands, is doing. He knows this man is healing people and teaching people. But still, John isn't sure. He's sitting in prison and wondering: *Am I here for a good reason? Am I following the truth? Am I following the Messiah?* And a bit of doubt crept into that prison cell.

And so, if John the Baptist can doubt, and still be called "the Elijah who was to come" (Matthew 11:14 NIV), then maybe we can have doubts too. We can ask questions and have them answered by the Son of God.

Messiah, thank You for answering my questions. Amen.

NEVER SHAKEN

Who may live on your holy mountain?

PSALM 15:1 NIV

The list of character qualities in Psalm 15 seems almost unattainable. Can any one of us put a checkmark beside them all? Is anyone's walk on this troublesome earth blameless?

But if that's what it takes to climb up the mountain—to dwell with the Lord—what should we do? We have to do what any good climber does—we keep trying. And each time we climb, we get a little closer. We get a little smarter. We get a little stronger. We get a little better. And somewhere along the way, we realize that we are not climbing alone—that we have never been alone, because the whole mountain is where the Lord dwells. God is not just sitting on the peak, like the man with the white beard in the cartoons, with His head in the clouds, waiting for someone to finally reach Him. God is in the valley too. God is in the hard places. God is in the ravines. God is in the footholds. And yes, God is in the high places.

So each time we try, we learn more about Him, and more about us. And each time we fail, we will be shaken. But we will try again.

*Lord, I can never live on Your mountain on my own merits.
Please shake me with Your truth, so I can never
be shaken away from You. Amen.*

REST

*Come to me, all you who are weary
and burdened, and I will give you rest.*

MATTHEW 11:28 NIV

Only a few weeks into the year, and you are already tired. Somehow, you weren't quite able to shake the problems from last year. And those resolutions you made on day one have already been forgotten. Rest sounds very good right about now, doesn't it?

But the rest that Jesus promises is not a retreat from the world. His rest requires work and education so we can live in the world. We will have to put effort into learning the lessons He has for us. But it will be a shared effort. That's what a yoke is for. It's not meant for just one person to carry on her own. Jesus wants us to be partners with Him in the work. And partners with Him in the rest.

Perhaps that is why God reveals hidden things to little children (see Matthew 11:25). Children tend to carry burdens lightly and drop them easily. They have not yet developed prideful hearts that wish to take on more than they can carry so they can show the world how strong they are. They share their loads as easily as they share secrets, or cupcakes.

Are you weary? Are you carrying more than you can support on your own? Come to Jesus. Take on a burden that is only light.

Lord, make my heart gentle and humble, like Yours. Amen.

TRUSTWORTHY

*The warden paid no attention to anything under
Joseph's care, because the LORD was with Joseph
and gave him success in whatever he did.*

GENESIS 39:23 NIV

Trustworthy employees are valuable. It's not easy to find people who will work hard on their own with little supervision. It's not easy to find people who will stay true to their word.

And who would think that a young man, betrayed and sold into slavery by his own family, would grow to become such a valuable worker? But through all his trials, Joseph held on to the truth, and he held on to God. Over and over, scripture tells us that the Lord was with Joseph, and because of that, everything Joseph touched turned into a success. Joseph trusted God, and God made Joseph trustworthy.

Even while he was in prison, charged with betraying his master, Joseph's character shone through so brightly that the prison warden gave Joseph the responsibility of managing the other prisoners. And there in prison God gave Joseph success. The prison was managed well, and the prisoners lived at peace with one another. At each step of his journey, Joseph brought glory to the name of the Lord by being a reliable servant.

Whether you serve in a prison or a palace, honor God by being honorable. Trust God and be trustworthy. And watch what God has in store for you next.

*Lord, help me be a trustworthy person,
no matter what my circumstances are. Amen.*

FORTRESS AND FIGHTER

The LORD is my rock, my fortress and my deliverer;
my God is my rock, in whom I take refuge,
my shield and the horn of my salvation, my stronghold.

PSALM 18:2 NIV

Inside ancient stone castles, when you place your hand on the stone walls, you can almost feel the centuries leaning in toward you. Walls so massively thick, it's hard to imagine them ever crumbling. At one time, they acted as the stronghold for entire villages. Women and children and the elderly would be rushed inside as the enemy approached. They would gather together to be held in strength—and to pray that the strong line of men defending their position would hold.

God is both our fortress and our deliverer. He is the massive wall surrounding us, protecting us from the arrows of the evil one. He is the fighter high up on the wall's edge, pushing back the enemy. And He is the comfort at the center of a community, spreading out in ripples of love and compassion and kindness.

Be secure within His walls.

Be confident in His ability to defend.

Be inspired by His love.

Mighty God, thank You for protecting me, even when
I didn't know I needed protection. Thank You for
defeating death so I can live forever with You. Amen.

WHOEVER HAS EARS

Whoever has ears, let them hear.

MATTHEW 13:9 NIV

J esus taught the large crowds who gathered around Him. He wanted to tell them what the kingdom of God was like—to get them to see this was a kingdom unlike any other. He used stories of familiar scenes and objects to draw them in and help them understand. But they still didn't always get it.

Martin Luther King Jr. also taught people. He often painted pictures and created poetry with his words to help people see and hear his vision of what the world could be if justice was shared with everyone, no matter what they looked like or where they came from. He wrote this: "People fail to get along because they fear each other; they fear each other because they don't know each other; they don't know each other because they have not communicated with each other" (from "Advice for Living," *Ebony*, May 1958).

Often, the ability of people to understand a message has very little to do with their mental capacity and everything to do with the construction of their hearts. On this day, let us all commit to open our ears and our eyes a little wider, and love a little better.

Lord, open my eyes. Lord, open my ears.
Lord, open my heart. Amen.

SENT

So it was God who sent me here, not you!

GENESIS 45:8 NLT

It's hard to imagine a reunion more dramatic than that of Joseph and his brothers. If it had happened today, it would have been shown on every television talk show. Joseph would have told his story of multicolored rags to riches—from the time he was beaten and thrown into a well by his jealous brothers, to his years in prison, to his rise to power as second in command of the whole nation of Egypt.

Then his brothers would talk about the fear that struck them when they realized this powerful man, who held their lives in his hands, was that same brother they had sold to merchants—like nothing more than a sheep or goat.

But Joseph had no desire to hurt them. He didn't want revenge. He had experienced redemption, and he wanted his brothers to know that, no matter what they had intended for him, God had intended for good to happen. God had a plan, and no brothers or slave owners or devious wives or prisons could change that. It was a plan to save the lives of many, which is exactly what Joseph did.

Are you standing in the way of God's plan today? Are you feeling like you're stuck in the bottom of a well? Consider Joseph's story and realize God is always in control.

God, help me to trust that You are sending me. Amen.

A STORY TOLD

The heavens declare the glory of God,
and the sky displays what his hands have made.
One day tells a story to the next.
One night shares knowledge with the next
without talking, without words,
without their voices being heard.

PSALM 19:1-3 GW

God's story is displayed in a million ways all throughout our world. In the beauty of the mountains, in the vastness of the sea, in the mysteries of the oceans, His creation speaks of the wonder and creativity of a master Designer. In the unexpected caring of strangers helping one another, in the memories of ones we've lost, in the hearts that break over communal sorrows, His powerful love reveals no human source—it comes from outside of us and is beyond us. In the rhythm of words woven into poetry, in the skill of a farmer's rugged hands, in the spark of insight of a scientist's discovery, His wisdom speaks into being unlimited inventions.

God tells His story, again and again. When Jesus walked on the earth, He, Yeshua, told the story with His life and His words: "I will open my mouth to illustrate points. I will tell what has been hidden since the world was made" (Matthew 13:35 GW).

God keeps telling His story. All we have to do is listen, watch, follow, and realize that we are part of His story too.

God, thank You for showing me Your story. Amen.

IN THE NAME

Some trust in chariots and some in horses,
but we trust in the name of the LORD our God.

PSALM 20:7 NIV

They look so strong—lined up, uniformed, fully armed, faces stern. Heavy tanks wait behind the lines and lines of soldiers. They seem ready to fight any battle.

But look closely and you'll see anxious eyes, a tremor in someone's lips, and shaking hands. The faces are young—so young. They are about to march into unknown horrors, when just a few months ago their biggest worry was who to take to prom.

When faced with the terrible struggles and suffering that exist in our world, some trust in armies. Some trust in heavy artillery. Some trust in the power of money. Some trust in the political process.

But all those systems are created by human minds. And all those systems are vulnerable to human failings. Even the strongest, bravest hearts can falter. Even the most intelligent minds can make mistakes. And there's always someone who is stronger or smarter or better.

There's only one person we can always count on. Only one mind that is perfectly in order. Only one Almighty God who is all-powerful and always the same, yesterday, today, and forever.

Lord, thank You for being the one thing in
my life that will never change. Amen.

IN THE STORM

When they climbed back into the boat, the wind stopped.
Then the disciples worshiped him. "You really are
the Son of God!" they exclaimed.

MATTHEW 14:32-33 NLT

This was not the first supernatural show the disciples had attended. They had seen Jesus heal many. They had just handed out dinners—which Jesus had created from some bread and fish—to more than 5,000 people. They had even watched Jesus calm a storm on a lake before. They were intimately acquainted with the power of this Man. They felt the press of the crowds of people seeking His healing touch. They picked up the leftovers from His miracle meals. Their faces were splashed with the waves that He then silenced. Yet here they were again—scared by a storm.

At least Peter knew Jesus' voice.

At least Peter trusted Jesus enough to step onto the waves.

And Jesus met him on the way.

We are so very much like those quaking disciples—knowing full well what our God is capable of, and yet still needing to see the wind stopped before we can trust Him. But if we just have at least enough courage to stick our toes into the stormy waters, we might feel the blessing of Jesus reaching down and rescuing us . . . again.

Jesus my Lord, help me trust You
enough to get out of the boat! Amen.

LETTING GO

*Then she placed the child in it and put it
among the reeds along the bank of the Nile.*

EXODUS 2:3 NIV

Can you imagine the desperation of this Hebrew mother? She couldn't bear to give up her infant. From the moment he arrived, she looked into his dark eyes and fell in love with his fine face. "Beautiful boy!" she might have whispered, as she soothed him so his cries would not alert anyone to his newborn existence. For three blessed months, she stared into his face, nursed him, rocked him, and kept him quiet. The whole family worked together to hide him, knowing that discovery would bring death, as ordered by the cruel ruler of the land.

Perhaps the pressure came closer to their home. Perhaps there were rumors. Perhaps she just couldn't bear to keep him any longer, knowing she might be forced to watch him being ripped from her arms.

She just wanted to give him one more chance. And this descendant of Abraham, this one of many promised children of God, decided to believe that God would take care of her child too.

What a sacrifice! It's so hard to let our children go, even when they are fully grown. To trust that God has a plan for them. But He does have a plan. And sometimes the children we deliver into this world end up delivering others into God's hands.

God of Israel, thank You for watching over our children. Amen.

SATISFIED

The poor will eat and be satisfied; those who seek the
LORD will praise him—may your hearts live forever!

PSALM 22:26 NIV

It's that time of day. Your stomach begins to growl. Your head aches a little. Your energy levels start to dip. You're a little grumpy. You're hungry!

Most of us feel a little hungry at some point every day. It's the body's way of telling us that it needs fuel. And for most of us, meeting that need is not a problem. Food of some sort is readily available. And if it isn't, we can go find some. We can eat and be satisfied. We can even eat and be extremely full.

But for many people, this is not the case. They either have no food or just barely enough to keep going. They never know that pleasant, filled-up feeling. Their hunger is never satisfied. They are glad if they can simply eat enough to survive.

The rulers of this world can be callous—like Pharaoh making the people's work even harder by taking away straw, one of the key brick-making ingredients. He wanted people to do more with less.

But in God's kingdom, Jesus takes the little that people have and makes it more. He takes their emptiness and fills it up. He takes the loaves and fish and serves a feast.

Lord, thank You for giving me so much.
Help me to be generous to others. Amen.

LEAVE YOUR CHAINS

So Moses spoke thus to the children of Israel; but they did not heed Moses, because of anguish of spirit and cruel bondage.

EXODUS 6:9 NKJV

His message was nothing but good news. The God of their fathers had heard their groaning! He was coming! He would rescue them and redeem them. They would be His people, and He would be their God.

But when Moses delivered this good news, the people couldn't hear it. They were so sunk down into pain and despair, so weighed down by their chains, they couldn't even imagine being anywhere else—much less having the God of heaven care about them.

The dying to self and loss of life that Jesus speaks of in Matthew 16:24-25 is not just aimed at those who are on top of the world and full of themselves. It's aimed at the lowest of the low as well. No matter where we are in our lives, we all have to be willing to set aside our cares, set aside the view that fills our sight, set aside the soundtracks that play over and over in our ears, and listen to the message of the Lord. We are sometimes like prisoners who have been given keys but won't leave our cells because we have grown so accustomed to our chains.

Leave your chains. Go out to what God has ready for you.

Lord, help me to accept my freedom in You. Amen.

STUBBORN

*But when Pharaoh saw that relief had come,
he became stubborn. He refused to listen to
Moses and Aaron, just as the LORD had predicted.*

EXODUS 8:15 NLT

By this time in Pharaoh's story, he must have known something was rotten in Egypt. Aaron's staff had become a serpent, right before his eyes. And the Egyptians had been digging for water, since their rivers turned to blood. Now he pulled back his sheets and found frogs in his bed!

But even as the plagues on his land became worse and worse, even when his own magicians claimed, "This is the finger of God!" (Exodus 8:19 NLT), even after destruction rained down on his land, Pharaoh was resolute. He refused to let the people of Israel leave.

Why? Because they were his.

So often we hold on tightly to the things in our possession, the relationships we are tied up in, the emotional rides we have ridden for years—we hold on so tightly, even if it hurts our own hands, or our hearts. We just don't want to admit defeat. Or we want to believe that we can somehow perform a miracle ourselves and change what's hurting us into something that heals. But only God can heal. And only God can work these kinds of miracles. And if God is telling you to let go, then it's time to let go.

Lord, help me to release anything that is keeping me from You. Amen.

WHEN?

All day long I put my hope in you.

PSALM 25:5 NLT

When you whack your alarm for the fifth time and rise in a haze of groggy bitterness, that's when.

After your second cup of coffee and your twenty-second mistake of the day, that's when.

At the busiest hour, when you just can't take it, that's when.

In the dusty stillness, when the loneliness settles like a heavy blanket, that's when.

As you close up and lock up and clean up and sigh a long, long sigh, that's when.

When you're walking away, and you want to just keep walking and never come back, that's when.

When you snuggle up at home, in your favorite spot and with your favorite people, that's when.

When things don't go as you planned them, that's when.

When things go better than you could have ever imagined, that's when.

When the chapter seems too hard to get through, that's when.

When the happy ending finally appears, that's when.

When you're on top of the world, that's when.

Or when you're in the very bottom corner of the pit of despair, that's when.

When all seems horribly, cruelly lost, that's when.

From the moment you open your eyes until darkness comes, that's when.

When can you trust God?

All day long, that's when.

Lord, I put every minute in Your hands. Amen.

UNLESS

Truly I tell you, unless you change and become like little children, you will never enter the kingdom of heaven.

MATTHEW 18:3 NIV

They are tyrants. They are unpredictable. They are easily distracted. They make messes. They tend to be rather self-focused. They are often confused.

Anyone who's spent a significant amount of time with small children might well be a little worried at Jesus' statement in Matthew 18. Be like a child? *That's* how we get into the kingdom of heaven? Really?

Yes, really.

In many cultures, children are not valued as complete persons. They count for half-price. Half a seat. Half a ticket. Half of our attention.

And yet, they don't seem to notice. They continue to live—fully engaged, with hands full of stuff and eyes full of wonder and minds full of creations.

And they love fully—with arms wide open and tears flowing and sloppy kisses and big smiles and even bigger hugs.

They don't care what their standing is. They just stand.

And they don't really care who notices them. They just like to be noticed.

And they love to be loved.

Unless you stop comparing and counting and judging by grown-up standards, and start living and loving and trusting like a child—unless you can do that, you might just miss out on the fact that you're already living with the King.

Jesus, let me love and trust You with the heart of a child. Amen.

BE STILL AND GO

"The LORD is fighting for you! So be still!"
Then the LORD said to Moses, "Why are you crying
out to me? Tell the Israelites to start moving."

EXODUS 14:14-15 GW

Flee, freeze, or fight. Those God-given responses have served humanity well when facing danger.

When they'd first left Egypt, the Israelites hadn't raised a weapon against their adversaries but "left with fists raised in defiance" (Exodus 14:8 NLT), applauding God's triumph. Now, seeing the Egyptian army approaching, they were ready to flee in panic.

But Moses put a "trust" spin on the freeze-in-place reaction. "Stand firm. Be still." After delivering his rousing words to Israel, he prayed to God. God gave His next instructions: "Don't freeze. Run."

Not run *away*. Run *forward*.

The Bible doesn't indicate how Moses expected to get the Israelites across the Red Sea. Perhaps he was aware of the problem from his experience of fleeing Egypt forty years earlier. Whatever the case, on their own, the Israelites couldn't cross the sea. On foot. With the Egyptian army breathing down their necks.

But God knew all along. "Trust Me. Stop wasting time, get going, and let Me deal with the problem."

Whether God says to go, to stand still, or to fight, He'll always win the battle.

Mighty God, how often I waste time when a problem overtakes me!
Let me present the situation to You in prayer and act on Your
instruction, knowing I can trust You to win the battle!

GOD AS MAGEN

The Lord is my Strength and my [impenetrable] Shield; my heart trusts in, relies on, and confidently leans on Him, and I am helped; therefore my heart greatly rejoices, and with my song will I praise Him.

PSALM 28:6-7 AMPC

If any image demands trust in God, Jehovah-Magen, the Lord our Shield, does. Everything God is protects the person who hides behind Him.

Throughout history God has acted as an impenetrable shield for His people. After Abraham emerged victorious over the five kings in Genesis 14, God repeated His covenant to the patriarch, saying, "I am your shield, your very great reward" (Genesis 15:1 NIV). After God delivered David from the hand of Saul, David sang of his shield and rock, "He is a Magen to all those who take refuge in him" (2 Samuel 22:31; Psalm 18:30 GW).

In a similar vein, Moses boasted of God his strength and his defense after the Israelites had crossed the Red Sea unharmed (see Exodus 15:2).

When the battle rages, God is both the best offense (strength) and the best defense (shield.)

Trusting in God as Magen means moving forward without hesitation. Relying on God as Strength keeps His people marching when they believe they have gone as far as they can go. When the expected victory comes, trust rejoices, in heart and song.

Blessed be the Lord.

God my Strength and my Shield, how I need You.
May I truly understand that nothing harmful
can reach me outside Your will. Amen.

AWAY FROM THE CROWD

*And Moses brought the people out of the camp to meet
with God; and they stood at the foot of the mountain.*

EXODUS 19:17 NKJV

Trusting God often draws people away from the things of this world.

After the Israelites crossed the Red Sea, they headed to Mt. Sinai to prepare to meet with God, as Moses had originally told Pharaoh.

They had already left their world behind, the certainty of the lives of slavery for the uncertainty of life on the road with no visible means of support. But that wasn't enough. God wanted *more*.

They had to leave the camp, the place where they carried everything most precious to them, and the treasures the Egyptians had heaped on them. Naked in spirit, the Israelites stood before God at the foot of the mountain.

Jesus made a similar request of the rich young ruler in Matthew 19. Until this man got rid of his wealth, he wasn't ready to follow Jesus.

God still calls His people to set aside everything that holds them back from a total trust in Him. Surrender all to Him today.

*Sovereign Lord, You will do everything and be everything we need.
You only ask that we make You first, alone, on the pedestal of our lives.
Forgive us when we cling to the things of this world. May we follow
You to the quiet corners of the desert and drink of Your holiness. Amen.*

WHEN TRUST IS SCARY

*Moses said to the people, Fear not; for God has come
to prove you, so that the [reverential] fear of Him
may be before you, that you may not sin.*

EXODUS 20:20 AMPC

I srael heard God for themselves and not through Moses, in the thunder and lightning, fire and smoke.

They were terrified. They had peeked behind the wizard's curtain and discovered God was everything Moses had said He was, and more.

God had given them every reason to trust Him, from the arrival of Moses at Pharaoh's court as a child through the crossing a sea on dry land while their enemy drowned.

Even so, the moment they heard God, they backed away.

Trusting God isn't always comfortable—and that's a good thing. God reconciles His people to Himself through Christ, that they might have eternal life and grow in holiness.

God also prods His people to correct and teach them. The reason? Moses stated it plainly: to keep His people from sinning.

Trust God to do whatever it takes to make you holy as He is holy.

*Holy God, trusting You in Your holiness can be downright scary.
Because You are not only sinless, You are also everything sin is not.
Purity. Light. Wholeness. You call me and equip me to be as You are.
Do Your work in my life, sovereign Lord. Let me trust and obey. Amen.*

BE SPECIFIC

"Be quiet!" the crowd yelled at them. But they only shouted louder,
"Lord, Son of David, have mercy on us!" When Jesus heard them,
He stopped and called, "What do you want me to do for you?"

MATTHEW 20:31-32 NLT

How those two blind men must have delighted Jesus. They understood what the disciples had failed to grasp.

Jesus had explained that leaders must first be servants, and pointed to His coming death. The disciples saw themselves in the framework of an earthly kingdom, deserving of honor and deference.

The blind men saw the servant King. "Lord, Son of David. Jesus, David's King. Have mercy on us."

Still, their trust fell short. Jesus asked for clarification. "What do you want Me to do for you?"

How long did they take to answer? Did they discuss this once-in-a-lifetime opportunity between themselves? Would they ask for a temporary fix of money?

No, they dared to ask for the impossible—for their sight to be restored. Jesus honored their faith. In turn, they followed Him.

Today God invites His children to trust Him in everything, both in general and specifics. He will provide your daily bread. But He also wants you to ask if today's bread needs to include restoring your sight.

Almighty God, I can trust You to do the impossible. Too often I
don't receive because I fail to ask exponentially, according to my
need. Let me bring each and every need—whether physical,
spiritual, emotional, or monetary—to You. Amen.

TRUSTING GOD WITH THE IMPOSSIBLE

*Absolutely everything, ranging from small to large,
as you make it a part of your believing prayer,
gets included as you lay hold of God.*

MATTHEW 21:22 MSG

Jesus used the absurdity of moving mountains to illustrate a principle: God can and will do "absolutely everything" in response to believing prayer, from fixing the smallest hangnail to stilling the most powerful storm.

Believers often don't count on this promise as God intends. They feel guilty when their prayers aren't answered in the way they expected and wonder if they didn't have enough faith. Preachers may say it's not about the size of their faith, but the size of their God. But still believers ask, *Why does prayer remain a hit-or-miss affair when God promised "absolutely everything"?*

Maybe the answer lays in laying hold of God—because God will lay hold of you at the same time. When God tells His people He's ready to move a mountain, they'd better start praying. That's a prayer God will honor.

Prayer is all about trust. Trusting God is listening. Trusting Him to reveal His will. Trusting Him to act according to His nature and to do as He promised.

Prayer is trust in action, even when we don't ask for a thing.

Listening God, let me set aside my doubts and my failures and simply wait before You in simple trust. You will take that tiny seed of faith, water it, nourish it, and cause it to grow. Thanks for the blessing of answered prayer. Amen.

GOD IS COMING

Be brave. Be strong. Don't give up.
Expect GOD to get here soon.

PSALM 31:24 MSG

The majority of the Israelites who left Egypt had spent their lives making bricks (see Exodus 5:6-9). Now God gave them a different project: building the Tabernacle (see Exodus 25:1-31:11).

The first item on God's work order was crafting the Ark of the Covenant from acacia wood and overlaying it with gold. Other temple furnishings required a variety of skills: constructing furniture and sewing curtains made of finely twisted linen and animals skins. The Israelites, brave and strong, eventually completed the place where God would dwell.

In Matthew 21:33-45, Jesus told a parable about less reliable workers. A landowner left his farm in charge of tenants. At harvest time, he sent servants to collect his share of the fruit.

When the tenants beat and killed his servants, the landowner sent his son, hoping the farmers would listen to him. Instead, they killed him and claimed his inheritance.

The tenant farmers—and the religious leaders listening to Jesus' parable—hadn't figured God into their plans for the future. They weren't staying brave and strong to the pattern God laid for their lives.

People today make the same mistake. Jesus will return. Until then, trust Him. Be brave and strong. Don't give up. Work according to God's plan.

Coming God, teach me to live each day in the light of Your return.
May Your faithfulness encourage me and strengthen my own. Amen.

SEEKING GOD'S WILL

Thus Aaron will always bear the means of making decisions for the Israelites over his heart before the LORD.

EXODUS 28:30 NIV

Seeking God's will about the big questions—what job you should accept, which person you should marry—comes naturally. Other everyday questions that snip at your heels—how to handle a disobedient child, how to react when you receive bad news—maybe not so much.

God gave Israel's priests the means of discovering yes-or-no answers: the Urim and the Thummin. Gideon's fleece was a similar device (see Judges 6). God welcomes that absolute trust, a willingness to accept yes-or-no answers and confirmation of the direction we believe God's pulling us.

Of course, God's word itself guides you in how to love Him—with all your heart, soul and mind—and how to treat your neighbor (see Matthew 22:37-38). It also directs much of how you should live minute by minute.

Above all, God promises to instruct you and teach you in the way you should go (see Psalm 32:8). His still small voice in your ear and His hand on your shoulder will point the way.

Trust God in your decisions, both big and small.

Wonderful Counselor, You teach me the way to go. Nudge me right and left, open and shut doors. As I go where You lead, let me always walk within the light You shine and never stray. Amen.

WHO TELLS YOU WHAT TO DO?

*Don't set people up as experts over your life, letting them tell you
what to do. Save that authority for God; let him tell you what to do. . . .
And don't let people maneuver you into taking charge of them.
There is only one Life-Leader for you and them—Christ.*

MATTHEW 23:9-10 MSG

Jockeying for position is as old as humankind. (Think back to Cain and Abel.) Yet it's as new as today's news, with politicians and leaders lobbying for control for position at home and abroad.

And then there are the so-called teachers and experts looking to lord over you with their knowledge, guidance, and expertise. Jesus warned His disciples against the hypocrisy of the scribes and the Pharisees of His day because in the school of discipleship, there's only one professor: Jesus Christ. All believers are fellow students learning at His feet.

As far as guidance, that authority belongs to God alone, because He alone is the heavenly Father. Don't be bullied or seek additional counsel when God has made things plain.

Jesus also warns against your telling others what to do. Don't let people talk you into assuming the responsibility and authority that belong to Christ.

Turn your gaze to the God who has proven Himself faithful, not glancing to the right or left—or inward to yourself.

Let God lead.

*Life-leader, help me look to You alone
for knowledge and guidance. Amen.*

STICK-TO-ITIVENESS

"Staying with it—that's what God requires. Stay with it to the end. You won't be sorry, and you'll be saved."

MATTHEW 24:14 MSG

About this time of year, people evaluate their New Year's resolutions. Did they practice the desired behavior until it became a habit? Or has it already fallen by the wayside? Failure to follow-through is fairly commonplace, and few get upset about it.

God holds believers to a higher standard. He will never leave or forsake them. He expects the same loyalty in return. Each of today's readings touches on the importance of a full-time, lifelong commitment.

Where others saw a period, David put a comma, waiting with hope in God's unfailing love for delivery from death (see Psalm 33:18-19).

God put a comma in Exodus 31:13 (NIV), saying, "You must observe my Sabbaths. This will be a sign between me and you for the generations to come."

In Matthew 24:14 (MSG), Jesus added a comma when He reminded His disciples of the urgency of continuing perseverance. "Stay with it to the end." The end of time. The end of the story.

There is no room in God's family for wishy-washy, here-today-and-gone-tomorrow believers. Stick with Him out of hope. Cling to Him because He will always cling to you.

Our help and shield, today and every day, direct my steps to follow You. Increase the glue of my faith that I may cling to You when a wall threatens to separate us. Amen.

TRUSTING GOD IN THE SILENCE

*Then the Lord turned from the evil
which He had thought to do to His people.*

EXODUS 32:14 AMPC

A month after their encounter with God at the bottom of the mountain, the people of Israel decided God and Moses had disappeared. The itchy Israelites demanded Aaron create an idol, a new god to worship.

Hadn't God earned their trust? He'd begun eighty years before, when He placed Moses in Pharaoh's court. God had demolished their enemies through the plagues, secured their freedom at Passover, and nailed it at the Red Sea.

People today, even Christians, sometimes lose their trust in God as easily as the Israelites did. When a mountaintop experience descends back into the valley, when God's presence doesn't shine in brilliant glory, they wonder where He went. When the impossible-to-ignore meeting with God fades back to everyday light, they seek their next spiritual fix somewhere else.

No wonder God wanted to start over with Moses. Yet God relented after Moses' powerful intercessory prayer.

God's plans for today began before time. He sent His Son so He could offer eternal life to every human being. All He asks in return is that each individual trust. Believe. Receive.

God has done the rest of the work.

*Lord, You're higher than my thoughts, Your ways are higher than mine.
When Your thoughts and ways seem to disappear into the clouds,
keep my gaze fixed on You—not on the things of this world.*

GIVING BACK

Those who were willing and whose hearts moved them
came and brought their contributions to the LORD.
The gifts were used to construct the tent of meeting,
to pay other expenses, and to make the holy clothes.

EXODUS 35:21 GW

After the mountaintop experience, God gave Israel two commands, one new, one old: keep the Sabbath and gather an offering.

The Sabbath was for everyone without exception. God's second command was only for those who were willing. (God still loves a cheerful giver. See 2 Corinthians 9:7.) Regarding offerings, He made specific requests, according to the needs for the tabernacle: gold, silver, and bronze; woven material in blue, scarlet, and purple; animal skins from goats, rams, dolphins; the gems needed for the priest's ephod; spices for incense and oil for lamps.

God wants more than money in an offering plate, although today money is exchanged for the kinds of gifts Israelites offered to God. One church sponsors missionaries and immigrants. Another ministers to inmates and their families. Many fill food pantries and gather necessities for families who lose everything in a fire.

Although churches corporately help the needy, individual Christians may hold back despite God's nudges to give.

May God's people search their homes and hearts for what they can give back.

God, teach me to be a cheerful giver. You gave Your Son to die for my salvation. Make me a person willing to give until it hurts. Exchange the sense of duty with a gratitude that results in generosity. Amen.

WHAT TO DO WITH GOD'S GIFTS

The master said, "Well done, my good and faithful servant. You have been faithful in handling this small amount, so now I will give you many more responsibilities. Let's celebrate together!"

MATTHEW 25:23 NLT

The man who said, "God doesn't give a writer a story to put it in a drawer" echoed the point Jesus made in today's parable.

A master gave three servants different sums of money. The servants with five bags and two bags of silver, respectively, invested them and doubled the original amount.

The third servant hid the money in a hole, choosing security over growth.

Bezalel and Oholiab, the men God put in charge of building the tabernacle, had the know-how for making "all sorts of things" (Exodus 35:31 MSG). They also possessed the ability to teach others. Their skills, creativity, and talent multiplied as they trained others, building the tabernacle as God had commanded. They didn't leave their skills in a drawer but used them, and so acquired more knowledge.

When Christians wonder why they don't get ahead, why better opportunities elude them, the answer may lay in the parable of the talents. When they are faithful in the small things, greater opportunities will come.

Lord and Master, You have assigned gifts to me according to Your will. Let me not long for someone else's gifts. Instead, let me put my skills to use where You have placed me. I trust You will give the increase. Amen.

LOVING OTHERS=LOVING CHRIST

*And the King will reply to them, Truly I tell you, in so far
as you did it for one of the least [in the estimation
of men] of these My brethren, you did it for Me.*

MATTHEW 25:40 AMPC

O n Valentine's Day, hearts turn to thoughts of love. Although romance is what we usually think of on this occasion, in today's reading, Jesus would have us consider God's love for humankind, and His call to be loved in return.

What does loving God look like? Rapturous worship? Saying, "I love you, God, for all You have done for me?"

Jesus gives a fuller answer. When Christians help a person in need—hungry, thirsty, naked, sick, imprisoned—they are in fact loving their Master.

In Psalm 35, David speaks of how he showed that kind of God-inspired care (and failed to receive it in return): "But as for me, when they were sick, my clothing was sackcloth; I afflicted myself with fasting, and I prayed with head bowed on my breast. . . . But in my stumbling *and* limping they rejoiced and gathered together [against me]" (PSALM 35:13, 15 AMPC)

On this Valentine's Day, embark upon a heavenly romance. Say "I love you" to God by reaching out to someone in need.

*Loving God, You demonstrated Your love for me by the
extreme act of sending Your Son to die. Open my eyes today
to the needy around me and open my hands to help. Amen.*

WHEN GOD DOESN'T ACT

LORD, you have seen this; do not be silent. Do not be
far from me, Lord. Awake, and rise to my defense!

PSALM 35:22-23 NIV

D avid's cry is as ancient as Job's, as modern as the Holocaust
and beyond: "Awake, and rise to my defense!"

"Abba Daddy, wake up! I need help."

Things were beyond bad for David. Although he'd done nothing
wrong, others gloated over him, hated him without cause, and
accused him falsely.

After unburdening his heart, David returned to an attitude of
praise. Placing full confidence in God's trust, he says, "My tongue
will proclaim your righteousness. . .all day long" (Psalm 35:28 NIV).

Centuries later, the Son of David, Jesus Christ, reached the hour
planned since before time began. Feeling overwhelmed, lonelier
than at any point in all eternity, He begged God, "Let this cup pass
from Me" (Matthew 26:39 NKJV).

Like David, Jesus circled back to trusting faith. "Nevertheless,
not as I will, but as You *will*" (Matthew 26:39 NKJV). His absolute
surrender is an example of trust carried to the extreme.

You may not be called to such extreme tests. But whenever it
seems God is taking a break, voice your fears and requests—then
fall back to trust God to do what's best.

Whenever Your silence adds confusion to the attacks of
the enemy, thank You for accepting my complaints and cries.
Let praise and trust rise up in me before I see You in action.

BIG WORDS

God's love is meteoric, his loyalty astronomic, his purpose titanic,
his verdicts oceanic. Yet in his largeness nothing gets lost.

PSALM 36:5-6 MSG

"Your love, O Lord, reaches to the heavens." Go ahead, sing along. Where are there words big enough to describe God? David painted a vivid word picture. *The Message* adjusts the brilliance by exchanging adjectives for nouns.

God's love is meteoric. It reaches to the heavens. It moves as swiftly as a meteor and blazes a path for all to see.

His loyalty is astronomic. It reaches to the skies. It's inconceivably great, stretching beyond earth's atmosphere to the most remote galaxy.

His righteousness is titanic. It's like the highest mountains. Its magnitude dwarfs everything surrounding it in force and power.

His purpose is oceanic. His justice is like the vast deep. Its greatness extends His purpose across the earth.

Yet that infinite God knows when a balding man loses hair. Regardless of His largeness, *nothing gets lost.*

Oh, to trust a God like that! How can His children fail to cling to Him?

When David saw people without fear of God, he reminded himself how much better it was to take refuge in the shadow of His wings (see Psalm 36:7).

God is timeless. What was true in David's day is true today. Amen.

Creator God, You are far greater than tongue can tell or
mind comprehend. Let me never doubt You. When trouble
comes, hide me in the shadow of Your wings. Amen.

I CANNOT TELL A LIE

If you are called to testify about something you have seen
or that you know about, it is sinful to refuse to testify,
and you will be punished for your sin.

Leviticus 5:1 nlt

Alas, the familiar legend about George Washington is a myth. But the virtue it taught, of honesty at whatever cost to the individual, remains true.

In the story, young George didn't confess to chopping down the cherry tree until his father confronted him. Would he have spoken up if someone else got in trouble for his actions?

That's the crux of today's passage from Leviticus. If people fail to trust God with the truth, they will be punished for their sin.

In our society, a witness to a crime may receive a subpoena. Perjury, failure to tell "the whole truth and nothing but the truth," is a crime.

Yet the principle of speaking up extends so much further. How about whistleblowers and tattletales? How about champions who speak out against injustice? How about when it becomes personal, between brothers and sisters, parents and children, husband and wife?

A Christian doesn't have a choice. Not to speak up is a sin.

O God who does not lie, You command me not only to speak
the truth but also to speak up about what I've seen and heard.
Forgive me when apathy or fear bind my tongue. Give me courage
to speak for You and on behalf of the innocent. Amen.

ACCIDENTAL HOLINESS

*The LORD spoke to Moses, "If any of you fail to do your duty
by unintentionally doing something wrong with any of
the LORD's holy things, bring a guilt offering to the LORD.
It must be a ram that has no defects or its value in silver
weighed according to the official standards of the holy place."*

LEVITICUS 5:14-15 GW

God pronounced many things holy: time (the Sabbath), objects (the temple's contents), people (the priests, Christians), places (Mt. Sinai), and worship rituals (offerings). And God calls His people to treat everything in a respectful manner. He commands them to be holy as He is holy. Even their bodies are to be respected because they are God's living temple.

Yet God knew His people would mistreat His holy things. Such errors were still a sin even if committed accidentally. But God provided a way out, an offering for those unintentional sins, so that you could "make peace with THE LORD for what you did wrong" and "be forgiven" (Leviticus 5:6 GW).

Given the seriousness God places on the command to holiness (see Leviticus 11:44), how reassuring it is to know you can trust God to forgive you when you miss the mark, whether intentionally or unintentionally.

Holy God, separate me and everything I touch as holy. Let me see everything in my life as You see it, and act accordingly. Forgive me when I sin through unawareness. In Jesus' name I pray, Amen.

WHY IS IT GOOD FRIDAY?

*Now when the centurion, and they that were with him, watching
Jesus, saw the earthquake, and those things that were done,
they feared greatly, saying, Truly this was the Son of God.*

MATTHEW 27:54 KJV

People who don't know the Lord sometimes ask why the day Jesus died is called *Good* Friday. They find the juxtaposition of the ultimate sacrifice with the awesome display of power as confusing as the first-century witnesses must have.

The ordinary Jewish citizen didn't make any connections between the earthquakes, three hours of darkness, and the man who claimed to be God.

The Jewish leaders who'd clamored for Jesus' execution thought His death settled the question of His claim.

Jesus's disciples fled in fear, even though He'd warned them ahead of time about what had to happen.

No, the faith heroes at the cross were the very soldiers who nailed Jesus to it. On the day He died, these outsiders saw, observed—and came to the obvious conclusion: The man known as Jesus of Nazareth must be the Son of God. They responded with fear and awe.

Almost two thousand years later, people around the world celebrate *Good* Friday. They testify to the miracle of how Jesus' death paved the way to life for all who receive Him.

*Son of God, words fail when I try to comprehend
what happened on the cross. Today, this minute, may I
cling to that same power and love at work. Amen.*

DON'T HOLD BACK

The moment they saw him they worshiped him. Some, though,
held back, not sure about worship, about risking themselves totally.

MATTHEW 28:17 MSG

The disciples had fled in fear of their lives when Jesus was nailed to the cross. What if the Jewish leaders lashed out at Jesus's staunchest supporters? In hiding, surely they grieved and sought solace from God.

Their reasons for holding back after Jesus's resurrection makes less sense. They weren't sure about risking themselves totally. But Jesus didn't criticize them. He knew Pentecost was coming, when the promised Holy Spirit would give them a boldness unparalleled in world history.

Leviticus 10 tells a different, sadder story. Nadab and Abihu had been holed up with their father, Aaron, and their brothers to be schooled in the priesthood. After they were trained and anointed, they went to work.

Immediately, matters went horribly wrong. Doing their own thing, regardless of what they knew God required, the brothers boldly offered "strange fire" to God and were incinerated by His hand.

In brief, don't hold back. Don't allow doubt to keep you from walking with God. Yet don't replace God's instructions with plans of your own. Obey His commands, even when you don't understand them. That's when God will exalt you to inherit the earth.

Father, help me not to hold back when worshipping You.
I will cling to Your trustworthiness even when I don't see
the evidence. Forgive my doubt. Increase my faith. Amen.

DO-IT-YOURSELF HOLINESS

*For I am the LORD your God. You shall therefore
consecrate yourselves, and you shall be holy; for I am holy.*

LEVITICUS 11:44 NKJV

The God who gave His Son expects believers to be as passionate about holiness as He is, but sometimes that central truth gets lost when reading the rules and regulations in Leviticus. God's command to the Israelites to consecrate themselves, or as *The Message* puts it, to make themselves holy, may be scary.

Yet *how* do we accomplish such a feat? Levitical holiness called for a lot of external actions meant to reflect an internal attitude. For instance, Jewish tradition teaches for people to wash their hands before meals, based on extrapolations of Leviticus 15:11.

But where can Christ-followers turn? To Romans 12:1-2 (NLT), where how to consecrate oneself is described: "Give your bodies to God because of all he has done for you. Let them be a living and holy sacrifice—the kind he will find acceptable. This is truly the way to worship him. Don't copy the behavior and customs of this world, but let God transform you."

Perhaps that's what holiness means. Turning ourselves over to God, trusting Him to renew minds and dedicate lives to living out that transformation.

*God, make me holy as You are holy. I want to be like You,
my Abba Father. As You transform my thinking,
show me how to change my ways.*

WHEN SILENCE SHOUTS

And so, Lord, where do I put my hope? My only hope is in you. I am silent before you; I won't say a word, for my punishment is from you.

PSALM 39:7, 9 NLT

Some people can't keep quiet. They dominate every conversation, raise their hands to answer every question asked. Other people naturally hold back. It takes a skillful conversationalist to get them talking. Still others are inconsistent, talking when they should be silent and not speaking up when their voices are needed.

In the Old Testament, David was in his own when-to-speak quandary. He zipped his mouth shut when in the presence of the wicked (see Psalm 39:1-2), the words of truth he wanted to voice burning within him. But he later broke down, pouring out his fears and disappointments to God (see Psalm 39:4-13).

In the New Testament, when Jesus promised forgiveness to a paralytic lowered through the roof, the minds of the Pharisees and scribes jumped to silent accusations: *Only God Himself can forgive sins* (see Mark 2:7). Their silence emphasized what their inner condemnations tried to hide. Jesus, knowing their thoughts, answered their unspoken doubt with a miracle of healing.

How much better it is to speak the truth and trust in God!

Omniscient God, You record my every thought and deed. Keep that in the forefront of my mind as I come to You in hope and trust. I confess my wrongdoings and ask for You to speak to me once again.

EXTERNAL ACTIONS DEMONSTRATE INTERNAL TRUTH

Which is easier, to say to the paralytic, "Your sins are forgiven you," or to say, "Arise, take up your bed and walk"?

MARK 2:9 NKJV

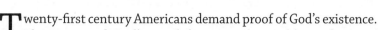

Twenty-first century Americans demand proof of God's existence. If science and God's word disagree, the visible evidence of experiments carries more weight than the word of the unseen God.

The age of science and reason has been both a blessing and curse. It's led to advancements and improvements of so many human miseries. At the same time, it has replaced faith in God for many.

However, the desire for proof is a human condition, not a contemporary one. The problem is, no experiment can demonstrate things like eternal life.

Jesus couldn't prove the paralytic man's sins were forgiven when the Pharisees doubted.

Instead He offered proof of His authority by healing the man's physical body. "I say, 'Your sins are forgiven,' but you don't know if that happened. But so you know I have the power to do what I say, I'll do something you can see. You there, on the mat. Get up and walk" (paraphrased).

Even that demonstration didn't convince everyone. The more Jesus proved His identity by teaching and miracles, the more they rejected Him.

Believers trust God by faith. They hope in His character as revealed in His actions and in their hearts. Pray that people walking outside of God's light might someday understand.

O unchanging, everlasting God, open my eyes to unseen truths, that I may put my hope solely in You.

HOLINESS IS COMMUNAL

Later Jesus was having dinner at Levi's house.
Many tax collectors and sinners who were followers
of Jesus were eating with him and his disciples.

MARK 2:15 GW

S inners. . .were followers of Jesus." What a contradiction. Didn't following Jesus involve a change of life? Did Jesus really permit people still involved in a sinful lifestyle to seek after Him?

No wonder the Pharisees questioned Jesus' ministry. They placed supreme value on following the intricacies of the law as the means to achieve righteousness. That involved not associating with anything or anyone who was unclean. Instead of helping sinners to return to God, the Pharisees "cleaned house" by sweeping sinners out of their presence.

Perhaps they meant well when they reprimanded Jesus for associating with men like the maligned tax collector Levi. But Jesus pointed out that just as the sick need a doctor, He came to minister to sinners. "I'm here inviting the sin-sick, not the spiritually-fit" (Mark 2:17 MSG).

Sinners needed God most of all. When Jesus appeared among them, He awakened a hunger in them for righteousness. When Jesus invited Levi to follow Him, he jumped at the chance.

When a brother or sister is caught in sin today, call for the Doctor instead of the housecleaner.

Dear Lord, let us call the Doctor for healing instead
of seeking a surgeon to remove the sin-diseased
organs within Your body, the church. Amen.

TRUSTING GOD WITH THE HARVEST

The farmer sows the word.

MARK 4:14 NIV

A sales rep makes dozens of cold calls to meet his quota. A writer sends multiple query letters to sell an article. The broker invests in the market to make his commission. A farmer sows seed to reap a crop. A mathematician might write an equation as A x B = Z, where A is the worker, B the effort, and Z the results.

Right? *Not exactly.* The better equation is (A x B) x C = Z, where C is the soil.

The place where the farmer sows his seed plays a major role in the harvest. No matter how diligently the worker labors, if the soil is poor, it won't produce large numbers of good fruit.

God asks Christians to trust Him, whatever soil they work with. They can rejoice because He has already prepared good soil in their hearts, soil that's received the seed of His word. God then puts some laborers to work in a fertile field, where they'll reap a large harvest.

God's equally pleased with those spreading the sparkling truth of His love among the rocky soil.

Whether working in rocky soil or fertile, trust God for the increase (see 1 Corinthians 3:6).

Lord of the Harvest, You know exactly what kind of response we'll get from the place You have set us to work. Keep us faithful in the difficult times, that we may rejoice together in the bad.

THE RIGHT KIND OF FEAR

You shall. . .[reverently] fear your God. I am the Lord.
LEVITICUS 19:32 AMPC

Katrina, Andrew, Harvey: say the names, and images of death and destruction tinged with remembered fear spring to mind.

It takes a special kind of storm to evoke that degree of terror. The experienced fishermen among Jesus's disciples wouldn't have been scared by thunder and lightning. But the fervor of this squall surpassed anything they had seen, and they feared for their lives. This was no ordinary storm. And Jesus, their miracle-working Rabbi, was asleep. Out of ideas, desperate, the disciples woke Him. "Don't you care if we drown?"

Jesus calmed the wind before He turned to the deeper issue. "Why are you such cowards? Don't you have any faith yet?" (Mark 4:40 GW).

Was He saying, "You didn't have to wake Me. I wouldn't have let you drown?" Did He mean, "Why didn't you wake Me before fighting it in your own power?" Perhaps He was asking, "Why did you doubt My concern for you?"

They didn't understand or trust Jesus enough. Man feared the nature God created more than the God who created nature.

The law and God's character commands a healthy respect and awe that lies at the heart of trust. The next time troubles come, gaze heavenward at your awesome, all-powerful God—not at the circumstances.

God, I know I can trust You precisely because of Your fearsome power. Let me walk with assurance in that knowledge.

THE WRONG RESPONSE TO FEAR

*Those who had seen it told the others what had happened to the
demon-possessed man and the pigs. At first they were in awe—
and then they were upset, upset over the drowned pigs.
They demanded that Jesus leave and not come back.*

MARK 5:16-17 MSG

E veryone ran away from the man who broke chains, lived among
tombs, and cut himself with stones. Everyone but Jesus.

As soon as He arrived, He restored the broken human being.
He demanded that the demons possessing the man leave him and
go into a herd of pigs. In turn, the animals stampeded over a cliff.

The transformation of the nightmarish ogre into someone calmly
eating his meal scared people more than his previous rants. In
addition to the people's fear, they were angry about their loss of
pigs and begged Jesus to leave.

Unlike the pig herders, when the once-shepherd David had a
setback, he "used to go to the house of God ... with shouts of joy and
praise" (Psalm 42:4 NIV). If a day brought loss, he said to himself,
"Put your hope in God, for I will yet praise Him" (Psalm 42:11 NIV).

When life takes an unexpected turn, do you turn away *from* God
or *to* Him? Be wise and yet praise Him.

*God of miracles, You work in my life in big and small ways. May I
accept and learn and praise You. Let me ever hope in You. Amen.*

WHEN FAMILIARITY BREEDS CONTEMPT

In God we boast all the day long,
and praise Thy name for ever. Selah.

PSALM 44:8 KJV

Jesus electrified Israel, attracting praise and criticism simultaneously. Common people loved the popular teacher and divine healer. But religious leaders couldn't accept His claims of being God.

At one point, Jesus took a break and went home. Instead of welcoming the public figure, the hometown Nazarenes rejected the carpenter's son who had left His family in a lurch.

The sting hurt worse than anything the Pharisees said or did, moving Jesus to remark, " 'A prophet is not without honor except in his own country, among his own relatives, and in his own house.' Now He could do no mighty work there" (Mark 6:4-5 NKJV).

When Israel treated their Redeemer God with contempt, He sent them into exile. When the people of Nazareth didn't recognize their hometown hero, He couldn't perform miracles there.

Still today, believers may not recognize God in their midst. They may respond to Jesus, incarnate divinity, but shy away from the Lord of the Heavenly Army. Or fall at the feet of the King of kings, yet overlook their heavenly Father.

Review God's acts in the past in order to recognize Him in the present. When you see and welcome God in all His aspects, He will not pass you by (see Mark 6:6).

Lord Father, You're both my Abba Father and my Brother.
Let me boast of and in all Your aspects. Amen.

CELEBRATE!

The Lord said to Moses, "Speak to the Israelites and say to them:
'These are my appointed festivals, the appointed festivals of
the Lord, which you are to proclaim as sacred assemblies.'"

LEVITICUS 23:1–2 NIV

D on't you wish you could travel back in time and join in these festivals with the ancient Israelites? It would be quite the adventure to see firsthand how our faith's forebears celebrated and commemorated everything God had done for them.

While we may be tempted to skim through these festival descriptions, thinking they don't apply to us, how amazing is it that God *commanded* His people to have times of special celebration throughout the year? In addition to the weekly Sabbath, God instituted special days of rest and worship for the Israelites to remind them of His work in providing for them (the Festival of the Firstfruits), in delivering them from sin (the Day of Atonement), and in bringing them out of slavery in Egypt (the Festival of Booths). When we dwell on God's gracious work toward us, our hearts can't help but respond in trust and worship!

Set aside time for your own "festival" to the Lord, whether on your day of rest or in your daily devotional time: kick up your heels in joyful praise and let your soul kick back in heart-deep rest, celebrating your loving, faithful Mighty God.

Father, as it was for the Israelites, let my days
be rounded out with intentional rest and praise.

BANK ON HIS GENEROSITY

*"You may ask, 'What will we eat in the seventh year if we do
not plant or harvest our crops?' I will send you such a blessing
in the sixth year that the land will yield enough for three years."*

LEVITICUS 25:20–21 NIV

Can you imagine regularly taking a year off work and having *no
worries* whatsoever? Today's Leviticus reading gives a fascinating
look at God's generosity and provision: Every seventh year, the
Israelites were to leave the land fallow, a "festival year. . .a year to
honor *the LORD*" (25:4 GW). If the Israelites were obedient in this,
God promised to provide extra for their needs, far beyond the bare
minimum, so they and the land could rest that year.

God's abundance is also seen in Mark, as Jesus feeds the
multitude (including five thousand men!) who had followed Him
into the countryside to hear Him preach. There were twelve baskets
of leftover food *after* the people had eaten "as much as they wanted"
(6:42 GW).

Jehovah Jireh, our Provider, is delighted to care for His people.
What have you been waiting for God to provide? All throughout His
Word is evidence of His generosity and compassion. He will provide
for your needs for today and for tomorrow—you can bank on it.

*Lord, You are a generous God. It's hard to wait for
Your answer, but I trust in Your promise that You
take care of Your children. (see Philippians 4:19)*

COMPARISON GAME

"Well did Isaiah prophesy of you hypocrites, as it is written: 'This people honors Me with their lips, but their heart is far from Me. And in vain they worship Me, teaching as doctrines the commandments of men.'"

MARK 7:6–7 NKJV

The Pharisees clucked officiously at Jesus, "Why do Your disciples not walk according to the tradition of the elders, but eat bread with unwashed hands?" (Mark 7:5 NKJV). *This upstart rabbi doesn't teach the whole Law! Disgraceful.* But Jesus revealed their wayward hearts, which were more interested in enforcing human commandments—and looking better than others—than honoring God.

The Pharisees were all about the comparison game. Armed with their good works, they judged everyone by their strict, self-righteous standard. But though they perched at the top of the spiritual pecking order, they'd missed the Law's heart—enjoying God's love and humbly showing their love through obedience.

Our standing before God has never been founded on "how well we're doing"—only grace. Even back in Leviticus 26:44–45 God promised to be faithful to the Israelites whether they were obedient or wayward. And today, our salvation rests solely on Jesus; we just humbly receive His gift.

So when tempted to find our worth by seeing where we stack up with one another, let's instead meet together on our real level: equally loved and accepted through God's boundless grace.

*Jesus, whether my self-confidence is strong or shaky,
I will trust Your grace as my foundation.*

HIDE IN HIM

God is a safe place to hide, ready to help when we need him.
We stand fearless at the cliff-edge of doom, courageous in
seastorm and earthquake, before the rush and roar of oceans, the
tremors that shift mountains. Jacob-wrestling God fights for us.

PSALM 46:1–3 MSG

There are weeks when trouble seems to be working overtime: a flat tire with your kids in the car, a midnight trip to the ER, your friendship with your neighbor unexpectedly and inexplicably gone cold. And as if trouble isn't hard enough ("All things work together for good," you mutter through clenched teeth), sometimes you struggle with guilty feelings. *I should be stronger than this! I should have more faith! God, why can't I keep it together?*

But God answers you with reassurance, not censure: "I'm a safe place to hide. I'm ready to help when you need Me." The psalmist sang fearlessly in the face of nature's fury not because of his own strength, but because he relied on God to fight for him. God's power is available to you too: He invites you to hide in Him, leaning on Him for help.

Today, whether you're fearfully or fearlessly standing at the "cliff-edge of doom," trust in the nearness of your powerful God and get ready to watch Him work. Trouble's got nothing on Him.

Father, so much feels upended in my life right now.
But I can trust You to hold it—and me—together.

KNOW AND GROW

Jesus took Peter, James and John with him and led them up a high mountain, where they were all alone. There he was transfigured before them. . . . Then a cloud appeared and covered them, and a voice came from the cloud: "This is my Son, whom I love. Listen to him!"

MARK 9:2, 7 NIV

Who knows what Peter, James, and John were thinking when Jesus led them to the mountain. They had seen Him feed the five thousand people, then four thousand more; they had watched Him silence the Pharisees with His wisdom about the scriptures. They and the other disciples had left all to follow Him, but was this outspoken yet compassionate rabbi truly the messiah Israel had been waiting for, or just a good teacher?

Their burning question was answered by none other than God the Father Himself. God's statement from the cloud affirmed Jesus' identity as the Son of God, beloved and trustworthy, telling them to "listen to Him!" God's declaration revealed a new truth to these disciples: Jesus was so much more than even the earthly messiah they had been hoping for.

Do you, like the disciples, have deep questions about Jesus and His ways? Follow the Father's words: listen to Him, through the Word and prayer, and your trust will grow as you get to know Him better. He is indeed more than you could ever hope for.

Jesus, deepen my trust by showing me more of You.

ENTRUSTED

*"I have taken the Levites from among the Israelites in place of the first
male offspring of every Israelite woman. The Levites are mine, for all
the firstborn are mine. . . . They are to be mine. I am the Lord."*

NUMBERS 3:12–13 NIV

The book of Numbers has long sections that are filled with, well,
numbers. In Numbers 3 the Levites are counted, named, and
set apart to serve God, each clan assigned a special duty in caring
for the tabernacle. The Lord set them apart for His special service,
declaring, "They are to be mine."

What a blessing it is to know that God has also declared that *we*
are His! In Christ we have the privilege of being "a royal priesthood,
a holy nation" set apart for God (1 Peter 2:9 NIV), and He has given
each of us talents and abilities to help grow His kingdom.

Regardless of your occupation, God wants you to work with
Him in mind, whether your job is creative, collaborative, mundane,
enjoyable, frustrating, or rewarding. Entrust your work to Him. Just
as God used the Levites' everyday work to lead Israel into worship,
we can be confident that our trustworthy, sovereign, loving God can
use our work to grow us and bless others.

*Father, I am Yours. I entrust my talents and work to You,
looking for ways to declare the praises of You who called me
out of darkness into Your wonderful light. (see 1 Peter 2:9)*

HOPE FOR THE DRY TIMES

*For this God is our God for ever and ever:
he will be our guide even unto death.*

PSALM 48:14 KJV

Two women waiting for their flight struck up a conversation after one noticed a Bible app on the other's phone. It turned out they were both believers. Feeling burdened, one began to share her heart with this just-met sister. "My times with God just feel so dry right now. They used to be so rich and deep, but now I'm struggling to even read my Bible."

The other woman nodded. "I've been there before. It can be so hard to keep going." They encouraged each other with what's needed most in spiritually challenging times—God's unchanging truth.

Today's psalm is full of truth about God's character: our righteous Lord is full of lovingkindness, His name endlessly worthy of praise (see Psalm 48:9–10). He chooses to be our guide, walking close to us "even unto death." No matter how distant we feel, He will not abandon us; even when we are disobedient He will restore us as a loving parent.

It can be so discouraging when your spiritual walk feels desert dry. But take courage, daughter of God. Press on, and even if you can only manage a whisper, declare, "He is my God forever and ever; He *will* guide me through this season and the rest, until I meet Him face to face."

*Father, help me trust Your truth and
encourage others to do the same.*

SERVE IN TRUST

*"For even the Son of Man came not to be served but to
serve others and to give his life as a ransom for many."*

MARK 10:45 NLT

In today's passage, the disciples were arguing about who would be the greatest among them, entirely missing the true character of God's kingdom. While we may chuckle at their misunderstanding, Jesus' words still have a salient message for us: service is the heart and mark of Christian leadership.

But is there such a thing as "too much" serving? Maybe you genuinely follow Jesus' example in serving others but constantly find yourself spent and worn out, more jaded than joyous. Perhaps you take on too much out of worry, thinking things just "won't get done right" (or at all) if you don't step in. But worries like these may mean you're depending a little too much on yourself. Remember, God is committed to the service you're involved in—even more than you are—and He will make His good work flourish.

We need to exercise our trust muscles to serve well as leaders in our churches, homes, and communities—and that may look like intentionally making time to rest or leaving work (maybe more than we're used to!) to others. Let's follow Jesus' model and stay connected to our Source of Life, trusting that no matter what, He has it all under control.

*Jesus, when it feels like it's all up to me,
remind me You're always at work.*

SHINE ON US

" "The Lord bless you and keep you; the Lord make His face
shine upon you, and be gracious to you; the Lord lift up
His countenance upon you, and give you peace.' "

NUMBERS 6:24–26 NKJV

Amid people waving palm branches, Jesus entered Jerusalem on a donkey's colt. Perhaps the celebrants crying "Hosanna" ("Save us!") in the streets remembered Aaron's blessing and thought, *Today God's face shines upon us at last, after so long.* They hoped against hope that Jesus would be the one to restore peace to David's kingdom.

They were right about God's blessing arriving, but it would not come in the way they expected. Humble and lowly, God the Son would lift up His human countenance upon them, face to face, to be gracious to them and give them peace. Through laying down His perfect life, Jesus would usher in something more precious than kingdoms and land: a no-holds-barred relationship with the Father, a God who is strong to answer His children when we pray (see Mark 11:24).

Daughter of God, Christ still blesses you and keeps you; He looks on you with radiant love and grants you daily grace after grace. When all looks dark, turn your face to the Savior's. Let Him illuminate your heart with lasting peace.

Jesus, Light of the World, I'm so thankful for Your saving grace.
I want to reflect Your light to everyone in my words and
actions. I trust You for the strength to do that.

IT'S ALL HIS

"The world is Mine, and all its fullness. . . . Offer to God thanksgiving,
and pay your vows to the Most High. Call upon Me in the day
of trouble; I will deliver you, and you shall glorify Me."
PSALM 50:12, 14–15 NKJV

In Numbers 7, the leaders of Israel consecrated the tabernacle with daily, costly fellowship offerings for twelve days, celebrating God's presence among them. What an amazing thing, that a holy God chose to rescue them, members of an imperfect, lowly nation, and dwell among them!

Psalm 50 echoes the language of offerings from Numbers but reveals what God desires more than sacrifices—His people's love and trust. For God has no need of the gifts we bring, because the whole world is His. The Old Testament sacrificial system was actually a gift to *Israel*, as it made a way for sinful people to interact with the holy God who loved them. How could Israel ever repay this gift with bulls and gold dishes? How could we ever repay God, who opened the way to fellowship with Him through His very life? We cannot and are not asked to repay it; instead, let's offer a continual sacrifice of praise (see Hebrews 13:15) and bring our requests before God with trusting hearts. For He will answer when we call, and the glory is all His.

Father, my generous Deliverer, I offer
everything—my life, my heart—to You.

ON THE MOVE

Whether the cloud stayed over the tabernacle for two days
or a month or a year, the Israelites would remain in camp
and not set out; but when it lifted, they would set out.

NUMBERS 9:22 NIV

In their wilderness wanderings, the Israelites saw God's presence in the form of a pillar of cloud or fire over the tabernacle. If the cloud moved, the people knew it was time to set out for the next place God would lead them. This transient life must have been rough—the Israelites were probably packing pros in no time!—but God knew best how to care for His people, even if it meant short stays.

Today we've no pillar of fire to lead the way but Someone even better: the Holy Spirit, who lives and guides us as we seek God's will through the Word and prayer. But we've all had moments when we wished that literal pillar of cloud was still around. Those times are opportunities to grow in trusting the Spirit.

God put the Holy Spirit in your heart to be your "Comforter (Counselor, Helper, Intercessor, Advocate, Strengthener, and Standby)" (John 14:16 AMPC). The Spirit works for your good, teaching you God's truth (see 1 Corinthians 2:10–12) and praying on your behalf (see Romans 8:26–27). You aren't on your own. No matter your situation, you can depend on the Spirit to guide you forward.

Holy Spirit, grow my trust and strengthen
my heart to follow Your leading.

A TERRIBLE SIN?

Have mercy on me, O God, according to your unfailing love;
according to your great compassion blot out my transgressions.
PSALM 51:1 NIV

Complaining's as natural as breathing, whether it's about traffic, the weather, or the mess someone left in the microwave. But did you know that complaining is a terrible sin in God's eyes? In Numbers 11 the Israelites did a *lot* of complaining: They grumbled about their hardships, lamented about the great food they'd had at "no cost" in Egypt, and wailed for meat (Numbers 11:5 NIV). Their grousing sparked the Lord's anger (in verse 1, He literally sent fire into the outskirts of the camp), bringing Moses to near despair over this burdensome people.

What makes complaining so bad? It's mistrust in action: when the Israelites complained, they were telling lies about God's character— "He hasn't and *won't* provide what we need"—and they implied that Egyptian slavery was preferable to God's freedom! Complaining ignores everything God has done and says, "God, since this didn't go the way I wanted, You aren't actually trustworthy, are You?" Yikes.

The Israelites needed the repentant heart shown in Psalm 51 to confess their sin and reaffirm God's unfailing love toward them. We, too, should repent when we complain, and God is faithful and just to forgive us (see 1 John 1:9). Better yet, let's make a habit of giving thanks instead of complaints.

Father, help me see all the blessings You give every day.

STAYING ALERT

"But about that day or hour no one knows, not even the angels in heaven, nor the Son, but only the Father. Be on guard! Be alert! You do not know when that time will come."

MARK 13:32–33 NIV

In Cixin Liu's sci-fi novel *The Dark Forest*, alien foes will arrive to take over Earth. . .in four hundred years. The twenty-first-century people of Earth wonder what good they can do to prepare for a battle they'll never see. "It's hopeless," many say, but a future-minded few encourage their fellows to keep working to create the foundations of Earth's space defenses for later generations.

Sci-fi situation or not, staying future-minded takes focus, faith, and doggedness. In Mark 13, Jesus exhorted His disciples to "be on guard" and "alert" regarding the Jerusalem temple being destroyed. The same command applies to us about His second coming—we don't know when "the Son of Man [will be] coming in clouds with great power and glory" (verse 26 NIV), but we're to live as if it's imminent.

What can spur us on to staying future-minded? Trusting in Him who holds that future: at Christ's return, all things will be made new, including us, and we'll live with Him forever. Let's do the work He left us—sharing His good news with everyone—so all can look forward to and take comfort in the promise of His return.

Father, teach me to be future-minded,
and show me how to build Your kingdom today.

WELL ROOTED

*But I am like a green olive tree in the house of God; I trust in
and confidently rely on the loving-kindness and the mercy of
God forever and ever. . . . . I will wait on, hope in and expect in
Your name, for it is good, in the presence of Your saints.*

PSALM 52:8–9 AMPC

After the ten spies gave a terrible report about Canaan's dangers, Caleb and Joshua urged the panicking Israelites to trust in God: "The Lord is with us. Fear them not" (Numbers 14:9 AMPC). But the people wouldn't hear it, even planning to stone these two faithful men! That generation was barred from entering the promised land for their unbelief (see verse 23).

How do we hold fast to our faith when the news reports have everyone in a panic? In Psalm 52 David paints a beautiful picture of steadfast trust: he is a "green olive tree in the house of God"— rooted deep in a secure place, confidently waiting for and relying on the good nourishment of God's love along with his fellow believers.

Is your confidence rooted in God as Caleb's and Joshua's was? Deep roots will not be swayed even as high winds howl. Show others the firm ground of your confidence, like these ancient brothers, encouraging people around you with God's solid truth.

*Father, like David, Joshua, and Caleb, help me stay well
rooted in Your loving-kindness rather than trembling
before the "giants in the land." You've got this.*

WHEN FEAR STRIKES

And the second time the cock crew. And Peter called to mind the word that Jesus said unto him, Before the cock crow twice, thou shalt deny me thrice. And when he thought thereon, he wept.

MARK 14:72 KJV

M eg froze, hearing her coworkers make disparaging comments about Christianity and the Bible. *God, if I speak up, will they want to talk about spiritual things—or anything—with me ever again? They know I'm a Christian, so I need to say something. But I'm scared it's going to be the wrong thing!* The coworkers moved on to other topics, and Meg's heart sank.

We can relate to Meg's situation. All of us, even Peter, one of Christ's closest disciples, have been afraid of what others think. Peter declared he wouldn't deny Christ (see Matthew 26:35), but when questioned, a fearful, blustering Peter denied Jesus in self-preservation—then bitterly regretted it. But in his dark moment, we know Christ still loved him and restoration was coming (see John 21:15–17).

Be comforted if you feel you've missed an opportunity to tell about Jesus or acted contrary to His Word before others—He is merciful and welcomes you home when you confess your shortcomings. You can trust Him to enliven you when fear would paralyze you. For Christ's love is greater than your fear—He will cultivate boldness in you for His Gospel if you ask.

Jesus, when I'm afraid to share,
bear me up with Your love and presence.

DARING RESCUE

*The leading priests and teachers of religious law also mocked
Jesus. "He saved others," they scoffed, "but he can't save himself!
Let this Messiah, this King of Israel, come down from the
cross so we can see it and believe him!"*

MARK 15:31–32 NLT

Christ was silent in response to the mocking of the chief priests,
Roman soldiers, and even those being crucified with Him—"Save
yourself!" Jesus knew the chief priests had seen His miracles and
still refused to follow Him; they'd chalked Him up as a revolutionary
and arrested Him to get Him out of their way.

The priests assumed Jesus' mission was to seize power from them,
the elite. But at Gethsemane, in great heart-shaking prayer, Jesus had
entrusted His life to the Father's plan. Rather than sparing Himself,
He shouldered sin's agonizing punishment to rescue everyone. . .
including those who stood there taunting Him. To save others, He
could not, would not, save Himself.

Jesus coming to earth constituted the most important rescue
mission of all time. Holy God took on humanity to come and save
lost people, no matter how far they'd gone or what they'd done. For
those who trust Him, Jesus is their "helper" and the "provider for
[their] life" (Psalm 54:4–5 GW). He delivered us from sin; let's trust
that our Rescuer will help us when we pray.

*Jesus, You know where I need rescuing today;
I trust You to be the Helper You promise You are!*

SAINT PATRICK'S DAY

Cast thy burden upon the LORD, and he shall sustain thee:
he shall never suffer the righteous to be moved.

PSALM 55:22 KJV

The life of Saint Patrick often gets lost among shamrocks, green beer, and leprechauns. This fifth-century evangelist from Britain had an exciting life. As a teen he was captured by Irish pirates, served for six years tending animals in Ireland, then escaped back to Britain. He later returned to minister to the Irish people as a cleric and bishop. One of Ireland's patron saints, Patrick is credited with spreading Christianity in Ireland.

"Saint Patrick's Breastplate," part of a longer prayer by the evangelist, is a fitting reminder of the believer's relationship with Christ:

Christ with me, Christ before me,
Christ behind me, Christ in me,
Christ beneath me, Christ above me,
Christ on my right, Christ on my left,
Christ when I lie down, Christ when I sit down,
Christ when I arise,
Christ in the heart of every man who thinks of me,
Christ in the mouth of everyone who speaks of me,
Christ in every eye that sees me,
Christ in every ear that hears me.

Using Saint Patrick's prayer and today's psalm, meditate on the reality of your Savior's nearness. Give Him your burdens, for He supports you on every side; He loves you perfectly and provides what you need: peace, victory, protection, community, and encouragement.

Jesus, I bless You, for You are good, and You
sustain me. I rejoice in Your nearness!

FULFILLMENT

But the angel said, "Don't be alarmed. You are looking for Jesus of Nazareth, who was crucified. He isn't here! He is risen from the dead! Look, this is where they laid his body."

MARK 16:6 NLT

Mary the mother of James, Salome, and Mary Magdalene went to Jesus' tomb after the Sabbath had passed, having followed the requirements that no work be done on that holy day. Their plan was to anoint Jesus' body with spices. They then most likely intended to purify themselves according to the laws for ceremonial cleansing (see Numbers 19:11-13).

But what a surprise for these women: Not only did they not have to worry about rolling the stone away from the tomb, they also found Jesus' body was gone! The angel told them the most unexpected news: "He is risen from the dead!" In that moment, they were (understandably) terrified, but little did they know they had received the most joyous news the world had ever heard: the way to God was fully open through Jesus Christ.

Gone was the need for purification rites, for Jesus had conquered the curse of sin and made His people clean. Gone was the need for sacrifices and the temple veil separating God and humankind, for God Himself laid down His life and took up the role of mediator. Jesus fulfilled all He came to do, and you are free because He lives!

Jesus, I will trust in You, my Living Savior, every day.

FAITHFUL IN OUR LONGING

*Soon afterward his wife, Elizabeth, became pregnant and went into
seclusion for five months. "How kind the Lord is!" she exclaimed.
"He has taken away my disgrace of having no children."*

Luke 1:24–25 nlt

For her and Zechariah's whole marriage, Elizabeth had been barren. Her culture deemed childlessness a disgrace, for the Lord opening the womb was a sign of blessing on the Israelites' obedience (see Leviticus 26:3, 9). No doubt the couple—who were described as "righteous in God's eyes" (Luke 1:6 nlt)—wondered why God hadn't given them children. Despite that, they continued serving faithfully into their later years.

Notice Elizabeth's response after she becomes miraculously pregnant: "How kind the Lord is!" There's no anger or resentment in her words—just praising God for His kindness in fulfilling her heart's desire. And He gave her the honor of bearing the one who would point the way to the Messiah.

Maybe you also have longings you've been praying about for years; maybe thinking of continuing faithfully, as Elizabeth did, feels too hard to bear. But you're loved. Your heavenly Father sees you, keeps track of all your tears (see Psalm 56:8). He'll remain faithfully by your side, to comfort and bind up your broken heart (see Psalm 34:18). Keep seeking His goodness, for you will find it; He'll give you strength to go on.

*Lord, whether You fulfill my longing or not, keep on showing
Me that You are my great reward (see Genesis 15:1).*

TRUE BLUE

"God is not a man, so he does not lie. He is not human,
so he does not change his mind. Has he ever spoken and
failed to act? Has he ever promised and not carried it through?
. . . God has blessed, and I cannot reverse it!"

NUMBERS 23:19–20 NLT

B alak, the king of Moab, didn't know what he was in for when he asked Balaam (a sort of "prophet for hire") to curse the Israelites. Balak seemed to think that if he made the proper number of sacrifices on the right mountaintop, then Israel's God would be willing to turn against His people. But when Balaam tried to curse Israel, God would only allow him to bless His chosen nation.

The Moabite king found out the truth: God keeps His promises, and absolutely no one can undo His blessings.

Sing of that truth with David, relying in all things on your Savior's care: "My heart is confident in you, O God. . . No wonder I can sing your praises!" (Psalm 57:7 NLT). Trust God's integrity when He calls you to join His work, so you can experience the blessing Elizabeth gave Mary: "You are blessed because you believed that the Lord would do what he said" (Luke 1:45 NLT).

Be confident in your God! His character is firm—He's true blue, through and through.

Father God, as spring renews the earth,
let my heart be renewed by Your blessing today.

QUIET DAWN

"A new day will dawn on us from above because our God is loving and merciful. He will give light to those who live in the dark and in death's shadow. He will guide us into the way of peace."

LUKE 1:78–79 GW

Today's scripture comes from Zechariah's prophecy about his son, John, who would prepare Israel for the dawning of "a new day," the Messiah, Jesus, who would liberate Israel from "the dark" and "death's shadow." The Light of the World dawned to bring humanity peace with God.

Perhaps your story of meeting Jesus was like a slow sunrise: His light spread over the landscape of your heart, the blazing warmth of His love overtaking where death and sin had formerly reigned. Because God's kingdom is both "here and not yet"—Jesus is victorious over sin and death but all things have not yet been "made new"— there are still places in your heart where you need His restoring light, whether it's to drive out icy fears, stormy anger, or the fog of nagging sins. In your times of confession, invite Jesus into those places. He will not condemn or criticize but will heal you and illumine the path to His ways of peace. Though the process of change can be long and tough, you can trust Jesus to shed His light, His truth, where you need it most.

Jesus, You know where I need Your light today.
Thank You for patiently teaching me Your ways.

BOLDLY ASK

The LORD spoke to Moses, saying: "The daughters of Zelophehad speak what is right; you shall surely give them a possession of inheritance among their father's brothers, and cause the inheritance of their father to pass to them."

NUMBERS 27:6–7 NKJV

Zelophehad's daughters were in a bind—they had no brother to inherit their father's land and possessions, and according to the laws of the day, they'd be disinherited. . .and their father's line extinguished. They boldly brought their concerns to Moses, asking that they be given "a possession among our father's brothers" (Numbers 27:4 NKJV). Rather than just telling these sisters, "This is how it's always been," Moses wisely took this matter to the Lord. God affirmed the rightness of the women's request, changing the laws so a man's inheritance could pass to his daughters if he had no sons (see Numbers 27:8).

Perhaps this situation feels far removed from your modern experience, but its lesson remains vital today: You can be bold and ask God about anything. This may include things that you feel called to do that don't necessarily match up with "how it's always been" in your community or church.

Instead of shrinking back, trust that "the LORD *is* near to all who call upon Him. . .in truth" (Psalm 145:18 NKJV). He's ready to hear your requests, and His answer just might surprise you.

*When I feel boxed in by cultural expectations,
Father, remind me I can ask You about anything.*

A UNIVERSAL EXPERIENCE

*His mother said to Him, "Son, why have You done this to us?
Look, Your father and I have sought You anxiously." And He
said to them, "Why did you seek Me? Did you not know
that I must be about My Father's business?"*

LUKE 2:48–49 NKJV

A military family was looking for a new church home after moving that summer. After visiting one Sunday, they miscounted their six kids (hey, it's a lot!) and accidentally left one behind. Once they realized it, Mom and Dad rushed back to the church but found their missing son as happy as could be: a church family had looked after him, fed him lunch, and encouraged him to play with their kids, knowing his parents would soon return. Embarrassed but thankful, the lost child's parents never forgot this family's kindness.

In the wild world of parenting, every family has a "lost kid" story, even Mary and Joseph, and their child was the perfect Savior of the world! So take courage, moms. Whether you accidentally left a kid at the store, feel like you can't clean up another mess, or are so tired you forgot your cold coffee in the microwave (again), you're not alone. Your Savior is still about His Father's business—providing hope, restoration, and strength to all who trust Him.

*Jesus, thank You for taking care of me and my kids—and for
being "my fortress, my refuge in times of trouble" (Psalm 59:16 NIV).*

FRUITFUL

"Produce fruit in keeping with repentance. . . . every tree that does not produce good fruit will be cut down and thrown into the fire."

LUKE 3:8–9 NIV

S tirred by John's words about repentance, his listeners asked him, "What should we do?" (Luke 3:10 NIV). While John gave general examples—being generous with your possessions toward those in need—he also gave occupation-specific examples when the tax collectors and soldiers asked the same question. John told the tax collectors (considered traitors to Israel for collecting taxes for the Roman oppressors) to collect only the required tax, instead of taking a little "off the top" for themselves. John then told the soldiers to be content with their pay and not take advantage of their position to extort and accuse people falsely. All of John's instructions showed concrete ways of loving your neighbor, something God loves.

How can you cultivate love-focused, God-honoring actions in your day-to-day work? Maybe it's by consistently doing your best work to support your team or choosing graciousness over grumbling when talking with a coworker. Or it could be practicing patience and forgiveness toward family members when they're on your last nerve. No matter your job, one thing is certain: God will strengthen you and guide you in living His way when you ask Him.

Father, I want to produce good fruit in my life. I'm ready to learn, and I trust You to accomplish Your good work in me (see Philippians 1:6).

VICTORY IN HIM

With God we will gain the victory,
and he will trample down our enemies.

Psalm 60:12 niv

In scripture, we're familiar with the clash of swords and shields in battle: In Numbers 31, the Israelites gain the victory over the Midianites who were utterly destroyed as a judgment from God for leading the Israelites into idol worship. In Psalm 60, David writes to instruct the people of Israel in how to pray for their army during battles. In Luke 4, we witness a quieter but still intense battle as Jesus strives against exhaustion, hunger, and Satan's temptations.

In all these scriptures, though, who was the real winner of the battle? It's God who gives Midian into Israel's hand; Numbers 14:39-45 showed how Israel did not do well in battle when God wasn't with her. David affirms this truth in Psalm 60:11 (niv): "Give us aid against the enemy, for human help is worthless." And when Jesus was tempted, He used God's Word to repel the devil, His God-breathed truth trampling the deceiver's lies.

Where's your battle today? Whether you struggle against your sin nature or the enemy's discouraging whispers, whether temptation strikes or the world's unkindness stacks against you, practice David's lesson: pray to see God's deliverance, His strength, His mastery over your circumstances. He's your victorious Savior! He'll hold you up.

Jehovah-Nissi ("the Lord is my banner"), when the battle is raging,
I will rally to Your banner of truth, looking for Your victory.

NO GUILT, JUST GRACE

*Yet the news about him spread all the more, so that crowds
of people came to hear him and to be healed of their sicknesses.
But Jesus often withdrew to lonely places and prayed.*

LUKE 5:15–16 NIV

"You make time for things that are important to you." Do you immediately feel guilty when you read that adage? *I know, I know. I should make sure I get family time, prayer time, and gym time, but I'm beyond stressed even thinking about trying to add one more thing to my schedule!*

You're not alone. You know, Jesus probably felt pressures in His work too. As His fame spread, actual *multitudes* of people came to Him to be healed. Showing compassion, Jesus healed their diseases and preached God's good news. But we also see He "withdrew to lonely places" to pray. Jesus, fully God, was also fully human—He got hungry, tired, and probably emotionally drained from witnessing the brokenness in His creation firsthand. He met with the Father for rest and strength *so* He could be prepared to help those who needed Him.

Get out from under the guilt and lean into His grace: God invites you to come to Him—no matter where you are or what you're doing in your day—to exchange your cares for His strength, peace, and joy. He will meet you where you are.

*Jehovah Jireh, my Provider, remind me
throughout today that I can always rest in You.*

FAITH-FILLED IMAGINATION

*Truly my soul silently waits for God; from Him comes
my salvation. He only is my rock and my salvation;
He is my defense; I shall not be greatly moved.*

PSALM 62:1–2 NKJV

Whether it's nagging daytime fears or Technicolor nightmares, worry is something all of us know. We're made to be creative thinkers, but all of us have wished now and then that our imaginations would just *slow down*. God knows the power of imagination, which may be why He gave us so many concrete pictures about Himself in scripture for us to hold on to. The Psalms are full of this imagery: God is a "rock," a "strong tower;" He even has "wings" to cover us as a mother hen does her chicks (Psalm 62:2, Psalm 61:3, Psalm 91:4). A vivid image of God's strength and safety can help in the moments our worries overwhelm.

You can also pick a physical "touchstone" to remind you of God's character. One man kept a rock on his desk to signal the safety and solidity of his heavenly Father. One author thanked God for His goodness every time she saw wild doves—reminders of God's Holy Spirit's continual presence—from her window. What touchstone could you use to turn your imagination to God's attributes on your worry-filled days?

*Father, thank You for the gift of imagination and creativity.
When I feel worried, help me dwell on things that
remind me of Your goodness and care for me.*

TIMELY REMINDERS

*The LORD your God has blessed you in everything you
have done. He has watched over you as you traveled through
this vast desert. For 40 years now the LORD your God has
been with you, and you haven't needed a thing.*

DEUTERONOMY 2:7 GW

As the wilderness wandering years drew to a close, Moses knew
he needed to instruct the Israelites one more time in God's
ways and laws. As disobedience had kept Moses from entering
the promised land (see Numbers 20:9–12), he knew this teaching
was crucial: his sermons in Deuteronomy feel like a loving father's
final talks with his grown children before they're on their own.
In addition to teaching God's law, Moses also recounted all God's
mighty work toward Israel—even as they sinned and struggled—
reminding the Israelites anew of God's love and grace to spur them
to obey Him out of love and gratitude.

It's important to recount where God has brought you in your
faith journey with Him, for it encourages you for the road ahead.
Look back on your life and, like Israel, see "how the LORD your God
carried you, as parents carry their children. He carried you wherever
you went until you came to this place" (Deuteronomy 1:31 GW).
Daughter of God, He'll carry you now and till the end.

*Father, I will recount Your goodness, relish the stories
of Your care toward me. I trust You will be with me
through everything ahead; Your grace goes before me.*

LOVE LIKE HIS

But love ye your enemies, and do good, and lend, hoping for nothing again; and your reward shall be great, and ye shall be the children of the Highest: for he is kind unto the unthankful and to the evil.

Luke 6:35 kjv

Laura was fuming. She'd been picking up the slack for an important project at work, and today she'd raced to drop off Brandon's forgotten science paper during her lunch break. She waited for thank-yous and got. . .nothing. *Really, guys? Do you not see everything I'm doing?*

No one likes their work being overlooked, including God. But here's what's amazing: God is radically kind and generous even when He receives no thanks in return. Matthew 5:45 says He sends rain and sunlight on the just and the unjust; in His "common grace," the Creator lavishes good over all the earth, not just the people who follow Him—and not out of obligation, but out of love for what He has made.

We're God's children when we reflect His love and generosity, doing things for Him, not for accolades. It isn't our first instinct to act this way: we need God-transformed hearts to be consistently compassionate and generous when we may never be repaid in kind. But we do it because God did the same for us—sending His Son to call unthankful people to Himself.

Father, You see my efforts. Help me open my hands and heart to those who need to see Your grace.

LIKE GLUE

*My whole being follows hard after You and
clings closely to You; Your right hand upholds me.*

PSALM 63:8 AMPC

When you were growing up, did you have a little brother or sister who followed you everywhere? If you were like most big kids, you probably wanted them to go play with their own friends and stay out of your room (good luck with that!). But little kids want to be just like their big brothers and sisters, and they can be awfully persistent.

In Luke, Jesus reminds us that we're to imitate God, being merciful as He is merciful (see Luke 6:36). We are to reflect Him in our whole being—words, actions, thoughts—just as a disciple learns to be like her teacher (see Luke 6:40). Perhaps you've been following hard after God but feel discouraged with your spiritual progress. *I'm still struggling with all this stuff! Am I really doing a good job following You, Lord?* But no woman walks alone in her journey with God; whether you feel strong or weak, His "right hand upholds" you, carries you through.

Just for a second, imagine you're a child again, following after your big Brother, Jesus. Instead of trying to ditch you, He invites you to follow Him into His next adventure: "Okay, lil sis. Stay close to Me!" You can trust He won't leave you behind.

*Jesus, I trust Your strength for my faith journey.
Help me cling to You and learn all Your beautiful ways.*

ALL YOUR LOVE

"Listen, O Israel! The Lord is our God, the Lord alone.
And you must love the Lord your God with all your heart,
all your soul, and all your strength."

DEUTERONOMY 6:4–5 NLT

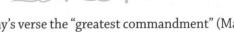

J esus called today's verse the "greatest commandment" (Matthew 22:38). It's also the hardest, as it asks for the totality of our love. While we show our love for God by following His Word (see Deuteronomy 6:1–2), we learn to love Him by meditating on His beauty and character.

So let's love the One whose power rescued a nation from four hundred years of oppression, through mighty wonders bringing her out safely to a good land (see Deuteronomy 6:20–25). Let's adore the Creator whose words wrought the earth, whose command silences the angry winds and seas. Let's bow in reverence before the God who drew near to His creation to restore it, who "gave himself for us to redeem us. . .to purify for himself a people that are his very own" (Titus 2:14 NIV). Let's sing of His daily provision, His food for the hungry, His comfort to the hurt and lonely, His mercies that are new every morning.

Hear, O daughter! The Lord is your God, the Lord alone! His salvation is greater than any gift you could bring Him. . .and yet it's your love, your heart, that He desires.

Father, I'll walk in obedience, secure in
Your love for me, responding in trust.

MIRACLE UPON MIRACLE

"Go back and report to John what you have seen and heard:
The blind receive sight, the lame walk, those who have
leprosy are cleansed, the deaf hear, the dead are raised,
and the good news is proclaimed to the poor."

LUKE 7:22 NIV

G od's in the miracle working business, even today. How easily we forget that all of creation serves as a daily reminder of this fact. The same Creator who spoke mountains and rivers into existence causes the sun to rise each morning and to cast its golden rays over us as we journey from place to place.

There are miracles in a baby's smile, the wrinkled hand of an elderly neighbor, the playful yap of a rowdy pup. There are supernatural reminders of God's grace in our bodies, as well—a heart that beats in steady rhythm, hands that bend and move, legs that take us where we need to go.

May we never forget God started all of creation with just a word. And, as we witness miracles in our lives, may we respond with words of awe and wonder, praising our amazing Father for all He continues to do.

Lord, I witness miracles every day of my life. From the rising of
the sun, to its setting in the evening, the miracles never cease.
My trust is ever-increasing as I witness one after the other!
May I never forget that even now You are a God of miracles. Amen.

AWESTRUCK WITH WONDER

The whole earth is filled with awe at your wonders; where morning dawns, where evening fades, you call forth songs of joy.

PSALM 65:8 NIV

We serve a remarkable God! His mighty hand is at work in creation around us. With the tip of a finger, He draws canyons out of rock. With just a breath, He moves ocean waves to and from the shore. With just a word, He bids the sun and moon to light our path.

The evidence of God's trustfulness is evident if we're paying attention. The tide continues to roll in, day after day. The sun continues to rise, morning after morning. Dew covers the earth in a cool, damp blanket, causing things to grow. Trees shoot up in magnificent splendor, shedding their leaves in autumn and springing back to life after snowy winter frosts melt away.

All of nature stands as a testimony to the fact that God is trustworthy, from the tiniest caterpillar to majestic mountain peaks. If He can take care of even the smallest creature, if He can remind the moon to cast its glow, surely He can care for you, even when you walk through dark valleys.

Lord, I'm awestruck when I think about Your creation! Ocean waves crash in joyous praise. Shimmering rays of sunlight cast their beams across waving fields of wheat. All of creation sings in grateful chorus, Father, and I'm overwhelmed at it all. What a mighty God You are! Amen.

CROSSING OVER

But you will cross the Jordan and settle in the land the LORD your God is giving you as an inheritance, and he will give you rest from all your enemies around you so that you will live in safety.

DEUTERONOMY 12:10 NIV

God promised the Israelites a land filled with milk and honey, a place they could call their own. He led them through the wilderness and pointed them toward their ultimate destination. When they reached the Jordan River, however, the Israelites hesitated.

How many times have we done the same? God brings us through wilderness experiences and points us toward a place filled with promise, but we hesitate, overcome with fear. We can see the fulfillment of promises ahead. We know our future is filled with possibilities. But we stand frozen in place, unable to move.

The same God who led you through the desert can be trusted to carry you to the next phase of your journey. He's got amazing things in store for you. Say goodbye to fear. Take hold of His hand, and cross the Jordan to an amazing new adventure.

Father, I'll admit it: There have been many "Jordans" in my life that I refused to cross. I got to the very edge and lost my nerve. I was afraid to step over the invisible line. Thank You for giving me the courage to cross over into new and exciting seasons in my life, Lord. From now on, I choose to trust You! Amen.

FROM CHAOS TO CALM

*And they came to Him and awoke Him, saying, "Master, Master,
we are perishing!" Then He arose and rebuked the wind and the
raging of the water. And they ceased, and there was a calm.*

LUKE 8:24 NKJV

Our hearts go out to the disciples who faced the storm while traveling in a small boat upon the sea. How terrified they must've been as the small vessel tipped this way and that, thunder crashing overhead, rain pouring down on their heads, lightning streaking across the sky.

Jesus was never afraid of the storm. In fact, He was able to sleep through it, completely at peace. How we long to be like Him! How wonderful, to trust Him so fully that we can be at rest, even when storms rage around us. With just a word, our precious Savior can calm the storms in our lives. He speaks, and thunder seals its lips. He lifts His hand, and lightning tucks itself away behind a cloud. Even drops of rain cease at His command.

There'll be storms. But you can trust Jesus to stay in the boat with you, even when you're tipping to and fro. He'll never leave you. He's right there, whispering, "Peace, be still!"

*Lord, so many times I've found myself in the proverbial raging
seas, and it's exhausting. Fear overwhelms me. Thank You
for the reminder that a simple word, a whisper from You—
and storms in my life cease. Speak now, Father, I pray. Amen.*

REFINED AS SILVER

For You, O God, have tested us;
You have refined us as silver is refined.

PSALM 66:10 NKJV

There's no way for precious metals to be refined without going into the fire. A lovely wedding band starts as an ugly lump of lead. It's placed into a fiery furnace, where the precious is separated from the nonprecious. Only the good remains while the bad is sloughed off.

The same is true in our lives. When we go through the fire (difficult or painful seasons), we undergo a holy refining. We become who we were meant to be. The good is separated from the not-so-good. When we are purified, we become stronger. Brighter. Purer. We will stand the test of time. No longer a lump of lead, we are bright and shining witnesses of God's transforming power.

The refining process is never easy. No one wants to go through fiery trials. But, oh, to shine like silver! To know that the work God is doing in us will last for all eternity. It makes the hard times worthwhile when we realize the Lord's purification process can be trusted.

Lord, I'll be the first to admit, I'm not a huge fan of
the "refining" process. Going through the fire can be
brutal. But when I come out on the other end, Father,
what joy! The purification process is worth it
all as my heart becomes sterling! Amen.

WITH US

*When you go out to battle against your enemies,
and see horses and chariots and people more numerous
than you, do not be afraid of them; for the LORD your God
is with you, who brought you up from the land of Egypt.*

DEUTERONOMY 20:1 NKJV

The Israelites squared off against their enemies more times than we can count. At nearly every turn, another tribe or nation reared its head against the people of God. The Israelites had to be ready for battle on countless occasions.

The Christian life is, at times, a bloody battlefield. We face a very real foe—the enemy of our souls. He stirs up situations that cause us to become afraid. We look across the battlefield and see our enemy looming, large and intimidating.

Today, be reminded that God (who resides inside of you) is greater than any enemy you might face. No matter how many chariots or horses look you in the eye, don't give in to fear. The Lord is with you and will fight your battles.

Stand firm. Don't back down. He brought you out of Egypt. He can cause you to triumph, even now.

It's easy to get overwhelmed, Lord. Those who're against me often seem greater than those who're for me. Thank You for the reminder that having You on my side tips the scale in my favor. You've brought me through so many scary places in the past, Father. I trust You to do it again.

TAKE UP YOUR CROSS

*"If any of you wants to be my follower, you must give up
your own way, take up your cross daily, and follow me.
If you try to hang on to your life, you will lose it. But if
you give up your life for my sake, you will save it."*

LUKE 9:23-24 NLT

"It's my way or the highway." This expression reeks of pride and
arrogance but has an even deeper root: lack of trust. When we
demand our own way, we're saying we don't trust God's way above
ours. How foolish to think we know best.

God has called us to a life that doesn't demand our way. In fact,
He's called us to lay down our lives (our will, demands, know-it-all
attitudes) and follow Him.

What's the Lord asking you to lay down today? Is there something
you're clinging tightly to that might be separating you from God? If
you cling tightly to the things that threaten to separate you from the
Lord, you'll surely lose your life. But if you give them up and follow
hard after Him, you will gain eternal life.

*Lord, it's so much easier to think of all I have to gain by following
You. Laying things (like my will, way, personality) down feels
like such a sacrifice. But I long to follow hard and fast after You,
Father! Today I commit to take up my cross daily, that I
may gain the best possible life in You. Amen.*

FATHER TO THE FATHERLESS

Father to the fatherless, defender of widows—
this is God, whose dwelling is holy.

Psalm 68:5 nlt

D oesn't your heart ache for the fatherless children in this world? Many of these little ones weep for the daddy they never had. Others have gone without for so long that they don't know any other way of life. They don't even know how to mourn for what they've never had.

As members of Christ's body, we've an obligation to care for those in need and fill in the gap when parents are missing. But we also have an obligation to share the good news that God is the best Daddy of all. Our Abba Father sweeps in like a knight on a white steed, ready to show His sons and daughters that He'll care for them, no matter what they're going through. He's a fierce protector, one who cares greatly about those who've been overlooked or abused.

Perhaps you're in need of a reminder that God is your Daddy. Lift your hands toward heaven and let Him sweep you up into His arms. Even now, He's dancing and singing over you, longing to fill the voids in your heart.

It does my heart good, Lord, to remember You are a Father to the fatherless. What a loving Daddy You are! How you defend the weak! How you care for those in need! How trustworthy You are! I stand in awe of Your tender care for Your children, Lord. Amen.

MAY WE NEVER FORGET

*When you cross the Jordan River and enter the land the LORD
your God is giving you, set up some large stones and coat
them with plaster. Write this whole body of instruction on
them when you cross the river to enter the land the LORD
your God is giving you—a land flowing with milk and honey,
just as the LORD, the God of your ancestors, promised you.*

DEUTERONOMY 27:2-3 NLT

Picture the Israelites crossing the Jordan River into the Promised Land. Can you see them scratching their heads as they listen to the Lord's last-minute instructions? Can you hear their questions: "Wait a minute, Lord. . .stones? Put them. . .where?"

Oh, but after-the-fact, when they looked back at the place where they crossed over, it all became crystal clear. What a tangible reminder of what the Lord had done! Those very stones stood as a memorial, a vivid reminder, so they would never forget their deliverance story.

When God works miracles on our behalf, delivering us from our proverbial (and often very real) enemies, He longs for our trust to grow as we remember all He's done on our behalf. May we lift our hearts and hands in praise for all He's brought us through.

*Lord, You've carried me through rough seasons and brought me into
new places where I can thrive in You. May I never lose my sense of
wonder over Your grace, provision, and love. I trust You, Father. Amen.*

BEARING OUR BURDENS

Praise be to the Lord, to God our Savior,
who daily bears our burdens.

Psalm 68:19 niv

So many times, we hyper-focus on our burdens. It's almost as if we choose to trust in the burden, not the burden-bearer. Our gaze remains fixed on the problem, not the problem-solver.

It's time to shift our focus! God has promised in His Word that He will bear our burdens, not just occasionally, but daily. Every problem we face can be placed into His mighty hands. He's more than capable. When we shift our attention away from our trials and onto Him, our perspective changes completely. The weight is gone! And when the weight is gone, we're better able to lift our hands and hearts in praise, which further strengthens our faith.

No matter what you're going through today, praise God! He's ready and willing to carry the load on your behalf. What a trustworthy and faithful God we serve!

Lord, there are so many days when I feel weighted down with life's burdens. How freeing, to know You want to lift those weights from my shoulders, to carry them for me. What a gracious and kind Father You are! I'm so grateful to You, my burden-bearer. Amen.

FEW THINGS ARE NEEDED

"Martha, Martha," the Lord answered, "you are worried and upset about many things, but few things are needed—or indeed only one. Mary has chosen what is better, and it will not be taken away from her."

LUKE 10:41-42 NIV

When you think of the word *many* what comes to mind? Many joys? Many sorrows? Many challenges? Many faith-moments?

Our lives are filled with "many" things to do. We're overwhelmed with tasks. And in this crazy fast-paced world, we work double-time to keep up with those around us. We want to prove our worth through our busyness.

In this story of Mary and Martha, we get God's perspective on busyness. "Mary has chosen what is better." Those words ring out as a reminder that God cares more about the "few" things that are needed. In fact, He boiled it down to one critical thing: spending time in His presence.

The next time you're tempted to do the "many" things (and at a rapid pace, no less) pause a moment and think about these two sisters. Has God called you to be a Martha. . .or a Mary?

Lord, I admit I often focus on the "many" things that need to be done and not on the" few" that're truly necessary. Spending time at Your feet is far more important than racing through each day, exhausted and frazzled. Shift my focus, Father, as I let go of the things robbing me of my time with You. Amen.

HE LEADS THE WAY

The LORD your God himself will crossover ahead of you. He will destroy these nations before you, and you will take possession of their land. Joshua also will cross over ahead of you, as the LORD said.

DEUTERONOMY 31:3 NIV

Remember how you loved to play follow-the-leader as a child? It was even more fun when you got to be the leader. As an adult, though, leading can be an overwhelming challenge. It's tough to be the responsible one, the one everyone looks to for guidance. The game isn't as much fun when the stakes are higher.

Isn't it wonderful to realize that God wants to assume the leadership role in our lives? We don't have to be the ones in charge, making all the decisions. He leads, guides, directs, and encourages. Our role? To listen and to follow. We can trust His leadership to be the very best.

Who (or what) are you following today? Your gut? Your friends? Your peers? Those on social media? There is one who leads the way, and He stands ready to guide you, even now. Shift your gaze to Him, and take possession of the land!

You're an amazing Leader, Father! I have nothing to fear as long as I stick close as You guide me into the promised land. I choose to follow closely, Lord, and to place my trust in You. I can't wait to see where You're leading me next, Father! Amen.

BECAUSE OF ME

*Don't let those who trust in you be ashamed because
of me, O Sovereign LORD of Heaven's Armies.*

PSALM 69:6 NLT

We are called by God to shine our lights as brightly as we can. Many times, we fall short, then run and hide, ashamed that we've given God a bad name. How can we go on calling ourselves Christians when our choices seem to contradict that?

Time to admit the hard truth: We're human. We make mistakes. But we can't let them define us. Instead of slinking off into the shadows when we fall short, we must fall on God's grace and mercy, then allow Him to use our stories (even the not-so-flattering parts) as part of our testimony.

God can use you, you know. Even if you've messed up. And while He doesn't encourage a rebellious lifestyle, He is more than able to point you in the right direction and set your feet on a straight path once again so that your light can go on shining in this dark world.

*Father, I want to be the best example I can possibly be so that
others will be drawn to You. Today I ask for Your forgiveness
for the times that I've inadvertently led people in the wrong
direction or left a sour taste in their mouths. May my life
be a reflection of Your heart for Your people, Lord. Amen.*

WHERE VALUE IS FOUND

"What is the price of five sparrows—two copper coins?
Yet God does not forget a single one of them. And the very
hairs on your head are all numbered. So don't be afraid;
you are more valuable to God than a whole flock of sparrows."

LUKE 12:6-7 NLT

Even as our Savior was being paraded into Jerusalem, heralded with cheers and shouts, He knew the reality: those same people would turn on Him and betray Him. In less than a week, He would be devalued in their sight.

Perhaps you know how it feels to be devalued. Maybe you think you're not worth much. People don't include you. They don't consider your feelings. They push you to the outer fringes. Look to Jesus as an example of how to respond. Even in the face of His worst accusers, He found His value in His Father.

God looks at you with eyes of love. You're His precious child, worth more than a flock of sparrows. He numbers every hair on your head and sees you as priceless—so much so that He gave His only Son to die in your place.

Lord, as I look forward to Easter, may Your sacrifice on the cross serve as a vivid reminder that I, Your child, am valuable to You. You haven't forgotten me! I am Your beloved, more valuable than I'll ever be able to comprehend. Thank You for the reminder that I matter, Lord. Amen.

PREPARING FOR THE MIRACLE

Then Joshua told the people, "Purify yourselves,
for tomorrow the LORD will do great wonders among you."

JOSHUA 3:5 NLT

I f you knew that God was going to perform a miracle for you tomorrow. . .what would you do differently today? If you were convinced He was about to move on your behalf, would it change your actions, your heart, or your mind? If so, in what ways?

The Israelites were called to purify themselves in preparation for God's great wonders. They were to focus on their hearts, even before the miracle occurred. This getting-ready-to-receive process was a critical part of the equation and provided ample opportunity to trust in the unseen.

When you think of preparing your heart to receive a miracle, what comes to mind? How would you begin the purification process? Today, as you pray for God's miraculous power to be revealed, ask Him to show you how to prepare. Then set yourself apart, purified, ready to receive His abundant blessings.

I often beg for miracles, Lord, without committing myself to
the process. I want to see You come through for me, but I don't
always want to put in the hard work of purifying myself in order
to pave the way. Today I choose to trust You, even in the fire.
I give myself over to the purification process, Lord, so that I
become a clean vessel, ready to be used in miraculous ways! Amen.

BE MAGNIFIED!

I will praise the name of God with a song,
and will magnify him with thanksgiving.

PSALM 69:30 KJV

Have you ever looked into a magnifying mirror? It can be rather shocking! It's one thing to see your image; another altogether to see every pore, wrinkle, and freckle up close. There are certain things that seem worse when enlarged.

Our holy and magnificent God, on the other hand, deserves to be magnified. He is worthy of our praise. When we see Him through the lens of His Word, we don't find anything ugly or perverse. Indeed, when we examine Him in detail, we find a loving, patient Father who cares about His children, no matter their sinful state. How wonderful He is!

Today, spend some time magnifying the King of kings and Lord of lords. Proclaim His majesty. Exalt in His goodness. Adore Him with a song. Give Him your highest praise, for He, alone, is worthy.

Father, how I love to magnify the things I care about. People, events, sports teams. . . I'm great at drawing attention to the things that matter to me. May I never forget to magnify You, Lord! May I sing Your praises at every turn. May I praise Your Name with each passing day. You are worthy of my praise, Father! Amen.

SPREADING HIS FAME

But they said to Joshua, "We are your servants." And Joshua
said to them, "Who are you, and where do you come from?"
So they said to him: "From a very far country your servants
have come, because of the name of the Lord your God; for
we have heard of His fame, and all that He did in Egypt."

JOSHUA 9:8-9 NKJV

If you were asked to make a list of your favorite actors, whose names would you include? If you were instructed to list the professional sports teams that set your heart racing, which teams would you list? If you were given the task of naming the people you most admire, who would come to mind first?

The world is filled with many people who've been made famous because of their talents and abilities. Some are to be admired; others set a poorer example. While we're quick to sing the praises of the celebrities we adore, we're often less willing to shout our praises for the Lord quite as loudly.

May we make a commitment to spread God's fame, that all might be drawn to Him!

Lord, this scripture excites me! I want to be so passionate about You, so ready to share stories of what You've done in my life, that people will hear of Your great fame and seek You out. You're the Creator of the Universe, the One we should all admire most of all. Take Your rightful place in our hearts, Father. Amen.

REMARKABLE GROWTH

Then He said, "What is the kingdom of God like? And to what shall I compare it? It is like a mustard seed, which a man took and put in his garden; and it grew and became a large tree, and the birds of the air nested in its branches."

Luke 13:18-19 NKJV

A mustard seed is a tiny thing—so small that you might look right past it and not see it at all. And yet, from that tiny seed grows a magnificent tree. The same is true with our faith. God can take even the smallest grain of faith and use it to bring about the greatest miracles. Mountains can be moved. Rivers crossed. Addictions broken. Brokenness healed. Mourning lifted.

What are you believing God for today? Does your faith feel small? Trust Him, even in your weakest moments, to accomplish great things. He has the ability to take the smallest thing and grow it beyond your wildest imagination. Best of all, He always carries through on His promises. If He said it, He will most certainly do it.

I have to admit it, Lord, I sometimes doubt the process. I see a tiny mustard seed and have a hard time imagining it blossoming into a magnificent tree. Today, Father, I place every "small" thing into Your hands and trust You will bring all things to fruition in my life. You're growing me into a mighty woman and I choose to trust You during the process. Amen.

THE NARROW GATE

And He went through the cities and villages, teaching, and journeying toward Jerusalem. Then one said to Him, "Lord, are there few who are saved?" And He said to them, "Strive to enter through the narrow gate, for many, I say to you, will seek to enter and will not be able."

LUKE 13:22-24 NKJV

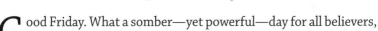

G ood Friday. What a somber—yet powerful—day for all believers, the day we're forced to look, eyes wide open, at the cross. We examine our Savior's body, hanging there. We hear His cries, see the blood spill from His side, imagine His final breath.

When we fully examine Jesus' great sacrifice, we must ask: "Why?" Why would He do all of that for us? Why not choose some other way?

God's plan to redeem humankind was driven by grace. He longs for all to know Him. But it begins and ends at the cross. To inherit eternal life, we must "enter through the narrow gate" which means we have to apply the spilled blood to our lives. We have to accept this gift and respond to it. What a perfect day to do just that!

Lord, I love the story of Good Friday for it reminds me of Your great sacrifice on my behalf. In exchange, You've asked for my heart, my commitment to follow after You. It's not always easy to walk the narrow road, Jesus, which You so beautifully demonstrated as You carried the cross toward Calvary. I'm forever grateful. Amen.

NEVER FORSAKEN

*O God, You have taught me from my youth; and to this day I declare
Your wondrous works. Now also when I am old and grayheaded,
O God, do not forsake me, until I declare Your strength to this
generation, Your power to everyone who is to come.*

PSALM 71: 17-18 NKJV

Have you ever known the pain of betrayal? Ever been badly hurt by someone who promised to stick by you, no matter what? Losing a friend can be gut-wrenching. No one enters a relationship hoping to be abandoned. This sort of heartache can linger and cause issues years after-the-fact.

No matter how badly broken your heart has been in the past, you can experience healing and wholeness again. Give that broken heart to the Lord and watch Him miraculously ease your pain. Best of all, He will stick close to you. In fact, He promises to never leave you. No rejection. No betrayal. No abandonment. When you enter a relationship with the Lord, it's for eternity. Now, that's a friendship worth having!

*You've always stuck with me, Lord, even when I didn't deserve it.
From the day I drew my first breath on planet Earth until this very
moment, You've been right there, gently guiding me and giving me
strength to overcome every obstacle. You've never left my side,
Father, and You never will. I can trust in You, Lord. Amen.*

WORTHY OF PRAISE

I will praise you with the harp for your faithfulness, my God;
I will sing praise to you with the lyre, Holy One of Israel.

PSALM 71:22 NIV

Easter Sunday is truly the most glorious day of the year for the believer. Just three days after witnessing the death of the Savior, a miracle that defies explanation—Jesus burst forth from the tomb. Resurrection!

Have you ever examined the word *resurrection*? To be resurrected means you're reborn, restored to life. It's a miraculous do-over, a second chance at life, an opportunity to try again.

Jesus was literally restored to life on Easter Sunday, and He offers restoration to us, as well. No matter what broken places you might be facing in your life at this very moment, our risen Savior can restore. Broken marriage? He can fix it. Broken heart? He's the best heart surgeon on the planet. Broken relationships? He's the mender of fences.

A God who restores is a God who can be trusted. And because of His great faithfulness, He is worthy to be praised! Lift your voice in grateful chorus! "Lord, You are worthy!"

What a glorious story, Lord! You came bursting forth from the grave, just as You said You would. Your story didn't end in death—for Yourself or for me. Easter is a message of Your faithfulness. I can trust in the one who gave His all for me. Thank You for Your resurrection power, Jesus! Amen.

LITTLE LOST SHEEP

"Suppose one of you has a hundred sheep and loses one of them. Doesn't he leave the ninety-nine in the open country and go after the lost sheep until he finds it? And when he finds it, he joyfully puts it on his shoulders and goes home. Then he calls his friends and neighbors together and says, 'Rejoice with me; I have found my lost sheep.'"

LUKE 15:3-6 NIV

I f you've ever misplaced your keys or lost something more valuable, then you know what it is to panic. You scour the house and don't give up looking until you find it.

In many ways, that's what God did for us. When we wandered from the fold—eager to do our own thing—He came looking for us. With His great love, He pursued us. And He didn't give up until He found us once again.

Isn't it remarkable to realize the God of the universe loves and cares enough about you to search for you? And when He finds you, a celebration takes place! Like a daddy lifting a child to his shoulders, God raises you up and carries you home again. Talk about a loving Papa!

Lord, You kept searching until You found me. . .and I'm so grateful! You brought me back home, brushed the dust from my back, and even threw a party in my honor! What an amazing shepherd You are! Amen.

PROMISES FULFILLED

*Not one of all the LORD's good promises
to Israel failed; every one was fulfilled.*

JOSHUA 21:45 NIV

Have you ever been lied to? Ever been on the end of a broken promise? There's nothing worse than waiting for someone to carry through. . .only to find they never planned to. The disappointment is like a knife to the heart, especially coming from one you trusted.

Perhaps you've been on the opposite end of the story. Maybe you made promises to someone—a child, a spouse, a friend—and then went back on your word. Now you're regretting the pain you caused and you're wondering how to make things right again.

Thank goodness, God isn't like us. He doesn't make promises and then break them. If He said it, He will carry through. You won't have to wonder if He will make good on His promises to you. He is who He says He is and He'll do what He says He'll do.

Today, look at several of the promises in God's Word. Put your name in each sentence, personalizing each promise. Then claim it as your own and watch in wonder as God brings every one of them to pass in your life.

*Lord, You carry through on every promise. If You speak something
in Your Word, You'll fulfill it. Knowing You're a promise-keeper
strengthens my faith and increases my trust in each new situation.
How good You are, my faithful God! Amen.*

FAITHFUL IN THE LITTLE THINGS

"If you are faithful in little things, you will be faithful in large ones. But if you are dishonest in little things, you won't be honest with greater responsibilities. And if you are untrustworthy about worldly wealth, who will trust you with the true riches of heaven? And if you are not faithful with other people's things, why should you be trusted with things of your own?"

LUKE 16:10-12 NLT

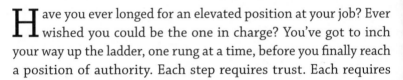

Have you ever longed for an elevated position at your job? Ever wished you could be the one in charge? You've got to inch your way up the ladder, one rung at a time, before you finally reach a position of authority. Each step requires trust. Each requires faithfulness.

God is watching as you take care of the details along the way. He's watching your heart, double-checking your attitude. He's smiling as you handle each task with a smile. You are proving your trustworthiness with every step you take.

Don't fret over whether or not you'll be placed in charge of the big things. For now, thank God for the small ones. . .and keep going.

Lord, You're teaching me to be faithful, as You are faithful. You've given me opportunity after opportunity with the small things, so that You can make sure I'm ready to handle the bigger things. Lord, may I be found trustworthy! I'm learning from Your example. May I be a ready student. Amen.

A SLIPPERY PATH

*Then I went into your sanctuary, O God, and I finally understood
the destiny of the wicked. Truly, you put them on a slippery
path and send them sliding over the cliff to destruction.*

PSALM 73:17-18 NLT

Psalm 73 is truly one of the most fascinating chapters in the Bible. It's a lament from a frustrated believer who can't seem to get over the fact that the wicked often thrive while he, the faithful, suffers.

Maybe you've sung this lament a few times yourself. Perhaps you've watched as ungodly acquaintances received riches, fame, or positions of power while you got tossed aside. Maybe you've cried out to God, "It's not fair!"

Like the author of this psalm, it's time to come to grips with reality. The ungodly might thrive during this lifetime, but unless they bow the knee to Christ, they won't spend eternity with Him. Instead of fretting over all they have during their stay on Earth, why not spend your time making sure they have the most important thing—a relationship with the King of kings that will carry them all the way to heaven.

*Life feels so unfair at times, Lord. People who disobey and
dishonor You often seem to have everything—wealth, fame,
relationships. It makes no sense. But You're teaching me,
Father, that many are on a slippery slope. They're headed for
destruction. Instead of envying them, remind me to intercede
on their behalf, that they might come to know You. Amen.*

A WOMAN OF WISDOM

*Deborah, the wife of Lappidoth, was a prophet who was judging
Israel at that time. She would sit under the Palm of Deborah,
between Ramah and Bethel in the hill country of Ephraim,
and the Israelites would go to her for judgment.*

JUDGES 4:4-5 NLT

Deborah served as a judge in Israel, a very unusual position for a woman of her day. She had a particular spot in the hill country of Ephraim, where she set up shop under a palm. People would come to her, share a story or concern, then ask for her wisdom and judgment on the matter. She was a godly woman who shared as the Lord led.

Are you the sort of person that others come to for wisdom? Or do you often seek out a friend or loved one who happens to have a double-dose? It's always a good idea to surround yourself with people who are wise.

The best way to obtain wisdom is to seek God's opinion on a matter. Don't make rash decisions. Listen carefully and follow as He leads. For the very best sort of guidance is the kind that comes straight from the heart of God.

*Lord, I want to be a woman of great wisdom, so tuned in to
Your Word, heart, and voice, that I make a difference in the
lives of others. I want to be a Deborah for my generation, Father.
Increase my wisdom that I might lead others to You. Amen.*

TENACITY

*Then Jesus told his disciples a parable to show
them that they should always pray and not give up.*

How many times have you thrown your arms up in the air and shouted to the heavens, "That's it! I quit!" Life gives us many opportunities to give up. When we feel defeated, or we're facing what feels like impossible odds, it's easier to slink away than to face the music.

Oh, but aren't you glad that God didn't give up on You? He never once looked at you and thought you were too much work. Instead, He saw you as a possibility, not an impossibility. Even when the musical notes on the page of your life were in chaos, He turned them into a beautiful symphony.

That's how you need to look at the situations in front of you, even now. They're not impossible. Keep on keeping on. Don't give up. God has big plans, and you don't want to quit when you're so close to victory! So, bend the knee. Pray. Then never ever give up.

Lord, in those moments when I feel like giving up, please strengthen my resolve. Deepen my trust in You and in Your Word. I don't want to be one who is driven by emotions. Help me to dig my heels in, square my shoulders, look fear in the face, and say, "I'll keep going, in Jesus' name!" Amen!

RECEPTIVE

*And Jesus said, "All right, receive your sight! Your faith
has healed you." Instantly the man could see, and he followed
Jesus, praising God. And all who saw it praised God, too.*

Luke 18:42-43 nlt

*R*eceive. What an interesting word. When we're handed a gift, we must take it into our hands, to receive it. The same is true when it comes to the things of God. He stands ready to answer our prayers, but asks, "Are you ready?" When we answer with a triumphant, "Yes!" He responds with the words: "Then, receive!"

How do we get into "receptive" mode? What role do we play? We must empty our hands of anything we've been holding on to, then lift them, palms extended, to Him. We have to set our hearts and mind on Him, not on the gifts He's pouring out. Most of all, we have to praise Him—to have a heart of thanksgiving—even before the gifts arrive.

What are you waiting on today? Prepare your heart. Put a song of praise on your lips. Get ready to receive from on high.

*A receptive heart is a trusting heart, Lord! That's the kind of heart I
want to have. May I be so ready, so filled with anticipation of what
You're about to do, that my heart is wide open to the miraculous.
I can't wait to see what You have in store, Father! Amen.*

STILL IN PURSUIT

*When Gideon came to the Jordan, he and the three hundred men
who were with him crossed over, exhausted but still in pursuit.*

JUDGES 8:4 NKJV

"Exhausted but still in pursuit." Ponder those words for a moment. Surely you've been in that position too—so weary from life's battles that you felt you couldn't put one foot in front of the other. But how can you stop when the battle continues to rage around you? To do so would surely mean death, not just for you, but the ones you're attempting to protect, as well.

There's nothing fun about fighting, at least not after that first tight-fisted punch. Eventually, you grow so weary you want to give up. But today God is reminding you that you must stand firm. The enemy of your soul would love nothing more than to see you quit. Don't.

Giving up and giving in are not in your vocabulary as a believer. God will give you all you need to keep going. Just ask Him. Whisper a prayer, then accept His invigorating power. Brace yourself and get ready to pursue the enemy so the battle can be won.

*What a marvelous reminder, Lord! Even when I'm weary
(and it happens a lot), I don't have to give up. My pursuit of You
can carry on, even on the most exhausting day. May I follow
hard after You, Father, that the battle might be won. Amen.*

A FRESH START

And the children of Israel said to the LORD, "We have sinned!
Do to us whatever seems best to You; only deliver us this day, we pray."
So they put away the foreign gods from among them and served the
LORD. And His soul could no longer endure the misery of Israel.

JUDGES 10:15-16 NKJV

It would be impossible to count the number of times the Israelites turned their backs on God and did their own thing. Time and time again they crawled back to God, begging for mercy. And though He warned them of their transgressions, God still never lost His love for His children.

Not much has changed over the years, has it? Though we've been offered grace in abundance, we often do our own thing. We wander away, then crawl back, begging for forgiveness and mercy. God is good enough to show us where we got off-track, but He never slam-dunks us. Instead, He brushes us off and puts us on the right path again. He gives us a fresh start.

What area of your life needs a fresh start today? Even if you've painted yourself into a corner, even if your troubles are self-inflicted, cry out to God. In His mercy, He will answer and deliver you once again.

You are a God of fresh starts. Oh, how grateful I am, Lord!
I lay myself at Your feet and ask for mercy, time and time again.
You brush me off, extend grace, and send me on my way,
as if it never happened. What a gracious Father You are! Amen.

GOD AS *SHOPET*

It is God alone who judges;
he decides who will rise and who will fall.

PSALM 75:7 NLT

Judging the worthiness of others is something we tend to do automatically, naturally. Yet God, the supreme *Shopet* or Judge, wants us to take a supernatural point of view of things, adopt an otherworldly attitude.

Jephthah, the son of a prostitute, was chased off his father's land and away from his inheritance by his half-brothers because they deemed him unworthy of being part of their family. Yet later, Jephthah became one of God's judges of Israel. He knew who the true judge was. In his attempts to settle a dispute, he told an Ammonite king, "The LORD is the judge who will decide today whether Israel or Ammon is right" (Judges 11:27 GW).

In Luke 20, the leading priests and teachers would have chased the unwanted Jesus off, if they could have figured out how. They judged Him as a blasphemer, a rebel, a usurper. Instead of kissing Him as God's Son, they wanted to kill Him.

Who are you deeming as unworthy? In what ways are you making yourself the ultimate judge of situations and people in your life? Why not adopt the supernatural attitude or perspective that God alone is judge?

Lord, I know You're the one who sees beyond all
appearances and preconceived beliefs. Help me trust
You as the ultimate Judge. To leave all things and people
to Your holy discernment—not mine. Be my Shopet.

OPEN TO RECEIVE

And the Angel of the LORD appeared to the woman and
said to her, "Indeed now, you are barren and have borne
no children, but you shall conceive and bear a son." . . .
And the Angel of God came to the woman again as she was
sitting in the field; but Manoah her husband was not with her.

JUDGES 13:3, 9 NKJV

God knows what's going on in the lives of His people. In this story of a nameless woman, known only as Samson's mother or Manoah's wife, God appears. He states her case and gives her a promise. Although she knows neither this Angel's origin or name, she recognizes Him as a Man of God and relays His promise to her husband. But Manoah needs verification from the Angel Himself—and later gets it.

God knows who you are and what you desire. When that desire fits in with His plans for you, He cannot help but deliver. Your job is to allow Him an opening so that you can receive His message. That means spending time alone, waiting for Him to come, to speak. And then when He does speak, you are to have no doubts but to trust God will do what He has promised. "So the woman bore a son and called his name Samson. . .and the LORD blessed him" (Judges 13:24 NKJV).

Lord, come to me now. I am open to receive. Speak into my life.

TRUSTING TO THE END

"Every detail of your body and soul—even the hairs of your head!—is in my care; nothing of you will be lost. Staying with it—that's what is required. Stay with it to the end. You won't be sorry; you'll be saved."

LUKE 21:18-19 MSG

Today's reading (Luke 21:1-19) begins with a poor widow having so much trust in God that she puts all she has to live on into the collection plate. Although her offering was much less in actual amount than what the rich people were willing to contribute, it was a much bigger percentage of what she possessed in total. As Jesus says, the widow "gave her all!" (Luke 21:4 MSG).

In the verses that follow, Jesus tells His disciples that no matter what's happening in the world—famine, war, earthquake, betrayals, persecution—they aren't to worry. For this world can take nothing from them—as long as they trust in God, His promises, and His love. He will never leave them.

From first to last, it all comes down to a matter of giving God your all and trusting in God for everything, "every detail," to the very end. For that is how you will "win the true life of your souls" (Luke 21:19 AMPC).

Jesus, I give You my all and leave everything, every detail, in Your hands. I trust You, knowing that only in You will I find and win the true life.

ONE THING

The sky and the earth (the universe, the world)
will pass away, but My words will not pass away.

LUKE 21:33 AMPC

There is one thing we can truly trust, one thing we can count on with all our heart, soul, strength, and mind: the Word of God. It tells us what to do, how to walk, run, fly, soar to the One who is and always will be. It teaches us how to treat each other and ourselves. It gives us guidance, a pathway to the divine authority, the One who knows who we are and what our lives are to be.

In the days of the book of Judges, "there was no king in Israel; every man did what was right in his own eyes" (Judges 17:6 AMPC). But we who live in the days after Jesus know there is a divine King. And He has a good word for us every day, one we can open and read to discover what is right in *His* eyes and do as *He* bids. Our job is to look, to seek that word. To trust it. To follow it. For that word is something that will never pass away.

Read the Word and get the vision you need to do what is right in God's eyes.

Thank You, Lord, for the gift of Your Word, for the
wisdom that lights my path and helps me to follow You.

JUST AS HE SAID

*I will [earnestly] recall the deeds of the Lord; yes, I will [earnestly]
remember the wonders [You performed for our fathers] of old.*

PSALM 77:11 AMPC

When we lack clear direction, have doubts as to what awaits us, we can think back to a time when God has done something so beyond what we could've imagined, pulling us out of our quandary and setting our feet down in a good, secure place.

In Jesus' last days, the disciples were unsure about where to go to prepare the Passover meal for Jesus. But He told them exactly what would happen, who they would meet, and what they should do and say. Taking Him at His word, "they went and found it [just] as He had said to them" (Luke 22:13 AMPC).

Instead of worrying, go to God. Remember what He has done, the wonders He has performed in the past. Know that He will give you the information you need. And that when you take Him at His word, you'll be sure to find things just as He said you would.

*Lord, I don't know what to do, but I know where to turn. I remember
the deeds You have done, the wonders You have worked in my life
in the past. And I go forth assured You will show me the path
to take and that things will happen just as You say.*

GOD'S WILL AND WAY

*He walked away, about a stone's throw, and knelt down and
prayed, "Father, if you are willing, please take this cup of
suffering away from me. Yet I want your will to be done, not mine."
Then an angel from heaven appeared and strengthened him.*

LUKE 22:41-43 NLT

There may be times of hardship in our lives. Times when things
don't go the way we think they should. But when we desire God's
will above our own, we can trust Him to help us—no matter what.
And when we do, we know He'll strengthen us by supernatural means.

Throughout His story, God has strengthened and directed those
who are following His will. Regarding the Exodus, the psalmist wrote,
"Your road led through the sea, your pathway through the mighty
waters—a pathway no one knew was there! You led your people
along that road like a flock of sheep, with Moses and Aaron as their
shepherds" (Psalm 77:19-20 NLT).

Trust the will of your Good Shepherd, the one who knows best.
Not only will He send you supernatural aid, He'll reveal a pathway
no one knew existed!

*I'm down on my knees, Lord. You know how I'd like this to work out.
But I want to be walking in Your will, not mine. So strengthen me,
Lord, for what lies ahead. I'm trusting that You know best. Send me
supernatural aid and open a door I'm not seeing! In Jesus' name, amen.*

CONSTANT COMPANION

Ruth replied, "Don't ask me to leave you and turn back.
Wherever you go, I will go; wherever you live, I will live.
Your people will be my people, and your God will be my God."
RUTH 1:16 NLT

Ruth's mother-in-law Naomi had seen hardship. During a famine, Naomi, her husband, and two sons had left Bethlehem for Moab. There they found food and the sons' wives. But ten years later, both husband and sons died.

Naomi, heading back home to a now-fruitful Judah, tried to send her two daughters-in-law back to their homes. But one, Ruth (which means "companion"), refused to leave Naomi's side. When they together reached Bethlehem, Ruth told the townswomen, "Don't call me Naomi [meaning "pleasant"]. . . . Instead, call me Mara [meaning "bitter"], for the Almighty has made life very bitter for me. I went away full, but the LORD has brought me home empty" (Ruth 1:20-21 NLT).

Naomi, focused on the past and her lack, missed seeing the possibility of the future *and* what she actually had in the present—Ruth, a daughter-in-law through whom Naomi's life would be (and was already) richly blessed. She'd stopped trusting God to help her through the good and bad—*and* seeing that He works for her benefit through both!

Know God is always with you. He'll never leave you, in good times or bad.

Thank You, God, for being my constant
companion, always seeking my good.

ENTRUST AND REMEMBER

Jesus cried out in a loud voice, "Father, into your hands I entrust my spirit." . . . Then the women remembered what Jesus had told them.

LUKE 23:46, 24:8 GW

Jesus knew how His life was going to play out. He'd already told His followers how He'd fulfill the prophecies. And now, during His most extreme trial, hanging upon the cross, He publicly entrusted His Father with His human spirit.

Afterward, His grief-stricken female followers embarked upon the societal routine prompted by the death of a loved one. "The women who had come with Jesus from Galilee. . .observed the tomb and how his body was laid in it. Then they went back to the city and prepared spices and perfumes. But on the day of rest–a holy day, they rested according to the commandent" (Luke 23:55-56 GW). The next day they went back to the tomb to complete the burial ritual but instead of finding Jesus, they stumbled upon two angels. Terrified, they bowed down and heard the angels say their Savior had risen, just as He said He would. Then they remembered His words and ran to tell the others.

What would your life be like if every morning you entrusted your spirit to God? What would happen if, in the midst of panic—or preferably before you got to that point—you remembered God's words of comfort, prophecy, hope, and peace?

Lord, today, I entrust my spirit, putting it into Your hands, remembering Your words of comfort, prophecy, hope, and peace.

THE SOLID *TSUR* ("ROCK")

Hannah prayed out loud, "My heart finds joy in the LORD.
My head is lifted to the LORD. My mouth mocks my enemies.
I rejoice because you saved me. There is no one holy like the LORD.
There is no one but you, O LORD. There is no Rock like our God."

1 SAMUEL 2:1-2 GW

Because she was barren, Hannah was mercilessly teased by her husband Elkanah's second and amazingly fruitful wife Peninnah. One day while at the temple, "Though [Hannah] was resentful, she prayed to the LORD while she cried. She made this vow, 'LORD. . .if you will look at my misery, remember me, and give me a boy, then I will give him to you for as long as he lives'" (1 Samuel 1:10-11 GW).

God granted Hannah's request and she became pregnant with Samuel. Years later, when she dropped the weaned Samuel off at the temple, she picked up the words of praise you find above, claiming: "There is *Tsur* like our *Elohim*," no Rock like our God. She later gave birth to three sons and two daughters.

Where do you go when you feel barren, resentful, lost, depressed? Be like Hannah. Go to God. Pour out your heart to the solid Rock, trusting He will give you the miracle you need. Then, go back and praise Him. When you do, you will become even more fruitful.

I'm crying out to You, Tsur, my solid Rock.

SPEAK, WAIT, HEAR

*Eli said to Samuel, "Go, lie down; and it shall be, if He calls you,
that you must say, 'Speak, LORD, for Your servant hears.'"
So Samuel went and lay down in his place.*

1 SAMUEL 3:9 NKJV

In the Old Testament, God dwelled in the temple and spoke to specific people at specific times. But in the New Testament, the Word took on flesh. It began to live among God's people. It took the form of a human being called Jesus. John wrote, "And the Word (Christ) became flesh (human, incarnate) and tabernacled (fixed His tent of flesh, lived awhile) among us; and we [actually] saw His glory (His honor, His majesty)" (1:14 AMPC).

Gone are the days when we have to travel to a church, temple, or tabernacle, to speak to the one who was, is, and always will be. For having accepted Christ, God now dwells within us, leading us, guiding us, hearing us. But are we listening?

You may know who God is, but have you ever heard Him speak into your life? If you have, you know how amazingly wonderful that can be. Ask God to speak through His Word. Let Him know you're listening. Trust that He is within you, around you, beside you. Speak, and then wait quietly and patiently until you get a response, until you see the light He is so longing to give.

Speak to me, Lord. I'm waiting to hear Your sweet voice.

RE-TURNING

Then Samuel said to all the people of Israel, "If you want to return to the LORD with all your hearts, get rid of your foreign gods and your images of Ashtoreth. Turn your hearts to the LORD and obey him alone; then he will rescue you from the Philistines."

1 SAMUEL 7:3 NLT

Sometimes our relationship with God is a little frayed. That's when we need to look at our surroundings, the things that may be standing between us and Him.

The judge, priest, and prophet Samuel gave God's people three points to consider to find their way back to God. The first was to get rid of their foreign gods and images. The second was to turn back to God with all their hearts. The third was to serve and obey Him alone. Then and only then would God come to their rescue.

Consider reviewing where you are with God, using these three points. What things or images—TV, Internet, money, status symbols, icons, etc.—are you trusting to save you other than God? With how much of your whole heart are you turning to Him, seeking His presence? Who or what are you obeying or serving—societal norms, family mores, religious traditions—other than God?

Once you wholeheartedly turn to the true God, obeying Him alone, you will find God's "mighty voice" (1 Samuel 7:10 NLT) thundering into your life and yourself being rescued.

*I'm wholeheartedly re-turning to
You and You alone, Lord. Rescue me.*

TENDER HEART, TRUSTING HOPE

The wine supply ran out during the festivities, so Jesus'
mother told him, "They have no more wine." "Dear woman,
that's not our problem," Jesus replied. "My time has not yet come."
But his mother told the servants, "Do whatever he tells you."

JOHN 2:3-5 NLT

Jesus and His mother Mary, along with the disciples, were enjoying a wedding feast in Cana. At some point in the festivities, Mary notices their hosts are running out of wine. Having a tender heart and knowing her Son is here to serve, Mary points this need out to Jesus who, up to this point, has kept His divine power hidden.

At first, it sounds as if Jesus intends to put the problem off. But Mary remains undeterred and filled with trusting hope that her Son will do something to remedy the situation. And He does, turning water into wine.

On this Mother's Day, remember Mary. When your heart is touched by a need—including your own—simply point it out to Jesus. But don't tell Him how and when to fix it! Instead, know that He will remedy the circumstance and meet the need in His own time. Your only role is to allow it to rest in His hands, remind the parties concerned to do whatever He tells them, and then watch God work a miracle.

Lord, give me the tender heart and trusting
hope of Mary. In Jesus' name, amen.

LEADING A LAMB TO SAFETY

*But [God] led His own people forth like sheep and guided
them [with a shepherd's care] like a flock in the wilderness.
And He led them on safely and in confident trust, so that
they feared not; but the sea overwhelmed their enemies.*

PSALM 78:52-53 AMPC

Some days you may feel as if you are being squeezed, wrung out, hung out to dry. You mind is so scattered, your being so anxious, that no solutions come to mind. Any relief on the horizon appears distant, at best. It seems as if you have one problem coming from behind and nothing but a nameless dark out in front of you, keeping you from moving forward.

This is when it's good to remember God. How He led His people to safety over and over again. When you remember the plagues of Egypt, the parting of the Red Sea, the water gushing from a rock in the wilderness, the manna coming down from heaven, the water turned into wine, the waking and walking of the dead, the calming of a storm, then you realize you're safe in God's hands. You can move forward in confident trust. You can have the courage you need to let God shepherd you out of your wilderness and into His light.

*I'm looking to You for all, Lord, my Shepherd, confidently
trusting You to show me the way through this
wilderness, to lead this lamb to safety.*

STEP BACK, STAND STILL

*"Now then, stand still and see this great thing
the LORD is about to do before your eyes!"*

1 SAMUEL 12:16 NIV

A million potential solutions are ricocheting around in your mind. You finally pick one, then another, but both fall short of the need. You're biting your lip, chewing your nails, then take action once again, doing all you feel you can in the circumstances. But still things aren't exactly right, it seems.

Here's where you might want to ask yourself a few questions. Have you talked to God? Have you brought Him into the situation, told Him all the particulars? Have you given Him any room at all in which to work? Or have you only done so up to a certain point, and then given up? Perhaps you've determined that you *do* have the answer after all and are taking the proverbial bull by the horns once more?

There are times when God asks you to do some things, when He needs your hands, feet, and mind in a situation. But there are also times when He wants you to just stand back and be still. Give Him time and space. Trust and rest in Him. And then watch and see the fantastic thing He's about to do—right before your eyes! In other words, don't just do something—stand there!

*Lord, I don't know what to do, but I know You do.
Help me step back, stand still, and watch You work.*

NOTHING CAN HINDER

Jonathan said to his young armor-bearer, "Come, let's
go over to the outpost of those uncircumcised men.
Perhaps the LORD will act in our behalf. Nothing can hinder
the LORD from saving, whether by many or by few."

1 SAMUEL 14:6 NIV

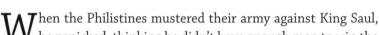

When the Philistines mustered their army against King Saul, he panicked, thinking he didn't have enough men to win the battle. So to win God's favor, he made an unauthorized offering to God (see 1 Samuel 13:5-16). Such panicked doings led to Saul's eventually losing the kingdom, all because he trusted earthly assets rather than God.

But in the next chapter, Saul's son Jonathan, trusting in God's power and presence, defeated twenty Philistines with only his armor-bearer by his side and caused the rest of the enemy army to flee in confusion. In fact, Jonathan's testimony of faith in God above prompted his armor-bearer to have faith in Jonathan himself, as the boy told him, "Do all that you have in mind. . . . Go ahead; I am with you heart and soul" (1 Samuel 14:7 NIV).

God wants you to have the faith of Jonathan. When you're facing a challenge, don't be concerned about the numbers or what you might have on hand. Instead, go forward trusting God, knowing nothing will hinder His power when He's willing to act on your behalf.

I'm trusting You, Lord, knowing nothing can
hinder Your power—in heaven or on earth.

GO IN PEACE

The king's officer pleaded with Him, Sir, do come down at once before my little child is dead! Jesus answered him, Go in peace; your son will live! And the man put his trust in what Jesus said and started home.

John 4:49-50 ampc

A Roman official's son was near death. So the officer approached Jesus and begged Him to come home with him so He could put his hands on the child and heal him. But Jesus told the king's man not to be anxious, to go home in peace, because his son would indeed live.

At that very moment, the officer took Jesus at His word. He believed what He said was reality. *He trusted Him.* And so the king's man started back home. On his way there, his servants came to tell him the boy had indeed recovered—at the same moment that Jesus had told the man, "Go in peace; your son will live!"

Put no limits on what Jesus and His word can do in your life. There's no amount of time or space He cannot reach across with His power. Believe in His words, that things are indeed, just as He says they are. Trust what He tells you, then go in peace, knowing His truth is yours.

Lord, with You there are no limits. You can reach across time and space. I believe and trust in what You say. I go in peace, knowing Your truths are my truths.

A WOMAN AFTER GOD'S OWN HEART

David said, The Lord Who delivered me out of the paw of the lion and out of the paw of the bear, He will deliver me out of the hand of this Philistine. And Saul said to David, Go, and the Lord be with you!

1 SAMUEL 17:37 AMPC

David, the shepherd-boy turned king, proved himself a champion over and over again. Why? Because he never lost sight of who God was—and who he himself was in the eyes of God. David was a man after God's own heart, wanting only what God wanted and trusting in Him with his whole being.

That desire and trust is what enabled David to turn away from his brother's discouraging remarks. His belief in God's power is what kept him out of the armor with which Saul attempted to outfit him. His memory of how God had worked in the past is what gave him the courage to face Goliath in the present. His understanding the battle was God's and God would rescue him once more is what gave him the ultimate victory (see 1 Samuel 17:47).

Armed with this same amount of trust in and knowledge of God, you too may call yourself a woman after God's own heart and face your challenges in His power.

Because I trust You, Lord, and want what You want for my life, I'm ready—just as I am—to take on all challengers in Your name and power.

SUCCESSFUL IN EVERYTHING

David was successful wherever Saul sent him. Saul put him in charge of the fighting men. This pleased all the people, including Saul's officials. . . . He was successful in everything he undertook because the LORD was with him.

1 SAMUEL 18:5, 14 GW

What made David successful was not just that Yahweh—the God of all creation, the God of the Exodus, the God whose name was not to be spoken—was with him. What made him successful was that David was *conscious* of Yahweh being with him. Yahweh permeated his very being. David tapped into His wisdom, knowledge, and power. David stayed connected through peace time and battles. He wrote poems about Yahweh, how He was his shepherd, protecting him, leading him, anointing him, blessing him.

The same thing that made David successful will make you successful. No matter where you go, no matter where you are sent, be conscious of the God who walks with you. Consult His knowledge and wisdom. Spend time in prayer, asking for guidance and protection. Be assured that He is within, spreading His light upon your path. Trusting Him with all, you can then go forward in confidence, knowing He will make you successful for His name and glory.

I know, Lord, that with You in my heart, body, and soul, and Your wisdom filling my mind, I can do all things—for Your glory.

LAUNCHING OUT

Jesus said . . .It is I; be not afraid! [I Am; stop being frightened!] Then they were quite willing and glad for Him to come into the boat. And now the boat went at once to the land they had steered toward.

JOHN 6:20-21 AMPC

We're ready to launch out on a new venture. We wait for Jesus but He seems delayed. So we decide to set sail in darkness. Unable to see what lies fore or aft, fear begins to creep in. We begin looking furtively around, wondering what threat may be approaching. Suddenly the wind rises and our boat rocks from unforeseen waves. We begin to lose our bearings, frantically trying guide our little craft, the oars held tight in our white-knuckled grip as we roll with every dip and crest of the waves. The cold seawater ripping across our faces, we begin to doubt our vision. Feeling as if we're making no progress at all, discouragement adds to our fears and loss of direction.

Then a ghostly figure approaches our craft. We scream in surprise but then hear a soothing voice, "It's only Me! Don't be afraid!" Deliriously relieved, we let Jesus into our boat. The next thing you know, we arrive at the destination for which we'd been striving.

When trouble arises, trust that Christ sees your struggle and is on His way. Your job? To let Him into your boat.

Thank You, Lord, for helping me reach the shore to which I'm heading!

OPEN WIDE

You called in distress and I delivered you. . . O Israel, if you would
listen to Me! . . . I am the Lord your God, Who brought you up
out of the land of Egypt. Open your mouth wide and I will fill it.

PSALM 81:7, 8, 10 AMPC

God is longing for His people to trust in Him. Over and over again, He's rescued the Israelites from peril. And over and over again, they turn away after His deliverance. Thus, He laments, "If only they would listen to Me!"

God can do anything, rescue us from any situation. He'll walk with us through our wilderness. He'll carry us like a mother does a nursing child. Like a hen, He'll cover us with His feathers until we're able to go on again. And most fantastic of all, if we open ourselves all the way up to Him, He'll overflow us, so boundless are His blessings.

All it takes on your part is belief, listening to Jesus, your "Bread of Life" (John 3:35 AMPC) and living water (see John 4:10, 14), trusting in Him above all else, and relying on Him more than your family, other people, society, institutions, or yourself (your abilities, knowledge, intuition, gut-feeling, intelligence, money, etc.).

Jesus is all you need for true fulfillment. Just listen. And get ready to receive.

I'm listening, Lord, my bread of life and living water.
I'm open wide. Fill me to overflowing!

WHISPERS

David's conscience began bothering him because he had cut Saul's robe.
He said to his men, "The LORD forbid that I should do this. . . ."

1 SAMUEL 24:5-6 NLT

David and his men, on the run from King Saul, found themselves hiding in the dark recesses of a cave. It just happened to be the *same* cave that Saul later entered to relieve himself. That's when David's men whispered to him, "Now's your opportunity! . . . Today the Lord is telling you, 'I will certainly put your enemy into your power, to do with as you wish.' "

Creeping forward, David lifted a hand against the king by cutting off a piece of Saul's robe. That's when that little voice, a *psst* from God, crept into the recesses of David's mind, and he knew what he'd done was wrong. So, once Saul left the cave, David told Saul what had happened and that David would not harm him—even though the king had been relentlessly hunting David down, aiming to kill him.

Many are the times people you trust will whisper things in your ear, urging you to take some action. You may or may not listen. But if you do, and your conscience kicks in, stop. Listen for God's *psst*. Consider what He would have you do. And trust His voice above any other.

Help me keep my ears open for Your voice, Lord—
and follow Your whisper and urgings above all others.

GO DEEP

Be honest in your judgment and do not decide at a glance
(superficially and by appearances); but judge fairly and righteously.

JOHN 7:24 AMPC

We're quick to rush to judgement based on appearances. We see a lawyer and think, *Shyster*. We pass a homeless person on the street and say to ourselves, *Hurry past—he might have some mental issues*. Our neighbor gets a new BMW and we mutter, "Yuppie." We meet a checkout girl with piercings and tattoos, and think, *What could she have been thinking?* We read God's edict in His word and think, *Archaic. Outdated. Old-fashioned morale. Can't apply to today's world.*

Yet that's not how Jesus wants us to think. Jesus says to "Look beneath the surface so you can judge correctly" (NLT). That means being more conscious of what your mind chatter is telling you. That means getting close to people or situations that may make you feel uncomfortable at first. That means getting all the facts before you rush to make any judgements. That means going deep so that you can see, hear, feel, and uncover all Jesus wants to reveal. That means having more compassion than suspicions.

What situations may you be going into with preconceived notions or judgements? Who do you need to look closer at today? Ask Jesus to help you go deep.

You know how quick I am to judge sometimes, Lord.
Help me see people and situations with Your eyes.

THINK TWICE

Jesus stooped down and wrote in the dust with his finger.
They kept demanding an answer, so he stood up again and said,
"All right, but let the one who has never sinned throw the first
stone!" Then he stooped down again and wrote in the dust.

JOHN 8:6-8 NLT

It is so easy to see the sin in the lives of others and not see it in ourselves. That's what happened to the scribes and Pharisees who were pulling out all the stops in their attempts to trap Jesus with His words. Adulterers themselves, the men found a woman committing adultery and brought her to Jesus. The Law of Moses said she should be stoned. They wanted to know what Jesus' sentence would be.

That's when He did the unexpected. He stooped to write some words in the dust. Impatient, they asked again for His judgment. That's when He—the one who sees and knows us better than we see and know our own selves—said that whichever man had never sinned should throw the first stone. Stabbed by their own consciences, the men left, one by one.

Jesus would have us spend more time tending to the missteps in our *own* lives than rushing to judge others. This passage, Matthew Henry says, teaches us that we are to "Think twice before we speak once."

Lord, help me spend more time examining my own
life than in looking for the missteps of others.

FOUND STRENGTH

*When David and his men saw the ruins and realized what had
happened to their families, they wept until they could weep no more. . . .
David was now in great danger because all his men . . .began to talk
of stoning him. But David found strength in the LORD his God.*

1 SAMUEL 30:3-4, 6 NLT

R eturning from the edge of battle, David and his troops find their
homes in Ziklag burned down to the ground and their wives and
children kidnapped. First, David was grief struck. Then he realized
he was in grave danger from his own men who were ready to thrash
him for what had happened. But the next eight words tell how David
triumphed over grief, panic, and destruction: "David found strength
in the LORD his God."

Instead of wallowing in sorrow, running away, freezing in panic,
or fighting his own men, David turned to God—asking Him what he
should do next. And then, with his men by his side, he did as God
instructed. At the end, "David got back everything. . . . Nothing was
missing" (1 Samuel 30:18-19 NLT).

When you are in sorrow or danger, don't take flight from your
problems, fight with others, or freeze and do nothing. Instead find
your strength in the Lord your God—and you, too, will triumph.

*I'm looking to You for the strength I need, Lord.
Show me the way You would have me take.*

STRENGTH TO STRENGTH

Blessed (happy, fortunate, to be envied) is the man whose strength is in You. . . . They go from strength to strength [increasing in victorious power]. . . . O Lord of hosts, blessed (happy, fortunate, to be envied) is the man who trusts in You [leaning and believing on You, committing all and confidently looking to You, and that without fear or misgiving]!

PSALM 84:5, 7, 12 AMPC

What joy there is for the woman who looks to God for her strength. Looking to Him isn't something she is forced to do but *pleased*—in fact eager—to do. God builds up not only her joy in Him, but her strength, increasing her power.

The key is trust. That's what brings a woman such joy, gives her such strength. She trusts God's watching out for her, watching over her. She stops along the way and waits until He turns her tears of sorrow and bitterness into a place of springs and replenishing rain. She cannot help but smile as she looks at God, seeing Him as her "sun and shield" (Psalm 84:11 AMPC), her light and protection. And she doesn't just slightly trust but commits everything to Him with confidence.

Trust God to take you from strength to strength.

I want to trust in You for everything, Lord, with my whole heart. No fear. Just confidence and a sense of expectation that You, my sun and shield, are walking with me!

THE LIGHT

"We must quickly carry out the tasks assigned us by the one who sent us. . . . While I am here in the world, I am the light of the world."

JOHN 9:4-5 NLT

Walking along with His disciples, Jesus sees a blind man. His followers ask, "Why was this man born blind? Was it because of his own sins or his parents' sins?" (John 9:2 NLT).

Jesus says it's neither. The man made of earth was born blind so others could see the power of God displayed. And Jesus proves His point by spitting on the ground, creating mud with His spittle, and spreading the concoction on the blind man's eyes. After He tells him to rinse his eyes in the pool of Siloam, the obedient man sees a whole new world.

Jesus, the constant Creator and re-Creator, reaches out for what is at hand. He makes a healing salve, providing a remedy that will open new vistas. Trusting Jesus, the blind man readily washes his eyes, and the Light of the world comes into his life. And all can now see God's power!

What is Jesus re-creating in your life? What remedy is He bringing to you that's already at hand? Do you trust Him enough to go where He's sending you? What power will God display when you do?

Light of my life, open my eyes to what You are re-creating in my life. Help me trust You and obey. Show me the Light.

POWER SOURCE

*David became more and more powerful, because
the LORD God of Heaven's Armies was with him.*

2 SAMUEL 5:10 NLT

David, now king over Israel and Judah, was a powerful warrior and commander. Yet he didn't let his power go to his head because he knew his power *Source*: the presence of God with him.

When the Philistines heard David had been crowned king of Israel, they came out against him in full force. Their army spread out in the Valley of Rephaim. Before moving an inch, David asked God if he should go out and attack the enemy and, if he did so, would God give him victory. God replied, "Yes, go ahead. I will certainly hand them over to you" (2 Samuel 5:19 NLT). David did go and defeat the Philistines, saying, "The Lord has broken through my enemies before me, like the bursting out of great waters. So he called the name of that place Baal-perazim [Lord of breaking through]" (2 Samuel 5:20 AMPC).

Know your power source: the presence of God with you. When something comes against you, ask Him what you should do and if He'll give you victory. Trust what He says. Then, depending upon the word He's given, either be still or move out with the confidence that He will breakthrough whatever stands against you.

*Lord, You are my power source. I'm standing
with You, looking to You for guidance.*

THE GATEWAY

Guard my life, for I am faithful to you; save your servant
who trusts in you. You are my God. . .I call to you all day long.
Bring joy to your servant, Lord, for I put my trust in you. You, Lord,
are forgiving and good, abounding in love to all who call to you.

PSALM 86:2-5 NIV

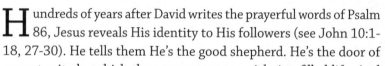

Hundreds of years after David writes the prayerful words of Psalm 86, Jesus reveals His identity to His followers (see John 10:1-18, 27-30). He tells them He's the good shepherd. He's the door of opportunity by which they may enter to a rich, joy-filled life. And He's also the door providing protection, the one that keeps out the wolves, the things and beings that would bring His people harm.

Jesus knows your voice. Come through the door and into His fold. Trust Him. Speak to Him. Call on Him throughout your day. Remind yourself *He* is God, your joy-giver, the love of your life. He's your front and rear guard, your gateway to security *and* an abundant life. Then listen for *His* voice. He'll call you out by name and lead you to where you are to go. He's also going on ahead, checking out the lay of the land, paving the path for your feet.

Thank You, Lord, for being my Good Shepherd and the
door through which I can find guidance and protection.
I'm calling for You now. Speak, Lord. I'm listening.

YOUR NARRATIVE

*"Anyone who walks in the daytime will not stumble,
for they see by this world's light. It is when a person
walks at night that they stumble, for they have no light."*

JOHN 11:9-10 NIV

In 2 Samuel 11, King David was hanging out at home when he should have been out with his soldiers. Bored, he took a walk around on his palace rooftop and happened to see the beautiful Bathsheba bathing on her roof. In this prosperous God-blessed king's quest to gain this married woman for his own, he manipulates his good friends, connives and conspires to kill Bathsheba's husband Uriah, and loses other good fighting men in the process. After Bathsheba mourns for Uriah, David takes her to wife. And in the very last verse of this chapter, we read of God for the first time: "But the thing David had done displeased the Lord" (v. 27 NIV).

What has your life story been like lately? How much is God mentioned in your narrative? Where might you be idle, wandering around, looking for something else to fill up your life, something that perhaps you have no business going after?

Wherever you are, instead of stumbling around through life, look for Jesus' light. And walk by it. Make God a substantial part of your own narrative.

*Lord, I want to walk in Your light. Help me
make sure You're always part of my story.*

DEEPLY MOVED

When Jesus saw [Mary] weeping. . .he was deeply moved in spirit and troubled. . . . Jesus wept. . . . Jesus, once more deeply moved, came to the tomb. . . . Then Jesus said, "Did I not tell you that if you believe, you will see the glory of God?"

John 11:33, 35, 38, 40 niv

Jesus' friend Lazarus has been laid in his tomb. And because of Lazarus's death, the sorrow of His friends and sisters, and the suffering of humankind, Jesus is deeply moved. He weeps. He mourns. Yet He knows that those who believe will see the glory of God. And so, He calls on Martha to have faith, and orders Lazarus to "Come out!" (John 12:43 niv). When Lazarus arises at Jesus' command, many believed.

The point? Jesus isn't immune to your suffering. He knows what you're going through. He has so much compassion for you that He cannot help but be moved, to hurt when you hurt, weep when you weep. But He also knows about the power of faith, the strength of God the Father, and the joy of the Spirit.

Trust that Jesus is walking with you through every trial and triumph. Know that no matter what happens, you, as a believer, *will see* the glory of God.

Thank You, God, for Jesus, the one who knows all about the human experience. With Him by my side, I'm never alone, in sorrow or in joy.

SHATTERED FEAR

"Do not be afraid, Daughter Zion; see, your king is coming, seated on a donkey's colt." At first his disciples did not understand all this. Only after Jesus was glorified did they realize that these things had been written about him and that these things had been done to him.

JOHN 12:15-16 NIV

In a world where it seems as if power-hungry and egocentric people are running amok, it's a relief to turn to the word of God for an attitude and outlook adjustment.

In the verses above, the word is telling us not to be afraid—because we have a king who isn't out just to increase his wealth or power or crush our spirits. No. Our King, our Jesus, our Savior is humble. He's one who's neither militaristic nor materialistic. He comes to us in peace and humility. He doesn't pound on the doors of our hearts and minds, demanding entrance. He does just the opposite. He knocks, hoping we will open *our* doors. He makes His word available, knowing that every day we delve into it, we come to another grand realization of who He actually is, what His word actually means. And because of all these things, our fear is shattered. We are filled with calm, relief, and gratitude as the more we get to know and love Him, the more we reflect His glory. And find our own selves becoming peace-loving, humble, and giving.

Help me, Jesus, become more like You!

WHATEVER SEEMS GOOD

Then the king said to Zadok, "Take the ark of God back into the city. If I find favor in the LORD's eyes, he will bring me back and let me see it and his dwelling place again. But if he says, 'I am not pleased with you,' then I am ready; let him do to me whatever seems good to him."

2 SAMUEL 15:25-26 NIV

King David was in dire straits. The hearts of his people had been won by his son and usurper, Absalom. So David had to flee Jerusalem. The people in the countryside cried as the king and his retinue passed by. Even the Levites had followed him with the ark of God. But David told the priest Zadok to go back to the city with the ark. Not knowing what was going to happen, David determined to leave his life in the hands of God, ready for whatever would happen, satisfied God would do what He deemed best. This sentiment is echoed later by Jesus who would one day, while in a Jerusalem garden, pray to Father God, "Not My will but Yours."

When all looks hopeless, when your dreams have become nightmares, how wonderful to be calm and content, rather than complaining. Have no fear of whatever the future may hold, knowing all events are in God's hands.

*Whatever You wish and will, Lord, I'm ready.
I and my life are in Your hands, knowing You know best.*

KNOWING GOD

Jesus shouted to the crowds, "If you trust me, you are trusting not only me, but also God who sent me. For when you see me, you are seeing the one who sent me. I have come as a light to shine in this dark world, so that all who put their trust in me will no longer remain in the dark."

JOHN 12:44-46 NLT

Not sure what God is all about? Uncertain as to His true character? You need not look any further than Jesus Christ. When you know Him, you'll know God. When you trust Him, you're trusting God. For Jesus was God in the flesh.

Study His compassion for the mourning, the lame, the weak, the blind, the leper, the sinner. Read of His attitude toward the political and religious leaders of His day. Walk with His disciples as they follow Him, forever trying to understand and often falling a little bit short. Allow Him to open up your eyes to what He reveals in the scriptures. Make a list of all the statements He begins with the words, *I am*. And then find proof of His identity in the word and in your own life.

Trust in Jesus. Love, worship, and believe in Him—and you'll find yourself living in His light, understanding God, and finding a peace beyond compare.

Jesus, show me God through You and Your life.
Open my eyes and heart to knowing You better.

LEAN BACK UPON JESUS

The disciples kept looking at one another, puzzled as to whom He could mean. One of His disciples, whom Jesus loved [whom He esteemed and delighted in], was reclining [next to Him] on Jesus' bosom. . . . Then leaning back against Jesus' breast, he asked Him, Lord, who is it?

JOHN 13:22-23, 25 AMPC

Some days can be confusing. We're a bit puzzled, unsure of what God's telling us. We look for answers in the world and people around us. But the true source of wisdom is found in the one who loves us—Jesus. It's to Him we can address our questions, in Him we'll find the truth. It's His answers we can trust.

To clear the confusion, come to a quiet place. Lean back upon Jesus' breast. Absorb His love and light. Bathe in the intimacy of His presence. Whisper the questions you want to ask. Then patiently and peacefully wait for His answer, for it will surely come.

Jesus isn't some god so far removed from you that you cannot reach Him. He's all around you, waiting for you to lean upon Him, ask Him questions, abide in His love. So, go to Him now, knowing He'll provide you with all the knowledge you need. Trust that you can rely on both Him and His word.

*Lord, I'm leaning back on You, ready to whisper
in Your ear, bathing in the intimacy of our love.*

IN YOUR POWER

Rizpah. . .the mother of two of the men, spread burlap on a rock and stayed there the entire harvest season. She prevented the scavenger birds from tearing at their bodies during the day and stopped wild animals from eating them at night.

2 SAMUEL 21:10 NLT

A three-year famine plagued David's kingdom. The Lord told him it had come because "Saul and his family are guilty of murdering the Gibeonites" (2 Samuel 21:1 NLT). To end the famine and appease the Gibeonites, David complied with their request to hang seven of Saul's sons.

Two of those sons were Rizpah's. This concubine had seen a lot of sorrow. After Saul had been killed in battle, Abner seduced her, then he himself was murdered. Now her two sons', slain for their father's sin, are hung out to dry.

But Rizpah doesn't cower. She doesn't rebel against King David's edict. She does what she has the power to do, and guards her sons' bodies from scavenging birds and wild animals—day and night—for five months! When David finds out, he buries the boys' remains. Then the rains came and the famine ended.

Sometimes in life there's no remedy for what befalls you. But you can trust God with all and unselfishly determine to do what's in your power to do for those you love. For this, you're rewarded.

Lord, help me determine to do what's in my power to do for those I love.

RELAX, RELY, REJOICE

David. . .said: The Lord is my Rock [of escape from Saul]
and my Fortress [in the wilderness] and my Deliverer . . .
As for God, His way is perfect; the word of the Lord is tried.
He is a Shield to all those who trust and take refuge in Him.

2 SAMUEL 22:1-2, 31 AMPC

Both Saul and David were the Lord's anointed. And that's where the similarity ends. For Saul never really and truly put his trust in God. Instead, he put his trust in himself and those around him. He feared the opinion and power of people more than he feared God and His law. That is why Saul's kingdom was torn from his hands, why he felt threatened by and so chased David, and why he, at the end, consulted the witch of Endor instead of God.

And then there was David, the man after God's own heart. Although he made mistakes, he was quick to confess to and humble himself before God. Because he trusted God, God became his shield and refuge. Because David trusted the word and promises of God, God continually delivered him in the wilderness.

When you trust and take shelter in God your Rock, He will become your impenetrable shield. And in following His word, you'll find your way perfect. Relax. Rely. Rejoice in the Rock that is your God.

Thank You, Lord, for being my Rock
and Fortress, my Deliverer and Shield!

MIDNIGHT CONFESSION

*After he had taken the census, David's conscience began to
bother him. And he said to the LORD, "I have sinned greatly
by taking this census. Please forgive my guilt, LORD, for doing
this foolish thing." The next morning the word of the LORD came.*

2 SAMUEL 24:10-11 NLT

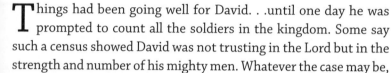

Things had been going well for David. . .until one day he was
prompted to count all the soldiers in the kingdom. Some say
such a census showed David was not trusting in the Lord but in the
strength and number of his mighty men. Whatever the case may be,
afterward David felt guilty. For some reason, his actions did not sit
right with him. His guilty conscience disrupting his sleep, he finally
turned to God, asking forgiveness for what his foolishness had
prompted him to do. The morning following his midnight confession,
the prophet Gad came and relayed the Lord's message to David.

Sometimes, when prompted by God only knows what, we, without
thinking, do something foolish. A guilty conscious and sleepless
nights may follow—and will most likely continue unless we, like
David, talk to God, tell Him what we've done, and ask forgiveness
for being such fools. When this is done, what will most likely follow
is an overwhelming sense of relief, and then a message from or a
mind-merge with the Lord—and a good night's rest.

How have you been sleeping lately?

Something is bothering me, Lord. Can we talk?

LISTENING IN PRAYER

*"Ask the Father for whatever is in keeping with the
things I've revealed to you. Ask in my name, according
to my will, and he'll most certainly give it to you."*

JOHN 16:23-24 MSG

Prayer—what a privilege! Yet how often do we take it for granted, simply mumbling our way through the emotions? Or asking for things that aren't even close to God's will for our lives?

Madeleine L'Engle wrote, "To pray is to listen, to move through my own chattering to God, to that place where I can be silent and listen to what God may have to say." *That's* the essence of prayer.

Prayer need not be boring or haphazard. It can be the adventure of a lifetime. And L'Engle has given us a good formula to follow. First, we must make the intention of listening to what we are saying to God. That helps us get some idea of where we are and where we think we might want to go. Listening in on our own requests to God also helps us recognize how aligned our prayer is with what Jesus wills for our life. Lastly, after moving through our chattering, we're to be silent and listen to what Jesus wants us to do. If we've truly made our request "in keeping with the things" Jesus has "revealed" to us, we'll happily receive what we've asked for.

Here I am, Lord. I'm ready to pray with and to You!

A PRAYER FOR YOU

"I am praying not only for these disciples but also for all who will ever believe in me through their message. I pray that they will all be one, just as you and I are one. . . . I have given them the glory you gave me, so they may be one as we are one. I am in them and you are in me."

JOHN 17:20-23 NLT

I magine this: Thousands of years ago, while He was in human form on earth, Jesus, the Son of God, prayed a prayer for you, a believer. He prayed that you and other believers would be one, just as He and Father God are one. And He didn't stop there! He who was the manifestation of God on earth, He who displayed every nuance of God's character, revealed all this to His followers—so that they could believe and reflect God's character themselves by walking as Jesus walked!

Make this awareness part of your daily walk. Know that Jesus has prayed for, is praying for, and will continue to pray for you. Know that He has been to you an example, and will help you reflect the character of Father God. And trust that you, the daughter, will never be parted from either Father or Son.

I am amazed at Your prayer for me, Jesus! Thank You for its power and purpose.

PARTICULAR CALLING

*Let us, your servants, see you work again; let our children see
your glory. And may the Lord our God show us his approval and
make our efforts successful. Yes, make our efforts successful!*

PSALM 90:16-17 NLT

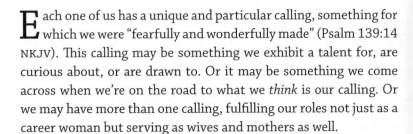

Each one of us has a unique and particular calling, something for
which we were "fearfully and wonderfully made" (Psalm 139:14
NKJV). This calling may be something we exhibit a talent for, are
curious about, or are drawn to. Or it may be something we come
across when we're on the road to what we *think* is our calling. Or
we may have more than one calling, fulfilling our roles not just as a
career woman but serving as wives and mothers as well.

The point is that no matter what we put our hand to—housework,
raising kids, working in an office, driving a school bus, or serving in
ministry—we're working for God's approval of our efforts alone and
entrusting the success of those efforts to Him. What a relief that
provides! All we need to do is our best as we follow opportunities
presented to us, and leave the rest in God's hands.

Because it's God alone you serve, your only true path to joy and
peace lies in pleasing Him.

*Lord, help me home in on the calling You have for my life.
And once I've found it, may I seek Your approval only.*

THE SECRET PLACE (PART 1)

He who dwells in the secret place of the Most High shall remain stable and fixed under the shadow of the Almighty [Whose power no foe can withstand]. I will say of the Lord, He is my Refuge and my Fortress, my God; on Him I lean and rely, and in Him I [confidently] trust!

PSALM 91:1-2 AMPC

What benefits are available to the woman who dwells in that "secret place" of God—"whose power no foe can withstand"—making Him her absolute Refuge and Fortress!

For once she makes God her dwelling and confidently trusts Him, she'll be delivered from every danger. She knows she can run under His wings and find shelter. Her shield shall be His truth. She'll fear no terrors, knowing they can never reach her. She cannot be destroyed, so disease and death don't scare her.

Find your way into that secret place where you'll find a calmness of heart and focus of mind. Constantly remind yourself there's no power greater than that of the Almighty. Trust that you can remain there always, that He is available to you 24/7, no matter where you are. Make the words of Psalm 91:1-2 your mantra. And reap the benefits—in heaven and on earth.

I'm looking to You for refuge, Lord. Beam me up to that secret place. Help me to remain in You—no matter what's going on in my life. In You alone I trust.

THE SECRET PLACE (PART 2)

He will order his angels to protect you wherever you go.
They will hold you up with their hands so you won't even hurt
your foot on a stone. . . . The LORD says, "I will rescue those
who love me. I will protect those who trust in my name. When
they call on me, I will answer; I will be with them in trouble."

PSALM 91:11-12, 14-15 NLT

When you're in that "secret place of the Most High" of Psalm 91:1-2, you can be sure God's angels are under orders to protect you—no matter where you are! They're going to watch over you so that you won't get lost. You might stumble in your spiritual walk, but you'll not fall or get hurt. For they'll lift you up.

When you love God, truly love Him, and totally trust His names—Deliverer, Provider, Defender, Protector, Fortress, and so many more—He'll rescue and protect you. He'll answer you when you cry out to Him. He'll be there, amid your trouble—and He'll bring you out in triumph.

Your God is not some abstract notion, some being that's out of your reach. He's within you, surrounding you, above you, below you, walking by your side. Reach out to your Abba God. Find your way into that secret place. And realize the amazing pleasure and power of His presence.

Lord, I love You like no other. Keep me in Your secret place!

FILLED WITH SPIRIT

*When the priests came out of the Holy Place, a thick
cloud filled the Temple of the LORD. The priests could
not continue their service because of the cloud, for the
glorious presence of the LORD filled the Temple of the LORD.*

1 KINGS 8:10-11 NLT

Imagine living in Solomon's day. After seven years of labor, the Temple was complete with all its magnificent pillars, basins, vessels, altars, and pedestals and with all forms of artistry worked in gold, silver, bronze, metal, stone, cedar, olive wood, and cypress. Solomon commands the ark and its sacred contents to be brought in by the priests. "There, before the Ark, King Solomon and the entire community of Israel sacrificed so many sheep, goats, and cattle that no one could keep count!" (1 Kings 8:5 NLT). After the Lord's presence filled the Temple, Solomon prayed to and praised the Lord.

Now come back to the present where you, a believer in Christ, are one with God. Know that "your body is the temple (the very sanctuary) of the Holy Spirit Who lives within you" (1 Corinthians 6:19 AMPC). Imagine all God's intricate artistry that makes you who you are in mind, body, spirit, and soul. Envision His Spirit filling you from the top of your head to the tips of your toes. Pray and praise God for the miracle of your faith.

*At times I cannot comprehend the miracle of my faith, Lord.
I'm awed by Your presence within me.*

WOMAN!

As she wept, she stooped down [and looked] into the tomb.
And she saw two angels in white sitting there, one at the
head and one at the feet, where the body of Jesus had lain.

JOHN 20:11-12 AMPC

Mary Magdalene hurried to the garden tomb, seeking her Lord. But instead of finding Jesus, she found the stone rolled away from the tomb's entrance. She ran to tell Simon Peter and John. They ran back, saw the empty tomb, then went back home, believing Jesus had somehow escaped death. But Mary stayed behind, sobbing.

She looked once more in the tomb and through her tears saw two angels sitting where Jesus had once lain. Their first word to her: *Woman.* They asked why she was crying. She said, "Because they've taken Jesus and I know not where." Then she turned, saw Jesus, but thought He was the gardener. His first word to her: *Woman.* He asks her not just why she's crying but who she's looking for. She answers His question with a statement: "Sir, if you carried Him away from here, tell me where you have put Him and I will take Him away" (John 20:15 AMPC). Jesus responds and reveals Himself, saying "Mary!" And gives her a message.

Woman, where are you hurrying to, whom are you seeking? Stop. Look. Recognize Jesus' presence. Listen. He's calling your name. He's got a message for you.

I come seeking You, Lord. Open my eyes as I turn to You.

BLESSED BELIEVER

*That Sunday evening the disciples were meeting behind locked
doors because they were afraid. . . . Suddenly, Jesus was standing
there among them! "Peace be with you," he said. . . . Eight days later
the disciples were together again, and this time Thomas was with
them. The doors were locked; but suddenly, as before, Jesus was
standing among them. "Peace be with you," he said.*

JOHN 20:19, 26 NLT

No matter where you are, Jesus can reach you. No matter what barriers, locked doors, or walls are surrounding you, Jesus can get through, stand beside you, show you His face, His hands, His feet, His love, His Spirit. No doors can shut out His presence.

And where Jesus gains entrance, His peace follows. He blesses you with peace with God, with your own conscience, and with others. His presence stills the storms of your life, the waves of anxiety, the eddies of troubles. He not only gives you His peace but asks you to carry it with you.

Although you have not yet met Jesus physically face-to-face, nor put your hands on His wounds, Jesus favors you because of your trust in Him, saying, "Blessed *and* happy *and* to be envied are those who have never seen Me and yet have believed *and* adhered to *and* trusted *and* relied on Me" (John 20:29 AMPC).

"Peace be with you."

*Lord, nothing can keep You from me! Thank You
for the calming peace Your presence provides.*

A VOICE FROM THE SHORE

*At dawn Jesus was standing on the beach. . . . He called out,
"Fellows, have you caught any fish?" "No," they replied. Then he
said, "Throw out your net on the right-hand side of the boat,
and you'll get some!" So they did, and they couldn't haul
in the net because there were so many fish in it.*

JOHN 21:4-6 NLT

You may, at times, find things aren't going your way. You're
surrounded by darkness, at a loss, hands empty, in despair,
adrift. As dawn breaks, you hear a voice from the shore, questioning
you: "What do you need? What are you looking for?"

You answer the questions as best you can, putting into words
the lack you feel. Then the same voice gives you direction, advice,
and you obey. As soon as you take action, you find so much of what
you'd been searching for that you have trouble taking it all in. And
that's when you realize that voice, that prompting, was from Jesus!

When you find yourself in a sea of despair, know that Jesus is
ready to call out from the shore and help you. Trust that His directions
will lead to your bounty. And after you've made your haul, celebrate
with the Master Fisher of men!

*I'm feeling adrift, Lord. Call to me from the shore.
Give me the direction I so desperately need!*

CELEBRATE AND REJOICE

Unless the Lord had been my help, I would soon have dwelt in [the land where there is] silence. When I said, My foot is slipping, Your mercy and loving-kindness, O Lord, held me up. In the multitude of my [anxious] thoughts within me, Your comforts cheer and delight my soul!

PSALM 94:17-19 AMPC

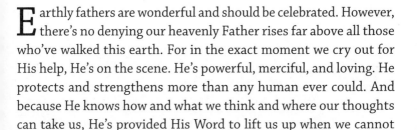

Earthly fathers are wonderful and should be celebrated. However, there's no denying our heavenly Father rises far above all those who've walked this earth. For in the exact moment we cry out for His help, He's on the scene. He's powerful, merciful, and loving. He protects and strengthens more than any human ever could. And because He knows how and what we think and where our thoughts can take us, He's provided His Word to lift us up when we cannot stand and to lighten our spirits when we cannot breathe.

God is not just the Father that will never leave you or forsake you. He's a being more than worthy of your absolute trust. When you exchange your thoughts with His words, you can say He "has become my High Tower and Defense, and my God the Rock of my refuge" (Psalm 94:22 AMPC).

So today rejoice in the earthly fathers you know and love. But above all, sing praises to the Father who loved you before you ever loved Him.

*Father God, thank You for making my footing
sure and my thoughts more like Yours.*

DECISIONS, DECISIONS

And they prayed and said, You, Lord, Who know all hearts (their thoughts, passions, desires, appetites, purposes, and endeavors), indicate to us which one of these two You have chosen to take the place in this ministry and receive the position of an apostle. . . .

ACTS 1:24-25 AMPC

Decisions, decisions. It's sometimes hard to know what to do in certain situations. Or who would be best suited for various scenarios. In Acts 1, the apostles were "[waiting together] with the women and Mary the mother of Jesus, and with His brothers" in the upper room in Jerusalem where they "devoted themselves steadfastly to prayer" (Acts 1:14 AMPC). And while they were waiting, Peter suggested they find someone to take the place of the now-dead traitor Judas. Not knowing whom to pick, they asked God to tell them whom *He* chose.

God knows all about each one of us. And because He sees what we cannot, there's no limit to His depth of knowledge about us and our circumstances.

Confused? Go to God. Ask Him for His advice. Know that He knows everyone's circumstances and thoughts, that He can fit anyone to do what He has purposed them to do. Your only job is to ask His choice and trust that He knows best.

I don't know what to do, Lord. So I'm coming to You. Look into all hearts involved in this matter. Tell me, who is Your choice?

LEAP OF FAITH

There was always enough flour and olive oil left in the containers, just as the LORD had promised through Elijah.

1 KINGS 17:16 NLT

Susan J. Decuir says, "Sometimes the only means of transportation is a leap of faith." That's exactly the kind of leap an on-the-run prophet and a starving widow had to make during a drought thousands of years ago.

Elijah had to take a leap of faith, trusting that if he did as the Lord instructed, God would provide him with water from a brook, and ravens would bring him food. Elijah took that leap and God provided the goods exactly as promised.

Then God told Elijah to find a widow in Zarephath who would feed him. So Elijah went, met the widow, and asked her for water. As she was fetching it, he asked her for bread. But she told Elijah all she had was a little flour and oil that she was going to throw together and bake. Then she and her son would eat it as their last meal.

Elijah said, "Don't fear. Make a cake for me, afterward make something for you and your boy. The Lord says your jars of oil and flour will not run out."

She leapt. And God's promise became reality.

What leap of faith are you waiting to take?

Lord, build up my trust as I look for ways to take leaps of faith when things seem impossible and Your solution sounds improbable.

GOD'S MESSAGE

*Elijah was afraid and fled for his life. . . . Then he went on alone
into the wilderness, traveling all day. He sat down under
a solitary broom tree and prayed that he might die.*

1 KINGS 19:3-4 NLT

E lijah usually trusted the Lord. In the past, God would perform some type of miracle to help him, no matter what he was facing. But perhaps this time things had gone too far.

Just before running away, Elijah had seen the Lord defeat the prophets of Baal. Elijah himself had killed several hundred of those prophets. Then he'd prayed for and seen the Lord bring rain, ending the drought. But Queen Jezebel, enraged over her prophets' deaths, sent a messenger to Elijah, threatening his life. So we find Elijah fearful, alone, on the run, and praying for death.

Sometimes exhaustion, shock, and fear can lead us to forget what we know. So caught up in our situation, we mistrust the one person we can always count on: God. Fortunately, He knows how fragile we are. When God sees we're suddenly listening to the wrong messages and "on the run," He sends one of His own messages supernaturally—through His word, angels, people, coincidence, or otherwise. Our role is to be as responsive to Him as Elijah was with the God-sent angel telling him to "Get up and eat!" (1 Kings 19:5 NLT).

Help me hone in on Your message, Lord, and trust You once again.

STRONG AND STEADY

Peter said, Silver and gold (money) I do not have; but what I do have, that I give to you: in [the use of] the name of Jesus Christ of Nazareth, walk! Then he took hold of the man's right hand with a firm grip and raised him up. And at once his feet and ankle bones became strong and steady. . . .

ACTS 3:6-8 AMPC

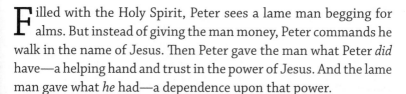

Filled with the Holy Spirit, Peter sees a lame man begging for alms. But instead of giving the man money, Peter commands he walk in the name of Jesus. Then Peter gave the man what Peter *did* have—a helping hand and trust in the power of Jesus. And the lame man gave what *he* had—a dependence upon that power.

Because of Peter's trust in and the lame man's dependence on Jesus, the man not only walked but began leaping. Peter tells the people, "Through faith in the name of Jesus, this man was healed. . . . Faith in Jesus' name has healed him before your very eyes" (Acts 3:16 NLT).

What answers do you look for when you need help? In what or whom do you trust when you're weak in the knees? When you're looking to stand, know the medicine for your malady is Jesus. Then pray, having faith He'll put you back on your feet.

Jesus, I need help standing strong and steady.
I trust in Your name and power! Raise me up, Lord!

MARKED BY THE SONLIGHT

When they saw the boldness of Peter and John, and perceived that they were uneducated and untrained men, they marveled. And they realized that they had been with Jesus. And seeing the man who had been healed standing with them, they could say nothing against it.

ACTS 4:13-14 NKJV

The Greek word for the "boldness" of Peter and John is *parresia*. It means that the two men were filled with the assurance and confidence given to them by the Holy Spirit. This new courage gave them the boldness to speak up for Jesus. Even though they were neither studied men nor ones who had been trained, their words and attitude made Jewish leaders marvel, and perhaps fear a bit. Their newfound assurance, their way of speaking, their exuberance, and perhaps the "Sonlight" upon their faces, clearly marked them as people who had been with Jesus.

If you do not have such assurance and confidence to share with others about Jesus—whether that sharing is exhibited by your speaking, writing, serving, crafting, singing, etc.—consider spending more time in the Son. Allow the Spirit to permeate your being. Snuggle up close to God. By so doing, you'll begin to glow. And others will not help but notice that you, too, have been with Jesus.

*Lord, I want to have the boldness gleaned by
being filled with the Spirit. Help me glow for You.*

PRAYING ON THE UPSIDE

"O Lord, . . .give us. . .great boldness in preaching your word. Stretch out your hand with healing power; may miraculous signs and wonders be done through the name of your holy servant Jesus." After this prayer, the meeting place shook, and they were all filled with the Holy Spirit.

ACTS 4:29-31 NLT

Sometimes we may find ourselves somewhat casual in our prayer frequency and intensity. Other days, our burden is so great, our crisis so deep, we find ourselves driven down to our knees in pleading before God. But how often do we pray intensely for more of what we already have?

That's what the apostles did. They'd already performed lots of miracles (see Acts 2:43; 3:7-11). They'd already demonstrated their courage and boldness before many people, including the Jewish courts. But they didn't rest on their reputations. Instead, they asked God for more boldness in preaching, more healing, more signs, and more wonders. Afterward, the place where they were meeting in prayer shook, they were filled by the Holy Spirit, and began preaching God's word with boldness.

Consider putting all your faith and trust in God and praying on the upside. When things are going well, pray even harder for God to work His will in your life. Shake up your world!

Make me bolder, Lord. Stretch out Your hand to heal. Show Your presence and power in my life. Shake up my world—for You!

A SIMPLE THING

"Thus says the LORD: 'Make this valley full of ditches. . . . You shall not see wind, nor shall you see rain; yet that valley shall be filled with water, so that you. . .may drink.' And this is a simple matter in the sight of the LORD; He will also deliver the Moabites into your hand."

2 KINGS 3:16-18 NKJV

Some days you may have no idea how to "fix" a situation. And so with your shoulders drooped, you come before the Lord. He tells you the impossible will happen in a way you never imagined. You'll be well-provided for. You're going to be victorious against whatever's coming at you. Not only that, but all these things are simple for the Lord! But you have to *trust* God will do as He says: you have to dig ditches to ready the dry earth to receive the water, full of faith that a miracle is imminent.

Jesus' apostles' readying work was to trust God and expect the miraculous. That's how it came to be that "at night an angel of the Lord opened the prison doors and brought them out" (Acts 5:19 NKJV). Their part was to then go and preach in the temple, bringing more believers into the fold.

Trust God. Expect Him to work. Know that for God, providing the miraculous is a simple thing.

Lord, I'm trusting You for a miracle.
What can I do to ease its entrance into this world?

VENTURE WITH GOD

Elisha said to her, What shall I do for you? Tell me, what have you [of sale value] in the house? She said, Your handmaid has nothing in the house except a jar of oil. Then he said, Go around and borrow. . .empty vessels—and not a few.

2 KINGS 4:2-3 AMPC

A widow had lost her God-fearing husband. Now creditors were coming to take her two sons to be slaves. So she goes to Elisha for help. And he asks what Jesus often asked His followers: "What shall I do for you?" His immediate follow-up question is, "What do you have?"

That's when the widow looks around, sees what she has, and offers this one asset—a jar of oil—to Elisha. He tells her to borrow vessels from all her neighbors—and not just a few. In other words, see plenty in this venture. Then she's to go into her house with her sons, shut the door, and start pouring the little oil she has into the other jars. She ends up filling all the vessels, selling the oil, paying off her debt, and living off the rest with her sons.

When you're in dire straits, tell God about it. Tell Him what you'd like Him to do for you and what you have on hand. Then follow His directions, seeing plenty in your venture, trusting that under His directions, all will come out well.

Here's what I have, Lord. What shall I do?

PRECONCEPTIONS

Then Naaman and all his attendants went back to the man of God. He stood before him and said, "Now I know that there is no God in all the world except in Israel."

2 KINGS 5:15 NIV

Naaman, commander of the Syrian army, took the advice of his wife's God-fearing servant girl. He headed to Israel to be cured of leprosy by the prophet Elisha. But when that man of God told him to wash in the Jordan seven times, Naaman balked because of his preconceptions of what Elisha's healing process would be: "I thought that he would surely come out to me and stand and call on the name of the LORD his God, wave his hand over the spot and cure me of my leprosy" (2 Kings 5:11 NIV). Fortunately for Naaman, his servants reasoned with him, saying, "My father, if the prophet had told you to do some great thing, would you not have done it? How much more, then, when he tells you, 'Wash and be cleansed'!" (2 Kings 5:13 NIV). Naaman then followed Elisha's remedy and received not only absolute healing but faith in God!

When you're looking to God for answers, trust Him to have the right remedy. Let go of any preconceived notions of what your "cure" should look like. Step out in faith, knowing no matter how out-of-your-realm His notions are, they are what will work for you.

Help me have more faith in You than in my own ideas, Lord.

SIGHTS AND SOUNDS

"Don't be afraid! . . . For there are more on our side than on theirs!"
Then Elisha prayed, "O LORD, open his eyes and let him see!" The LORD
opened the young man's eyes, and when he looked up, he saw that the
hillside around Elisha was filled with horses and chariots of fire.

2 KINGS 6:16-17 NLT

In 2 Kings 6:8-23, the Syrian army came to attack the city of Dothan. When Elisha's servant saw the army of chariots and horses surrounding them, he yelled, "Oh, sir, what will we do now?" (2 Kings 6:15 NLT). Elisha told him not to fear, then asked God to open his spiritual eyes. And the servant saw God's army. When the Syrian troops began closing in, Elisha prayed again, asking God to strike them with blindness. God did—and Elisha led the army out of the city.

Later, in 2 Kings 6:24-7:20, the Syrians sieged Samaria. But God routed the besiegers by causing "the Aramean army to hear the clatter of speeding chariots and the galloping of horses and the sounds of a great army approaching. . . . So they panicked and. . .fled for their lives" (2 Kings 7:6-7 NLT).

Open your spiritual eyes. God's using His supernatural means, including sights and sounds, to defeat the powers coming against you. Just watch—and you'll see.

I don't know what to do, Lord. But I know
that with Your help, I need not fear.

UNCHANGEABLE

LORD, hear my prayer! Listen to my plea! Don't turn away
from me in my time of distress. Bend down to listen, and answer
me quickly when I call to you. . . . [The Lord] will listen to
the prayers of the destitute. He will not reject their pleas. . . .
You are always the same; you will live forever.

PSALM 102:1-2, 17, 27 NLT

The world changes so quickly around us—places, faces, technology, relationships, mores, values, wars, boundaries, battles, surrenders, earthquakes, hurricanes, fires, and famine. . . . We can barely keep pace. Somedays we find ourselves breathless, not knowing what's sure and certain. We find ourselves feeling untethered, doubting the permanence of the very ground beneath our feet.

Yet we're believers in a God who never changes. He's always ready to help, teach, correct, and save. He's the one place we know we can go when we have problems and pleas. He's the one person who'll never turn from us when we're in distress.

Pray. And know that when you do, God will bend His ear. Know that He'll find coherence in your babbling. Know that He'll never reject you—but protect you.

In this world of constant change, remember that you're enveloped by the permanence of your Rock and Refuge, standing on Him and trusting in Him alone.

I pray to the unchangeable source and Lord of my
heart and life, knowing You will hear and answer.

STRENGTH, FAITH, AND COURAGE

Jehosheba, the daughter of King Jehoram, [half] sister of Ahaziah, stole Joash son of Ahaziah from among the king's sons, who were to be slain, even him and his nurse, and hid them from Athaliah in an inner storeroom for beds; so he was not slain.

2 KINGS 11:2 AMPC

After her husband (King Jehoram of Judah) and her son (King Ahaziah) were killed, Athaliah "arose and destroyed all the royal descendants" (2 Kings 11:1 AMPC). But Athaliah's step-daughter, Jehosheba, stole her nephew Joash so he wouldn't be killed. For six years, Jehosheba kept the boy and his nurse hidden in the house of the Lord while his power-hungry grandmother ruled Judah. Eventually becoming king, "Joash did what was pleasing in the LORD's sight" (2 Kings 12:2 AMPC) and Athaliah bit the dust.

Jehosheba was like Moses' mom. Jochebed had the faith, courage, and tenacity to hide her son Moses from the wrath of a blood-thirsty pharaoh *and* was able to give him the godly training and instruction he'd need to fulfill his calling. For these two women, strength, faith, and courage went hand in hand, enabling them to extend God's kingdom.

By following Joshua 1:7-9, you, too, can "be strong and very courageous" (verse 7 AMPC). But to be so takes hiding the word of God in the inner storeroom of your heart and mind.

Lord, by Your word, give me the strength, faith, and courage to do what You call me to do.

FROM GLOOM TO BLOOM

Let all that I am praise the LORD; may I never forget the
good things he does for me. . . . He fills my life with
good things. My youth is renewed like the eagle's!

PSALM 103:2, 5 NLT

Some days it's easy to feel we are sinking beneath the waves of bad news flowing out to us. To have the negativity of the world become like seaweed wrapped around our minds. But God would have us look not to our circumstances but to Him. To trust not in events but in His power. To focus not on our afflictions but our blessings. For when we change our perspective from one of "me" to "He," everything looks better and brighter.

What if you looked at the things that happen as neither good nor bad? What if you constantly remembered God is in your corner, on your side (see Psalm 118:6)? What if you understood and kept in mind the idea that God has everything rigged in your favor?

To be sure, there are times when you need to grieve the loss of someone or something. Times when you need to regroup and take stock of what's happening. But the majority of the time, looking at things as being rigged by God in your favor may just change your life from gloom to bloom!

With You on my side, Lord, I can't lose!

THE WAY

[Saul] went to the high priest and asked him for letters. . .so that if he found any there who belonged to the Way, whether men or women, he might take them as prisoners. . . . As he neared Damascus on his journey, suddenly a light from heaven flashed around him.

ACTS 9:1-3 NIV

Persecuting Saul was hunting down Christians, those "who belonged to the Way." This phrase referred to people who belonged to the "way" of salvation or walked the true "way" in relationship to God. Simply put, they were followers of Jesus.

This Way contrasted sharply with the direction Saul was going. He was headed his *own* way when he was suddenly blinded by a light from heaven and encountered Jesus who quickly rerouted him. As the persecutor began trusting Jesus, Saul went from being a follower of his own way, to being led away, receiving his spiritual vision, and becoming apostle Paul of the Way.

When God sees you losing your way, He sometimes does something drastic to remove the scales from your eyes. But before it gets to that point, you might want to stop in your tracks. Look around. And change your ways, follow His lead, and get back on His Way.

Which way are you heading lately?

Lord, show me where I may be stepping out of the Way.
Open my eyes to what You would have me see.

RECONCILER TO THE BROKEN

But the love of the LORD remains forever with those who fear him.
His salvation extends to the children's children of those who are
faithful to his covenant, of those who obey his commandments!

PSALM 103:17-18 NLT

Kimi's parents had divorced when she was ten and her relationship with her father was far from what she'd hoped. It had been over a decade, since just before her sixteenth birthday, that she'd last seen him *or* her grandmother.

When Kimi mentioned to her husband, Landon, that she wanted to reach out and try to reconnect with her grandmother, he encouraged her. Nervously, she glanced at him as she held her cell phone in her hand. He nodded and gently whispered, "Go ahead."

She pushed the receiver icon on her cell and waited as the phone rang. Seconds later she heard, "Ah, hello!"

"Grandma, this is Kimi."

"Kimi! It's so good to hear your voice," her grandmother said. And their long conversation began, followed by plans for Kimi, Landon, and their son to fly out to see Grandma.

Just as God is faithful to restore His relationship with you, He also is faithful to help you restore and repair those broken relationships you have with others.

Thank You, heavenly Father for your faithfulness to repair the broken
places in my life. I know I can depend on You to help me repair
the rifts I've had with others, if they're willing to reconcile.

ADVENTURES WITH GOD

Hezekiah put his whole trust in the God of Israel. There was no king quite like him, either before or after. He held fast to God—never loosened his grip—and obeyed to the letter everything God had commanded Moses. And God, for his part, held fast to him through all his adventures.

2 Kings 18:5-6 msg

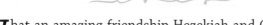

What an amazing friendship Hezekiah and God must have enjoyed. Today's reading is packed with details about their life together in just a few words. Hezekiah "put his whole trust" in God. He put everything he had, all that he was, and all that he did, completely on the line for God. And, because of his commitment to trust God in all things, there was no king like him—ever. Wow! Can you imagine God saying something like that about you?

Hezekiah held fast to God. Imagine him following right in step with God, going wherever He led. Not once did Hezekiah let go but did exactly what God told him to do, when He told him to do it.

In return, God held fast to him too—like two best friends always together—in all their adventures.

The Bible says God doesn't play favorites (see Romans 2:11). That means you have the same opportunity to share adventures with God if you follow Hezekiah's example.

God, I put all my trust in You. By faith I will hold tight to You and obey all Your commands.

HE HEARS YOU AND SEES YOUR TEARS

"Return and tell Hezekiah the leader of My people, 'Thus says the Lord, the God of David your father: "I have heard your prayer, I have seen your tears; surely I will heal you.'"

2 KINGS 20:4-5 NKJV

Hezekiah was one of the most faithful kings of Judah. His faith and prayer made a difference in his own life, his family, and in the lives of the people of God he led.

When Hezekiah became very ill, the prophet Isaiah gave him a message from the Lord instructing him to put his things in order because he was going to die. What a horrible message to receive! Imagine the emotions he must have felt. Immediately Hezekiah prayed, reminding the Lord of his faithfulness and devotion to Him. The scripture says, "Hezekiah wept bitterly" (2 Kings 20:3 NKJV).

But God! Before Isaiah even made it out of the palace, the Lord instructed to him to go back to Hezekiah with another message: "I have heard your prayer, I have seen your tears; surely I will heal you" (2 Kings 20:5 NKJV).

God looked upon His child and loved him, just like He looks upon you and is moved with compassion about the things that concern you.

Lord, I want to be a catalyst that makes a difference in my family, my city, and the world. Thank You for hearing my prayers and perfecting those things that concern me as I give them to You.

FREEDOM FOR ALL

"If therefore God gave them the same gift as He gave
us when we believed on the Lord Jesus Christ,
who was I that I could withstand God?"

ACTS 11:17 NKJV

D ad, what's a Gentile?" six-year-old Darlene asked as she walked into the living room, scratching her head.

Max smiled at his daughter, knowing the question must have been rolling around in her head since children's church that morning. He paused his football game on TV and motioned for her to sit next to him.

Darlene sat sideways on the end of couch, facing her dad, poised to hear another lesson.

"You probably heard about the Jews and the Gentiles this morning, right?" he began.

Darlene nodded.

"Well, some of the Jews thought Jesus' message was only for them and not for other people. 'Gentiles' are what they called people who didn't live the way these believing Jews thought you should live."

"So, in the Bible, it was like all the different people we have today?" she asked.

"Yes," Max continued. "Jesus came to give all people spiritual freedom. It's like how the Constitution of the United States says all the people in our country should be given the same rights and treated equally. Jesus wanted everyone to have the right to choose to invite Him into their hearts and live for Him."

Jesus, thank You that Your gift of eternal life is for all of us.

WALKING IN STEP WITH HIM

And the hand of the Lord was with them,
and a great number believed and turned to the Lord.

Acts 11:21 nkjv

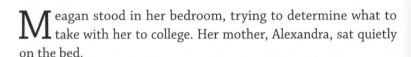

Meagan stood in her bedroom, trying to determine what to take with her to college. Her mother, Alexandra, sat quietly on the bed.

Meagan turned to her mother. "Mom, you know I've always believed I had a God-given purpose. . . But I've never felt so misplaced as I do right now. I just don't want to miss God's plan."

Alexandra said, "Honey, Dad and I have had those times in life when we felt like we weren't where we should be, but we prayed and pressed in to hear God. We listened and watched for His perfect will."

"I know, but you had each other. I'm going off to a place I've never been, with people I don't know," Meagan said. "I've prayed and believe I'm headed in the right direction, but sometimes—like today—I have doubts."

"Well," her mother responded, "I think you've done all you can do to hear from God, so you have to trust He's with you. I truly believe if you do your very best to follow Him, you'll never miss anything He has for you."

God, thank You for Your hand on my life. You have a plan
and purpose for me. In times of doubt, help me to hold
tight to You and trust that I'm walking in step with You.

TRUST HIS ABILITY IN YOU

One day as these men were worshiping the Lord and fasting,
the Holy Spirit said, "Appoint Barnabas and Saul for the special
work to which I have called them." So after more fasting and prayer,
the men laid their hands on them and sent them on their way.

Acts 13:2-3 nlt

You have abilities to do great things. It's when you allow God to infuse you with His strength that you can do more than you could on your own.

In today's reading (Acts 12:18-13:13), God gave Barnabas and Saul a special work. Their brothers in Christ laid hands on them, imparted faith, and believed God to do greater works than the two men could do on their own.

In 1652, Richard Baxter wrote in his book, *The Saints Everlasting Rest*: "They who seek this rest [to cease from striving] have an inward principle of spiritual life. God does not move men like stones, but he endows them with life, not to enable them to move without him, but in subordination to himself, the first mover."

God calls you to a higher place—a place where you can let go and allow Him to give you His direction. Trust His ability at work in you.

Lord, it's often difficult to only move when You move me, but I want to completely surrender—even in the smallest little detail—to all Your plans. I will not lean on my own understanding, but trust in You.

SIGNS OF HIS PRESENCE

Keep your eyes open for God, watch for his works; be alert
for signs of his presence. Remember the world of wonders
he has made, his miracles, and the verdicts he's rendered—
O seed of Abraham, his servant, O child of Jacob, his chosen.

Psalm 105:5-6 msg

L ife is busy—on purpose! The enemy of your soul wants to keep you preoccupied, filled with any distraction that would keep your eyes off the great works God is doing.

Yet God would have you do otherwise. As writer and pastor Henry Blackaby advises, "Watch to see where God is working and join Him."

Put down your busy schedule and take a deep breath! What's God doing in your life? Perhaps at first glance you saw His fingerprints on your life as coincidence. Look a little closer. Where has He blessed you lately? When has He poured out His favor on you and given you opportunities you otherwise might not have had?

Where's He at work in the lives of your loved ones? How has He intervened? Has someone escaped a car wreck untouched, or not been in the place they planned and so escaped tragedy?

What great work is God doing now, and how can you join Him? When you see Him at work and join Him there, your soul is awake to His presence and in tune with Him.

God, open my eyes to see Your works.
Help me be watchful and recognize Your presence.

SALVATION FOR ALL

"I have set you as a light to the Gentiles, that you should be
for salvation to the ends of the earth." Now when the Gentiles
heard this, they were glad and glorified the word of the Lord.
And as many as had been appointed to eternal life believed.

ACTS 13:47-48 NKJV

Forgiveness of sins and freedom from guilt are provided for all. Although it was always God's plan for the whole world to know Him through the saving knowledge of Jesus Christ, the promise of salvation was first given to the Jewish nation.

God desired for the Jews to be the light of the world. Jesus was born through Jewish lineage to be the light for all. But, heartbreaking to God, many Jews refused to believe Jesus was the promised Savior and Son of God.

As a follower of Christ today, you are a light pointing all people of every nation, tribe, and tongue to a relationship with God. Just as the disciples stood and shared the Gospel, you are called to do the same. While you may experience rejection as they did, some will hear about God's greatest gift and rejoice just as the Gentiles did in today's reading.

Lord Jesus, thank You for the gift of salvation. I choose to
be a light to the world. I rely on You to give me the words
to say and the courage to share Your love with others.

GRACE AT WORK

*The believers there had entrusted them to the grace
of God to do the work they had now completed.*

ACTS 14:26 NLT

Thirteen-year-old Natalie let the screen door slam behind her. She plopped down on the couch and sighed loudly.

"What gives?" her mother Kathi asked.

"Mom! Allie Baker is going to summer camp with us next week. I don't think I want to go now."

Kathi paused, silently asking the Lord to give her the right words. "Oh, honey, I'm so sorry you're disappointed to hear that news," she started.

"Mom, disappointed is an understatement," Natalie retorted.

Kathi's mind was spinning. This classmate, this mean girl, had made her daughter miserable the entire school year. Kathi's stomach felt a little sick, recounting those experiences. "I hate for you to miss camp. Have you prayed about it?"

"No, I'm kinda mad at God for letting her go," Natalie admitted softly.

"Well, you know you're going to have to talk to Him about it. And then decide what to do. It'd be just like God to use something like this for His glory. Sometimes we have to trust His grace to do the work in the hearts of others."

"I know. You're right," Natalie said as she got up and headed upstairs to her room. "I'll talk to Him. I promise."

*Jesus, above all, I want to show others—even the
most difficult people—Your love. Help me trust
Your grace to do the work in their hearts, and mine.*

HE REMEMBERS

He opened the rock, and water gushed out; it ran in the dry places like a river. For He remembered His holy promise, and Abraham His servant. He brought out His people with joy, His chosen ones with gladness.

PSALM 105:41-43 NKJV

"I hate it," Kristen complained to her best friend, Carmella. "It's just so hard to trust God because I've not had a lot of people in my life who kept *their* promises."

"I get that!" Carmella replied as she adjusted the hose before watering the next pot of flowers on her deck. "But, the Bible shows you how God faithfully kept every single promise He made. Abraham waited twenty-five years for God to keep His promise of a son. David waited over twenty years before he became the king of Israel. And look how long the prophets waited for Jesus to be born. . . ."

"Well, hopefully I won't have to wait two decades to see God's promises," Kristen joked.

"No," Carmella replied, "you won't. You're already seeing His promises at work. You're saved. He's a forever friend, always with you. You never have to be alone again. He comforts you when you're down. He gives you blessings and favor. The list goes on and on."

"Yes, I do see His promises around me. Like, the friend He's given me in you! A great friend who'll tell me like it is."

You, God, are my hope. Help me to always remember You keep Your promises.

IN HIS HANDS

Then [Israel] believed His words [trusting in,
relying on them]; they sang His praise.

PSALM 106:12 AMPC

After visiting their friends Tim and Jess, Cameron and Ryleigh traveled back through Dallas on busy Interstate 635.

"I am so glad you're driving," Ryleigh commented. "This is a crazy road. It just seems like if you don't drive fast and stay with the flow of traffic, you could get run over."

Minutes later they heard a crash. Cameron shifted their car slightly to the left, so as not to hit the sedan in that lane. He watched in the rearview mirror as the white SUV in the right lane beside them hit the retainer wall.

Ryleigh looked back through the passenger window to see the SUV suspended in the air next to their car. *It's like we're living in slow motion*, she thought.

Miraculously the SUV landed in its own lane, upside down, without damage to anyone else on the interstate. "Should we stop and help?" Ryleigh asked. But they soon realized there was no way to stop since traffic on both sides was still moving very fast.

Cameron and Ryleigh sat silently for a moment, both very shaken. Then she spoke, "Our angels were definitely at work. I'm so glad Tim and Jess prayed for our safety before we left."

Heavenly Father, thank You for always being with me.
You know every situation before me, long before
I get there. Thank You for keeping me safe.

A CONTENTED HEART

One woman, Lydia, was from Thyatira and a dealer in
expensive textiles, known to be a God-fearing woman.
As she listened with intensity to what was being said,
the Master gave her a trusting heart—and she believed!

ACTS 16:14 MSG

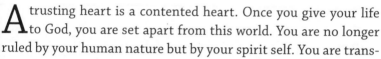

A trusting heart is a contented heart. Once you give your life to God, you are set apart from this world. You are no longer ruled by your human nature but by your spirit self. You are transformed by God's power and can gain contentment in the middle of a world filled with discontentment.

That's why Paul said: "I have learned in whatever state I am, to be content: I know how to be abased, and I know how to abound. Everywhere and in all things I have learned both to be full and to be hungry, both to abound and to suffer need. I can do all things through Christ who strengthens me" (Philippians 4:11-13 NKJV).

Would you say it's easy for you to trust God? What about trusting others?

As you grow in faith and trust in God's strength working through you, your heart becomes more contented. You come to know God and who He is. You have confidence in His character, believe in His wisdom, and trust that whatever He does is for your good.

Lord, I want to know You better. I want to have a contented
heart, trusting in You unconditionally and becoming more
and more aware of Your strength working through me.

FREE AT LAST

Along about midnight, Paul and Silas were at prayer and singing a robust hymn to God. The other prisoners couldn't believe their ears. Then, without warning, a huge earthquake! The jailhouse tottered, every door flew open, all the prisoners were loose.

ACTS 16:25-26 MSG

Chances are you've experienced hurt of some kind or another. Sometimes the scars and debilitating wounds are visible, but often they remain hidden deep inside, shared only with the few you think you can trust, or perhaps no one at all.

Paul and Silas were beaten and unjustly thrown into jail, simply for sharing their faith. In today's reading (Acts 16:16-40), they found themselves imprisoned with bruises and pain, no doubt on the inside as well as the outside. While they praised God through their suffering and heartbreak, God delivered them from their chains. He set them free, literally. In a difficult place, Paul and Silas chose to praise God anyway.

God's deliverance can happen rapidly or it can take some time. Either way, God will set you free you from the pain. While you're waiting, praise God. Doing so can comfort your heart and soothe the broken places in your life. Praise can give you the strength you need to let go, forgive, and break out of the chains.

Lord, I'm in one of those difficult places now. I open my heart and my mouth in praise to You today. I trust You to set me free from the pain.

FAITH FLASHCARDS

*Study GOD and his strength, seek his presence day
and night; remember all the wonders he performed,
the miracles and judgments that came out of his mouth.*

1 Chronicles 16:11-12 MSG

Faith grows with each obstacle you overcome. Even sometimes when you feel like you've failed, you still learn something that propels you forward. Still, when a challenge to your faith arises, it's a new opportunity to either stand firm or doubt God.

Imagine you had a set of flashcards, each one representing a time when God came through for you. You could pull out a card with a memory from your past and read about how God was there for you then. Doing so would give you the confidence you need to stand strong in your current faith crisis, reminding you that He can help you make it through any difficulty staring you in the face right now.

What amazing and miraculous things has God done for you or for those you love? Think of those times in your life when He faithfully brought you through the storm. Begin to build some faith flashcards from your life and use them to build your faith, to trust Him to once again to see you through.

*Heavenly Father, You are faithful. Thank You for the many
times You were there when I wanted to give up. I am encouraged
in my faith as I remember each one of those times today.*

FAITH TAKES ACTION

*Nevertheless He regarded their affliction, when He heard
their cry; and for their sake He remembered His covenant,
and relented according to the multitude of His mercies.*

PSALM 106:44-45 NKJV

Ginger found the perfect job, and she loved it, but the distance between her and her husband, Luke, was becoming impossible to handle emotionally. In the beginning, they'd agreed to live apart until Luke found a job in their new community. But that was nearly a year ago, and there were still no opportunities in sight.

Luke drove into town every other weekend to see Ginger and their two middle school-aged daughters, but the couple could tell the grace for their season apart was coming to an end. Finally, one evening while the girls were at a party, Ginger told Luke their family needed to be together. "We can move back; I'll give up my job if that's what you think the Lord will have us do."

Luke took her hand and they prayed, asking the Lord to reveal His will and wisdom. The next morning Luke decided he'd resign his job and Ginger would keep hers. They'd trust God to open the door for his new job. Five weeks after his resignation, God connected Luke with a new position in his new community.

*God, thank You for showing me that faith requires action.
Show me what I need to do next to see Your plans
become even more of a reality in my life.*

HIS MERCY IS GREAT

David said to Gad, I am in great and distressing perplexity;
let me fall, I pray you, into the hands of the Lord, for very great and
many are His mercies; but let me not fall into the hands of man.

1 Chronicles 21:13 ampc

In 1 Chronicles 21, Satan tempted David to take a census, for he was beginning to put his confidence in his army, instead of in God.

Once David realized his sin, he took responsibility for it and asked God's forgiveness. And even though God forgave David, there were consequences for what he'd done. God allowed David to choose: "Either [1] three years of famine, or [2] three months of devastation before your foes, while the sword of your enemies overtakes you, or else [3] three days of the sword of the Lord and pestilence in the land, and the angel of the Lord destroying throughout all the borders of Israel" (1 Chronicles 21:12 ampc).

David chose option 3. After 70,000 Israelites died from the plague, David cried for mercy for his people. He admitted the fault for taking the census was his alone. Then, after David built an altar and made an offering to God, the angel of death sheathed its sword.

Just as God extended His mercy for David, He extends it to you!

Lord, Your mercies are new every morning. I'm grateful I
can depend on You to show me mercy as I keep my heart right.

FROM DEATH TO LIFE

Paul said, "John's baptism called for repentance from sin.
But John himself told the people to believe in the one who
would come later, meaning Jesus." As soon as they heard
this, they were baptized in the name of the Lord Jesus.

ACTS 19:4-5 NLT

A favorite summer blooming shrub of locals in Tucson, Arizona, the red bird of paradise decorates landscapes with a stunning parade of orange-red flowers, the shrub reaching heights of ten feet or more. The dazzling individual flowers bloom from March to October.

The red bird of paradise has astonishing abilities of recovery, or even what seems to be a rebirth. In the winter, some homeowners cut the shrub back to a foot or so to the ground, leaving the plant looking devastated and completely irrecoverable. Even when the plant experiences a frost, it can seem to be lost, only to resurrect into flourishing blooms the next summer. In fact, the shrubs can sometimes spring back to life, twice the size they were before, as if they died and rose again.

As you surrender your life to Christ, you die to sin and all your old ways, becoming much like a shrub that has been cut back in the winter. Then your new life of Christ brings you up more lovely and beautiful than ever before with the promise of life with Him forever.

Heavenly Father, thank You for the gift saving
me from death and giving me eternal life.

MIRACLES STILL HAPPEN

And God did unusual and extraordinary miracles by the hands
of Paul, so that handkerchiefs or towels or aprons which had
touched his skin were carried away and put upon the sick,
and their diseases left them and the evil spirits came out of them.

ACTS 19:11-12 AMPC

Why do so many children who were raised in faith wander off into the world?" Kendra asked her neighbor, Sarah. "It's like my daughter Jane's forgotten the God of her childhood."

Sarah refilled Kendra's tea glass. "Children have to find their own way. There comes a time when their parents' faith isn't enough. Their relationship with God must become personal and real for them. They need to see that miracles still happen—for them!"

Later that day Kendra's phone rang. She recognized the ringtone. It was Jane. "Hey baby," she answered.

"Mom, you're not going believe it," Jane said excitedly. "Remember you always said there's no such thing as coincidence. . .and when I see coincidence I should look for God working in my life? Well, He's working. It's like all these things I've been asking Him about, well, they all worked out in the same day. I got answers from heaven one God-coincidence after the other."

Tears streamed down Kendra's face. Her own prayers were answered in her daughter's few words coming across her phone.

God, I believe in miracles. Thank You for the miracles,
big and small, that You perform for me each day.

TRUST EQUALS FAITH IN ACTION

*They sow their fields, plant their vineyards, and harvest
their bumper crops. How he blesses them! They raise large
families there, and their herds of livestock increase.*

PSALM 107:37-38 NLT

Kay and her new neighbor, Shelly, sat on Kay's back patio as their toddlers splashed in the kiddie pool. "Kay," Shelly said, "it just seems like everything you touch turns to gold."

Kay laughed, "I just approach my faith in a certain way. I believe faith requires action and sometimes means stepping out of your comfort zone."

"So, what does that look like?" Shelly asked.

"Well, we really needed new carpeting in the living room. I couldn't image the baby crawling around on that old rug. I asked God what I could do. One Saturday morning I got a box cutter and started ripping up the carpet. Thankfully my husband, Matt came in and finished the job. We prayed together and asked God to make a way for the money as we stood on that cement floor."

"Oh my gosh!" Shelly exclaimed.

"Yes, some people might think that was crazy, but I trusted God to make a way. Two weeks later, Matt's unexpected bonus and some overtime covered the cost of a new carpet. I believe I took action and my faith brought what we needed into reality."

*Heavenly Father, thank You for the many blessings You've given me.
Show me how to put action to my faith each day.*

ASKING RIGHTLY

God answered Solomon, "This is what has come out of your heart: You
didn't grasp for money, wealth, fame, and the doom of your enemies;
you didn't even ask for a long life. You asked for wisdom and knowledge
so you could govern well my people over whom I've made you king.
Because of this, you get what you asked for—wisdom and knowledge.
And I'm presenting you the rest as a bonus—money, wealth, and fame
beyond anything the kings before or after you had or will have."

2 CHRONICLES 1:11-12 MSG

The young King Solomon could have asked God to increase his earthly status in some way, but instead he asked Him for wisdom and knowledge. He wanted a heart of understanding so he could effectively lead God's people.

Knowledge is great but wisdom—the capacity to integrate that knowledge into decisions that benefit everyone—is better.

Solomon's unselfish and thoughtful request for wisdom and knowledge pleased God. Not only did God grant Solomon's request, making him the wisest man to ever live, but He also gave Solomon the things he *didn't* ask for—wealth, honor, and a long life.

When you ask God for something rightly—know that you'll not only receive something better—but beyond what you imagine.

Heavenly Father, it's easy to want what others have.
But I'm determined to ask rightly, knowing when I do,
You'll give me beyond what I imagine—for Your glory.

DREAM GIVER

*So the LORD has fulfilled His word which He spoke,
and I have filled the position of my father David, and sit
on the throne of Israel, as the LORD promised; and I have
built the temple for the name of the LORD God of Israel.*

2 CHRONICLES 6:10 NKJV

Is there a promise of a dream that has gone unrealized? Perhaps you didn't let go of the dream intentionally, but rather just set it on a shelf for another time and the dream slipped away.

God's plan for your life seldom happens in the sequence of events you imagine them to occur. And yet, your heavenly Father is the great dream giver. Even if your once big dream seems impossible, if He placed the seed of that dream in your heart, you can trust Him to bring it to fruition no matter how much time has passed since it began to grow.

Is it time to reexplore the dream God's given you? Are you willing to open a forgotten place in your soul? Will you stir up the passion and excitement again?

Those dreams God put in your heart make you who you were created to be. When you trust God to take your life and do with it what He purposed, He'll make your dreams a reality in His time.

*God, You are the dream giver. You know the dreams I've
set aside and even forgotten. Help me to see those
dreams again and bring them to reality.*

GOD COMES DOWN

When Solomon finished praying, a bolt of lightning out of heaven struck the Whole-Burnt-Offering and sacrifices and the Glory of GOD filled The Temple. The Glory was so dense that the priests couldn't get in—GOD so filled The Temple that there was no room for the priests!

2 CHRONICLES 7:1 MSG

It is often in those silent moments, when you're taking in God's creation, that you feel close to Him. The sand, the beach, the rushing sound of the ocean coming in to kiss the shore stirs something deep within your soul. Taking in an evening sunset on the beach or a slow walk down to the water's edge somehow compels you to connect with the one who created all of this for you. Even the sound of rushing waves, no matter how loud, can serve as a calming roar and settle every stressor weighing on you.

Times like that, it often feels that God comes down and you can experience His presence in a tangible way. Life's busyness fades away and all of who He is envelops you like a waterfall, washing away the stress.

Take time today to step back from the traffic, the turmoil, the loud shouts of life, and into the calm of His creation. Embrace the silence and step into the peace right now.

Savior, You are welcome in this place. My body is Your temple. Come and visit me today. Wash over me and fill me with Your peace.

PRIVATE AUDIENCE

Thus Solomon finished the house of the LORD and the king's house; and Solomon successfully accomplished all that came into his heart to make in the house of the LORD and in his own house. Then the LORD appeared to Solomon by night, and said to him: "I have heard your prayer, and have chosen this place for Myself as a house of sacrifice."

2 CHRONICLES 7:11-12 NKJV

You've no doubt experienced someone being distracted while you're trying to have a conversation with her. That person may drift off in her own mind, get a phone call, hear the annoying bleep of an incoming text message or the tiny voice of a child calling her name.

Your human audience may lose its attention but Your heavenly one won't. Father God is always listening. His eyes are ever on you, never looking above your head to see who's walked into the room. He gives you a private audience any time you want to talk with Him. You're His focus and He values every moment you give Him.

Even when you feel you're alone, you can trust God's there. He's an audience that never leaves the auditorium of your life. When you speak, He hears every word. And as you return the favor by listening to Him, He'll lead you, guide you, and show you things you'd never discover on your own.

Heavenly Father, thank You for listening to me.
Show me the plans You have for my life.

GOD'S GOT THIS

The word of GOD to my Lord: "Sit alongside me here on my throne until I make your enemies a stool for your feet." You were forged a strong scepter by GOD of Zion; now rule, though surrounded by enemies!

PSALM 110:1-3 MSG

Robyn was struggling with aspects of her husband's job. The pressure on Frank was overwhelming, making it hard for her to watch him bear the strain of it. His working late evenings and most weekends didn't make it easy on their marriage either. Worried and frustrated, she'd asked some friends to pray around the situation.

One evening Robyn got a call from Linda, a trusted friend and prayer partner, who said, "I've been praying for you this evening. I heard the Lord saying to you, 'I've got this.'"

Robyn's voice couldn't hide her frustration. "What does *that* mean?"

"It means He's taking care of it. That's all I know." Linda hesitated. "Listen. . .I know you want details, but God doesn't always provide them. Just know He's working things out for your good."

As Robyn crawled into bed, alone for the third evening in a row because Frank was working late, she thought about what Linda had shared. *Okay, God,* she prayed silently, *I have no other choice but to trust You.* "You've got this," she said aloud.

Peace fell over her as she drifted off to sleep.

God, You know the challenge before me.
Help me trust that You've got this!

COUNT ON HOLY STRENGTH

*Then Asa cried out to the Lord his God, "O Lord, no one
but you can help the powerless against the mighty! Help us,
O Lord our God, for we trust in you alone. It is in your name
that we have come against this vast horde. O Lord, you are
our God; do not let mere men prevail against you!"*

2 Chronicles 14:11 nlt

When you have strengths, abilities, and resources within yourself,
it's easy to look to yourself to solve problems and make things
happen. But God created you so that He could do life *with* you all
the time, not just when you need His help. When you include God
in your daily ups and down, that fellowship allows Him to fill you
with His power.

Complete dependence on God doesn't mean you're weak, passive,
or unproductive. It means you're allowing His power to make you
more effective for Him, enabling you to do so much more, often
with eternal value.

If you're facing battles you feel you can't possibly win, don't
give up. Study Asa who, when standing against immense throngs of
enemy soldiers, realized how incapable he was without God's holy
power. When He prayed for God's intervention, God came through,
supernaturally and stupendously. In all things, trust in God alone.

*God, I recognize my limitations and ask for Your help
in all things as You join me on my journey each day.*

GOD-GIVEN DREAMS FULFILLED

"The eyes of the LORD search the whole earth in order to strengthen those whose hearts are fully committed to him."

2 CHRONICLES 16:9 NLT

Andy could tell his teenage daughter, Livy, was struggling in her relationship with God. She had become disinterested in youth group and offered every excuse imaginable as to why she shouldn't have to go to church with the family. He followed her into her bedroom after another confrontation about house rules and church attendance.

Andy sat on her bed, motioning for her to take a seat next to him. "I need help understanding this whole disconnect from youth group, church, and God," he said.

Livy was still for a few minutes and then her eyes filled with tears. "Dad, I love God. You know that," she said softly. "But what if. . ." her voice trailed off.

Andy waited.

"If I give God control, then He'll make me do things I don't want to do and have to give up my dreams."

Relieved, Andy hugged her and replied, "God will definitely ask you to do things you don't feel like doing. That's when you have to do things by faith. But I promise, if you completely surrender to Him, He'll give you the strength to see your dreams realized because He's the one who gave you those dreams to start with."

Heavenly Father, I'm committed to You. Thank You for giving me the strength to make Your dreams for me a reality.

LEARNING TO REST IN HIM

He shall not be afraid of evil tidings; his heart is firmly fixed,
trusting (leaning on and being confident) in the Lord.

PSALM 112:7 AMPC

How often have you wanted God to open things up in your life and show you what He's working on? Just as the curious child is compelled to take something apart so she can look inside to see how it all works, you may have desired to see God at work, reassembling things in your life so that they come together better than before, working for your good.

Pause for a moment and look back on your life. What things could you have done better, or perhaps just a little differently? What would it have looked like if you would have trusted the Lord more? What if you'd let go and given Him control, especially knowing Him better now than you knew Him then?

How had God faithfully put things back together for you in the past? What are some examples of His faithfulness to you and to your family? What changes could you make today in your thinking that would help you to lean on and rest in Him even more when difficulties arise?

Thank You, Lord, for always being at work in my life. Help me
walk by faith and rely on You even when I can't see all the
details ahead, knowing You're working things out for my good.

GOD OF YOUR UPS AND DOWNS

Hallelujah! You who serve GOD, praise GOD! Just to speak
his name is praise! Just to remember GOD is a blessing—
now and tomorrow and always. From east to west,
from dawn to dusk, keep lifting all your praises to GOD!

PSALM 113:1-3 MSG

As you read through the psalms, you gain a glimpse of the highs and lows from the writer's soul. In the lowest points of his life journey, he pours out his heart, hopeless and distressed, maybe even feeling disconnected from God, thirsting for His presence.

Yet, through prayer, the writer finds comfort in God for his brokenness and pain. He reminds himself of God's faithfulness and unfailing love, and how it refreshes his spirit. Then he pulls himself up, encourages himself in the Lord, and becomes determined to experience the joy that only God can give. He rises again through faith in God, climbing ever higher with praise and thanksgiving.

Like the psalmist, you too can trust God with your ups and downs. Allow Him to go with you to the mountaintops and back down into the valleys. Wherever you are in your journey, you can safely and freely bare your soul to the God who listens and knows you like no other.

God, You are always with me. You faithfully walk with
me no matter what situation I face. I will rejoice in
You at all times because I know I can count on You.

GOD'S LIVING SANCTUARY

When the Israelites escaped from Egypt—when the family of Jacob left that foreign land—the land of Judah became God's sanctuary, and Israel became his kingdom.

PSALM 114:1-2 NLT

Maggie's parents made her go to church almost every Sunday. Once on her own, attending church never really crossed her mind again until her husband, Charlie, started going. He didn't ask her to go with him—at first. Once the children were old enough to go with him, he invited her and she refused.

For months, she enjoyed the quiet house all to her herself, but she began to feel like she was missing out. So, one morning she surprised herself, got dressed, and announced she'd join them.

Once inside the church, Maggie immediately noticed something very different. *Was it the church?* She sat quietly through the service and cried softly. Wet, hot tears dripped from her checks, but she didn't wipe them. Her husband noticed the gentle cleansing rain from her heart but said nothing. Instead, he took her hands and smiled.

Maybe the change wasn't the church, she thought. *Maybe it's me.* She felt differently inside.

What is God's sanctuary? Wherever you experience Him becomes His sanctuary, and it starts in the heart (see Matthew 5:8).

Lord, may I experience You deep in my heart, and not just on Sundays, but every moment of my life.

HELP FROM THE HOLY SPIRIT

O Israel, trust the LORD! He is your helper and your shield.
O priests, descendants of Aaron, trust the LORD!
He is your helper and your shield.

PSALM 115:9-10 NLT

Jim stepped out on the deck to put the hamburgers on the grill. "Honey, did you ever find my big, metal spatula for the grill?" he called.

Jill cringed at his question, remembering the last few times they'd both looked diligently through the kitchen, trying to remember where they'd seen it. This time she asked for help from the Helper: "Holy Spirit," she prayed, "help me find that thing," as she once again searched.

Within seconds of her request, she saw the tip of the metal spatula sticking out from behind some plasticware in the pantry. "Here it is!" she called as she took it to Jim.

The Lord remembers us. He sees us, thinks about us, and perfects those things that concern us. In His extraordinary love, He cares about everything—even the little things that we've lost track of. And He sent the Helper (see John 14:26 NKJV), the Holy Spirit, to assist us in everything, even in finding things we perceive to be lost.

Heavenly Father, thank You for sending the Holy Spirit
to help me with all things. Remind me that You care
about even the littlest things that concern me.

DEPEND ON GOD FOR EVERYTHING

*You who [reverently] fear the Lord, trust in and
lean on the Lord! He is their Help and their Shield.*

PSALM 115:11 AMPC

With an unrelenting trust in God, David stood courageous against a giant enemy that dared to mock his Lord. Through faith in the God he'd trusted since he was a child and while armed with a sling and a stone, he took down the giant Goliath.

David's faith training began as a young boy out in the field, protecting his father's flock of sheep from predators. His early days as a shepherd wandering the fields probably gave him a lot of time to think, pray, and unite with God. The battles he faced out there alone, taught him to depend on God for everything.

Throughout David's life, he often called on God to protect him from those who desired to end his life, including Saul, the king of Israel. Once King Saul stood just outside the cave where David hid. Easily David could have taken Saul's life, but he refused to touch the king God had anointed. Instead, he relied on God to keep him safe.

You may not spend your days battling enemies with a sword or a sling and stones, but you have an enemy. Yet you also have a God who stands ready to shield you, protect you, and keep you in all of His ways.

My Help and Shield, my safety and security are found in You.

CAN YOU HEAR GOD NOW?

"Therefore let it be known to you that the salvation of God has been sent to the Gentiles, and they will hear it!" And when he had said these words, the Jews departed and had a great dispute among themselves.

ACTS 28:28-29 NKJV

"Can you hear me now?" In the fifteen years since that ad campaign launched, those words have been a catchphrase in American English.

Up in heaven, God asks a similar question. "Do you hear Me?" Yet some people, listening for a thunderous shout, end up missing His still, small voice.

When the apostle Paul first arrived on the Italian peninsula, "the brethren" (Acts 28:15 NKJV), probably Jew and Gentile alike, urged him to stay with them in Puteoli for seven days before he traveled the final leg of his trip to Rome.

What a contrast to Paul's later arrival in Rome. When the Roman Jews couldn't come to an agreement (about whether or not to believe in Jesus) and left, he preached the message of salvation to the Gentiles. "And they will hear it!"

How sad God must be when people deliberately tune Him out.

When God speaks to you today, do you put ear plugs in—or do you listen with an open heart?

Universal God, how I praise You that You accept people from every race and tribe and nation on earth. And how I praise You for accepting me! When You speak, may I be found listening. Amen.

GIVING BACK TO GOD

*Then Hezekiah and all the people rejoiced that God had
prepared the people, since the events took place so suddenly.*

2 CHRONICLES 29:36 NKJV

The account of King Hezekiah is a welcome respite during Judah's unhappy journey to eventual exile. He brought about national revival in the first year of his reign. It took less than a month to clear the temple and reconsecrate the buildings, furnishings, and priests for worship. Temple worship was reestablished—and Hezekiah and the people realized only God could make it happen so quickly. Proof that God not only *expects* worship—He *enables* it!

Worship is the natural response of a heart that trusts in God. The psalmist asks, "How can I repay the LORD for all the good He has done for me?" (Psalm 116:12 GW). Then with a list that is suggestive, not all-inclusive, he names several methods of repayment. Accept salvation (see verse 13). Keep vows (see verses 14, 18). Sing a song of thanksgiving (see verse 17). Join with others in worship (see verses 18-19).

As God's people spend time reviewing all the good God has done, they will respond as individuals, and as a community, through spontaneous acts of worship and during appointed times.

*My good God, let me never forget all You have done for me.
All that I have, all that I do, comes from You. Let me offer
it all back to You, which is the only true form of worship.*

CENTER TRUTH

Praise the LORD, all you nations; extol Him, all you peoples.
For great is His love toward us, and the faithfulness
of the LORD endures forever. Praise the LORD.
PSALM 117:1-2 NIV

Consisting of only two verses, Psalm 117 is the central chapter of the Bible. The awesome, sovereign God arranged that His words be handed to twenty-first-century believers with these truths at their heart:

Praise the Lord. Exalt Him.
Whoever, wherever, whenever you are.
Great is His love toward you
His faithfulness endures forever

The Westminster Catechism asks and answers, "What is the chief end of man? *To glorify God and enjoy Him forever"* (emphasis added).

Praise God for His great love that created humankind and gave His only begotten Son so people might have eternal life. His love does not change and never fails.

Praise God for His eternal faithfulness. He always has been and always will be faithful. What He says, He'll do. Who He is doesn't change (see Hebrews 13:8).

King Hezekiah trusted the eternal God. When Sennacherib's army surrounded Jerusalem, Hezekiah told his people, "There is a greater power with us than with him" (2 Chronicles 32:7 NIV).

Whatever's going on in your life today, pause to praise the Lord. The God who rescued Hezekiah, who loves you and is faithful forever, is with you today.

Eternal God, You have loved me since before time began.
Today and always let me glorify and trust You.

KINDNESS DOESN'T MEAN SOFTNESS

Better think this one through from the beginning.
God is kind, but he's not soft. In kindness he takes us
firmly by the hand and leads us into a radical life-change.

ROMANS 2:3-4 MSG

Too often, people take God's kindness for softness, a permission slip to continue sinning. They don't recognize God's calling them to repentance.

Precisely because God is kind, He doesn't lead His people over smooth seas, at least not all the time. As an African proverb states, "Smooth seas do not make skillful sailors." Radical life-change happens in people when they face the waves and billows of the stormy sea.

That was certainly true of Judah, in spite of three of her better kings. Manasseh started out bad but repented while in exile, and God brought him back. His father Hezekiah and grandson Josiah "did what was right in the eyes of the LORD" (2 Chronicles 29:2; 34:2 NIV).

To the degree Manasseh, Hezekiah, and Josiah recognized Israel's unchanging, trust-worthy God, they prospered. Problems bubbled up when they turned away.

The same is true today. God's kindness will not allow His people to continue sinning. He will take whatever steps are necessary to bring them back.

Unchanging God, I confess I'm fickle. I presume upon
Your kindness and wonder why problems come.
Forgive me. May I follow You with all my being. Amen.

SOLA SCRIPTURA

[Hilkiah] reported. . . . "I've just found the Book of
GOD's Revelation, instructing us in GOD's way—found it
in The Temple!" When the king heard what was written in
the book, GOD's Revelation, he ripped his robes in dismay.

2 CHRONICLES 34:15,19 MSG

A popular bumper sticker reads, GOD SAID IT, I BELIEVE IT, THAT SETTLES IT. Perhaps it should read, GOD SAID IT, THAT SETTLES IT. For God's Word stands alone. It's a living instrument God uses to judge the human heart (see Hebrews 4:12).

King Josiah discovered the Word's power at a young age. After he commanded the cleansing of the temple, Hilkiah the priest uncovered the lost scrolls of the law, and Josiah's secretary shared them with his ruler. Josiah feared immediate judgment and pled for God's mercy.

Millenia later, a monk also discovered the power of God's Word. Martin Luther's formulation of *sola scriptura* ("Scripture alone"), *sola gratia* ("grace alone"), and *sola fide* ("faith alone"), shook the world. Scripture was his only defense at his trial for excommunication and possibly his life.

That same Bible, the best-selling book of all time, too often sits unread on a bookshelf.

Get busy and dive in. Discover the power of God's Word.

Living Word of God, teach me. May Your pages convict me, Your
promises encourage me, Your history inspire me. May I use Your
own words to speak of You, to praise You, to learn of You. Amen.

WHAT GOD SAYS, HE WILL DO

Abraham never wavered in believing God's promise. In fact, his faith grew stronger, and in this he brought glory to God. He was fully convinced that God is able to do whatever he promises.

ROMANS 4:20-21 NLT

I f anyone understood God's faithfulness from the bottom of his heart, and took that faithfulness as an irrefutable fact in spite of all evidence to the contrary, it was Abraham.

Abraham's faith remains unparalleled to this day. Unlike other people of his time, when the Creator God spoke, Abraham listened and acted on what He said.

Abraham didn't waver during the long years separating the call to leave his home and travel to a new land (see Genesis 12), God's first promise of a son (see Genesis 15:4), and Isaac's birth (see Genesis 21:3). Instead of growing weaker, Abraham's faith grew stronger. He gave glory to God before the fact, "*fully convinced*" (emphasis added). God had the power to do what He'd promised. Unfortunately, most of Abraham's descendants lacked his faith and ended up in exile.

Christians today have the same two choices: to believe God and trust Him, not depending on sight or immediate answers; or to give up and miss out on God's best. What choice will you make?

Unchanging God, Your purposes never change.
Ground my steps on the foundation of Your Word,
not on my feelings and shortsighted perceptions. Amen.

EVERLASTING LIFE AND LOVE

*They sang responsively, praising and giving thanks to the Lord,
saying, For He is good, for His mercy and loving-kindness
endure forever toward Israel. And all the people shouted
with a great shout when they praised the Lord, because
the foundation of the house of the Lord was laid!*

EZRA 3:11 AMPC

What a celebration Israel held after beginning the restoration of temple worship. Trumpets sounded, cymbals crashed, voices raised in song.

Most shouted for joy. Some wept, remembering the glory of Solomon's temple, destroyed during the exile of the Israelites.

Solomon's temple had replaced the tabernacle built under Moses's direction. And the offerings God commanded for Moses' tabernacle pointed back to the offerings made by Cain (given out of obligation) and Abel (given out of love), and the difference between them.

God has always weighed the heart of the giver more than the offering. The temple offered hope of forgiveness and redemption, but it was only temporary. A permanent change of heart was needed.

Fast forward to the final sacrifice, given once for all: Jesus' death on the cross. His blood covers our sin and runs through our hearts, rejuvenating, renewing, giving new life.

"God demonstrates his own love for us in this: While we were still sinners, Christ died for us" (Romans 5:8 NIV).

That's a love story for the ages. That's a reason to celebrate!

*Merciful and loving God, I fall at Your
feet in repentance and with joy. Amen.*

LIFE, NOT DEATH

*Likewise reckon ye also yourselves to be dead indeed
unto sin, but alive unto God through Jesus Christ our Lord.*

ROMANS 6:11 KJV

Some people see God as an old man on a throne, eyes flashing in judgment, ready to send them to hell. Others see Him as the gentle Savior who welcomes "whosoever will" to sit like a child on His lap.

Both views are correct. The same God who welcomes all believers won't hesitate to condemn unbelievers (see John 3:18). He's a God of opposites: the beginning and the end, Alpha and Omega; loving and just; strong yet gentle. He holds the keys to life—and death.

Paul discusses that tension in Romans. In 5:20 (NIV), he says, "where sin increased, grace increased all the more." He anticipates his audience's reaction: "Shall we go on sinning, so that sin may increase?" (6:1 NIV). Paul slams the door shut. Absolutely not. You died to sin. Period. No questions. You're now alive in Christ. Live like it! Paul doesn't ignore the practical problems—he addresses them throughout the remainder of Romans and his other epistles—but the bottom line: Christians are alive in Christ.

God doesn't want you to worry over how to die to self. He wants you to revel in your new, spirit-filled life.

*God thank You for the new life You've given me in
Christ. May I live, celebrate, and dance in my spirit,
not walk with a burden on my back. Amen.*

PASSING IT ON

*The gracious hand of his God was on him. For Ezra had
devoted himself to the study and observance of the Law
of the Lord, and to teaching its decrees and laws in Israel.*

EZRA 7:9-10 NIV

Ezra was the first in a long tradition of scribes—men who loved the law, meditated on it day and night, and taught it to others. Like the psalmist, he testified, "I run in the path of your commands, for you have broadened my understanding" (Psalm 119:32 NIV).

Yet Ezra did more than study the law. He obeyed its commands to the smallest jot and tittle—every small detail had been examined. He taught the law not only to his family, but also to all of Israel. He helped kindle the passion for God's Word in others.

God had devoted Himself to His people. And Ezra devoted himself back to God by diving into His Word. God responded to Ezra's faithfulness by placing His hand on his life. When people met the scribe, they knew they'd seen God at work.

The world today needs more people like Ezra. The more time you spend with God, the more His work will be evident in your life, showing itself in your obedience, the words you speak, and your recognition of His faithfulness.

*Lawgiver and Living Word, thank You for Ezra's example.
Give me running feet and broaden my understanding as I
study Your Word. Then help me pass this passion on. Amen.*

A LONG OBEDIENCE

God, teach me lessons for living so I can stay the course.
Give me insight so I can do what you tell me—
my whole life one long, obedient response.

PSALM 119:33-34 MSG

How long? Study the journey.

Long before Eugene Peterson wrote his study of the Psalms of Ascents. . . Two millennia before the apostle Paul described all of creation as groaning until God's glory is fully revealed and perfect order restored (see Romans 8:19). . . All the way back to Abraham and even before. . . Believers trusted God. Their faith all the more amazing, since they died without receiving "the promise" (see Hebrews 11:13).

In the verses above, the psalmist clearly understood that trust isn't a one-time event; it's a way of life. And it doesn't come naturally. He asked God to teach him so he could finish the course, for insight so he could obey his whole life long.

Teaching implies the student will be given a problem to solve, but the test isn't a theoretical question. It occurs in real time, the report card written on her heart.

The place to start learning is God's Word. It offers delight, not selfish gain nor worthless things. It exchanges promise for disgrace. It preserves life.

Loving Lord, open my eyes that I may see glimpses of truth You have for me. Shine Your bright life on my life as I read Your Word. Amen.

FOUR-DIMENSIONAL LOVE

For I am persuaded, that neither death, nor life, nor angels, nor principalities, nor powers, nor things present, nor things to come, nor height, nor depth, nor any other creature, shall be able to separate us from the love of God, which is in Christ Jesus our Lord.

ROMANS 8:38-39 KJV

Take all of human history. Every birth, death, kings and kingdoms, to the end of time. God's love is that big.

Go beyond that, to the beginnings of the universe, before humanity was no more than a speck in God's eye. God's love was there.

Go to the edge of the universes, to the place of nothingness— God's love is there.

Right and left, above and below, before and after: in every way man and woman has learned to measure existence, God's love is there.

Nothing can separate God's children from that love. While enduring a Nazi concentration camp, Corrie ten Boom declared, "There is no pit so deep, that God's love is not deeper still."

There's no end to the supply, and it's contagious. It's seen in a woman praying for a friend, "May your blessings be as abundant as the leaves blowing through an endless forest of God's love."

Explore that forest. The fruits may vary in taste and texture but all take their nourishment from God's love.

Jesus, Your love flows underneath me and all around me. Fueled by that love, let me live in peace whatever my circumstances. Amen.

THE SECOND-CHANCE GOD

Lord God of heaven, great and awe-inspiring God, you faithfully keep your promise and show mercy to those who love you and obey your commandments. Open your eyes, and pay close attention with your ears to what I, your servant, am praying.

NEHEMIAH 1:5-6 GW

Everyone loves hearing how Nehemiah rebuilt the walls of Jerusalem and fought off Sanballat, his greatest adversary.

The first few verses of his book give Nehemiah's background. Although he lived in exile, he knew what was happening back in Judah. His brother brought news that the walls of Jerusalem were broken down and ravaged by fire.

Nehemiah didn't storm off to the king. Instead, he spent several days weeping, mourning, praying, fasting. It boiled down to a single prayer request: give us another chance. And God said yes.

When you encounter a roadblock, God will always direct your way, whether it's a detour around the obstacle or setting a course that faces the problem head on. Either way, God will glorify His name. You simply need to follow. When you do, He will make the riches of His glory known.

God of Glory, You have faithfully kept Your promises and shown Your mercy to me. But I don't always see it in the hustle and bustle of life. Open my eyes to what You are doing. Give me a second chance. Show me the road You have paved before me. Amen.

GRINDING DOWN OR LIFTING UP?

*Then I pressed further, "What you are doing is not right!
Should you not walk in the fear of our God in order
to avoid being mocked by enemy nations?"*

NEHEMIAH 5:9 NLT

Nehemiah had led a successful effort to redeem his fellow countrymen from slavery. He might have expected gratitude from the population.

Instead, some officials and nobility raised prices, called in their debts—and forced recently freed men back into slavery. Enraged, Nehemiah pointed to the mockery arising from their actions. The Israelites didn't need an enemy to defeat them. They were too busy tearing each other down.

The writer of Psalm 119:74 (NLT) hoped his own behavior would bring joy to others, and not mockery: "May all who fear You find in me a cause for joy, for I have put my hope in Your word." Like Nehemiah, the psalmist received a mixed reaction. Some accused him without cause (see Psalm 119:78)

Instead of giving up and backing away, the Jews fought back against the unfair practices and criticism. God made them overcomers.

If godly people and great presidents have their detractors, how much more so ordinary people? Whenever someone strikes to tear down what you're building up, you can choose to give up—or to stand up, with joy and confidence in God.

*O Father, how I hurt when others unravel the progress I've made.
Strengthen me with joy and hope according to Your Word. Amen.*

WITH GOD'S HELP

When all our enemies heard about this, all the surrounding nations were afraid and lost their self-confidence, because they realized that this work had been done with the help of our God.

NEHEMIAH 6:16 NIV

In his first hundred days in office, Franklin D. Roosevelt set up his promised New Deal by passing fifteen pieces of major legislation.

Nehemiah the administrator beat FDR's standard for effective leadership. Less than a week after his arrival in Jerusalem, he challenged the residents to rebuild the walls. They didn't contract with a local builder. Instead, every man and woman living in the city took bricks and trowels in hand to build. They alternated bricklaying with standing guard so they could continue undisturbed. They finished in fifty-two days.

Their neighbors complained to the king, not realizing, perhaps, that Artaxerxes had already agreed to the project. Nehemiah reported that their enemies lost their self-confidence when they saw the work was done with the help of God.

Perhaps Nehemiah was taking the psalmist's words to heart: "All your commands are trustworthy; help me, for I am being persecuted without cause" (Psalm 119:86 NIV). As long as God had designed the plan, no persecution could overcome it.

Whatever God calls you to do can be completed with His help.

God my Helper, I need You today. Help me obey You when You first prompt me and continue obeying when the going gets tough. I depend on You because You are trustworthy. Amen.

PLEASE SPEAK UP

But how can people call for help if they don't know who to trust?
And how can they know who to trust if they haven't heard of the One
who can be trusted? And how can they hear if nobody tells them?

ROMANS 10:14 MSG

When people are in trouble, they need to know who to call. If someone's having a heart attack, they call 911, easy enough for a child to remember.

But what about other attacks of the heart and spirit, leaving a person cold and afraid, wondering what next? Whom can they trust? Who will listen, help, provide an answer?

Christians know the answer. The problem is, too often they neglect to share the emergency contact information with others. The numbers 911 would be useless if no one knew about them.

The Levites and scribes of Nehemiah's day must've spent time reading, meditating, and memorizing the law. When the exiles celebrated the completion of the wall and their return, priests "read from the Book of the Law of God, making it clear and giving the meaning so that the people understood what was being read" (Nehemiah 8:8 NIV).

The world still needs to hear about God's character, to see God at work in the lives of His people. Be a speaker and doer of the truth (see James 1:22).

Word of God, make me a trustworthy spokesperson
to share the good news to a world in need of You. Amen.

WHEN NOTHING MAKES SENSE—GOD DOES

Oh, the depth of the wisdom and the knowledge of God! How unsearchable His judgments, and His paths beyond tracing out!

ROMANS 11:33 NIV

G od's light shines brightest in the darkest place.

At the time this devotional was written, Americans were recovering from Hurricanes Harvey and Irma and battling massive fires in Montana and Colorado. Amid the devastation, the media reported acts of goodness, kindness, mercy, and compassion, all pointing to the greatest Giver of good gifts.

Paul battled a heart broken because (most of) his fellow Jews rejected their Messiah (see Romans 9:30-10:1). After explaining the special relationship between Jews and Gentiles, he turned from his personal pain to a praise of the Father. Although God's judgments are unsearchable, He's the most Supreme Court justice. Bottom line: His decisions can be trusted.

People throughout history have discovered this rock-solid truth. God spared generations of Israelites from destruction because of His compassion, mercy, and goodness (see Nehemiah 9:28, 31, 36). In the nineteenth century, the great preacher Charles Spurgeon said, "We cannot always trace God's hand, but we can always trust God's heart." Contemporary lyricist Kierra Sheard describes God as indescribable, uncontainable, incomparable, unchangeable.

God may not reveal the end, but He will always direct your next step.

God above my wildest imaginations, open my eyes to what part of Your glory I can bear to see. May You shine brighter on my life so I may better see my path to Your goodness. Amen.

DICTATED BY LOVE

*Let Your love dictate how You deal with me; teach me from
Your textbook on life. I'm Your servant—help me understand
what that means, the inner meaning of Your instructions.*

PSALM 119:124-125 MSG

These two verses from Psalm 119 read like a perfect prayer, that God's love will dictate how He deals with sin, human frailty, and steps of faith. Thanking God because His love permeates everything He does. Asking God to teach from the Bible and by the Spirit, during prayer and meditation. Requesting specific instructions on how to be a servant.

Fast forward to Romans 12, Paul's imminently practical guidelines for what a living sacrifice looks like. Just as believers plead for God's love to govern His dealings with humankind, God tells believers to devote themselves to each other in love (see Romans 12:9-10). Their love reflects His love.

Among other factors, that devotion shows itself in prompt, cheerful giving to each other what is owed. Yes, it's important to pay bills and taxes. But Paul also mentions the importance of other, less measurable gifts: honor and respect (see Romans 13:7).

Believers who grow deep roots in the love of God will know He is trustworthy and will throw themselves into emulating His example.

*Lord God, may Your love dictate how You deal with me.
May I study the Bible as my assigned textbook, preparing me
for life exams. I call You "Lord." Make it so in my life. Amen.*

DARKEST BEFORE DAWN

Besides this you know what [a critical] hour this is, how it is high time now for you to wake up out of your sleep (rouse to reality). For salvation (final deliverance) is nearer to us now than when we first believed (adhered to, trusted in, and relied on Christ, the Messiah).

ROMANS 13:11 AMPC

The proverb "The darkest hour is just before the dawn," first used in print by theologian Thomas Fuller in 1650, is meant to inspire hope in adverse circumstances.

To rally his troops to action amid war, Prime Minister Winston Churchill said, "This is no time for ease and comfort. It is the time to dare and endure."

Paul wrote with a similar urgency to Christians in Rome. The time of darkness and sin was drawing to an end. Born-again believers were to cloth themselves daily in Jesus Christ, until their salvation reached its fulfillment in heaven.

If God's salvation was near in Paul's day, how much nearer two millennia later! Blessed with eternal life, Christians have already been redeemed. Yet they also look to the future. One day they'll be perfect, without sin, in a glorified body.

Until then, they live out their salvation by setting aside darkness and putting on the armor of light, thus illuminating the way to heavenly glory.

Glorious Lord, inspire me with hope. Polish me inside and out until Your salvation shines in me. Not because I'm worthy, but because You are. Amen.

A QUEEN'S HOSPITALITY

May God, who gives this patience and encouragement,
help you live in complete harmony with each other,
as is fitting for followers of Christ Jesus.

ROMANS 15:5 NLT

God isn't mentioned by name in the book of Esther. It's strange, because her story rings with evidence of God's sovereignty and providence at work.

Take Mordecai's challenge to Queen Esther after telling her of the evil Haman's plot to exterminate her people. "Who knows if you have come to the kingdom for such a time as this?" (see Esther 4:14).

After a period of fasting and prayer, Esther determined to risk the king's displeasure by approaching the throne without an invitation. When he extended his scepter toward her, accepting her approach, she invited him and Haman to a dinner party—and later another feast. Esther not only chose her battles, but also the battlefields: the dining room, not the royal hall.

Esther might not have been queen for a long time, but she learned a lot about living in harmony. She used the silk glove, not a sword, to accomplish God's work of protecting her fellow Jews from Haman's murderous schemes.

God calls His people to live in "complete harmony," in the way Jesus showed His disciples. Together, we can overcome anything the world throws at us.

Father God, I thank You for the gifts of patience and encouragement.
Let me be hospitable and live in harmony with all. Amen.

KINGDOM CITIZENS

*And all the king's servants who were at the king's gate bowed
down and did reverence to Haman, for the king had so commanded
concerning him. But Mordecai did not bow down or do him reverence.*

ESTHER 3:2 AMPC

No one ever said obeying God would be easy.

As Christians are in this world but not of it (see John 17:16), the Jews in exile were in the center of the Persian empire but not of it. The deported Mordecai, Daniel, and the three men in the fiery furnace, took these words of Jeremiah to heart. "Seek the peace and prosperity of the city to which I have carried you into exile" (29:7 NIV). None of those heroes allowed their commitment to their new home outweigh their obedience to God. They refused to bow to anything or anyone—but Him.

People noticed Mordecai's refusal to bow to Haman and brought it to King Xerxes attention. Mordecai's commitment to honor God alone led to a plan to annihilate his people.

No one bows down in a literal sense to American politicians. Instead, people prostrate themselves in front of the false gods such as political correctness and popularity.

When you bow down to worship, make sure you're facing in the right direction.

*Lord, give me eyes to see the nature of that which asks
for my admiration and honor. Make me pure in my dedication
to You, that no other idol clouds or eats away at it. Amen.*

THE WIND AT YOUR BACK

*In every province and city, wherever the king's decree arrived,
the Jews rejoiced and had a great celebration and declared a public
festival and holiday. And many of the people of the land became Jews
themselves, for they feared what the Jews might do to them.*

ESTHER 8:17 NLT

According to Persian law, an edict couldn't be repealed once set into motion. Even after Xerxes learned of Esther's Jewish heritage, he couldn't change the law ordering the assault on Jews in his empire.

Instead, he found an alternative: Jews could arm themselves and fight back.

Perhaps one of the strangest events of the story is that *even before* the day the new edict was to take effect, many non-Jews converted out of fear.

Maybe God planned it that way. His people escaped unharmed, their enemies killed. And Gentiles aligned themselves with Israel's God, fearful because they recognized Him at work.

God's protection in tough times often resembles that of Esther's day. He doesn't always halt trials and difficulties, but He gives His people the necessary weapons to fight back. In the process, people are drawn to the demonstration of His glory and power.

Whatever your problems today, pray for God's glory to spread in and through them.

*Overcoming God, when battles come—for they will—
dress me in Your armor and be the wind at my back, that
I may stand, a beacon of light to those around me. Amen.*

GOD'S LULLABY

He will not allow your foot to be moved; He who keeps you will not slumber. Behold, He who keeps Israel shall neither slumber nor sleep.
PSALM 121:3-4 NKJV

Suppose a house or business owner decides to hire a security guard. How would either feel about an applicant with these qualifications?

Protects physical safety

Doesn't fall asleep on the job, not even for a quick catnap

Provides shelter from the elements

Keeps a record of every entrance and exit

Doesn't take a day off, ever

Sounds pretty impressive, doesn't it?

Suppose the same security guard offers to provide the service for free, no payment necessary, only a complete trust in his services and a recommendation to others in need?

That security guard's name would be GOD.

No wonder the psalmist said, "Where does my help come from? My help comes from the LORD!" (Psalm 121:1-2 NIV). Salvation guarantees the kind of security described above. God is with believers always, to the end of the age (see Matthew 28:19). Anyone can obtain that security: whosoever will may come (see Revelation 22:17).

When plodding through a morass of fear or depression, hum this psalm of God's love and protection. When sleep remains elusive, listen to His voice singing this lullaby.

That's where true freedom lies.

God, I rest in You, knowing You're awake and alert on my behalf, never taking a break. May I awake, refreshed, to move and act in the security of Your loving protection. Amen.

CALLED

God is faithful (reliable, trustworthy, and therefore ever true to His promise, and He can be depended on); by Him you were called into companionship and participation with His Son, Jesus Christ our Lord.

1 CORINTHIANS 1:9 AMPC

God calls all to walk in their unique path and ministry.

Sometimes that calling is obvious and unmistakable. Isaiah had a vision of God and angels in heaven, then heard God's voice. Jesus called the twelve publicly. He accosted Paul on the road to Damascus.

Others discover their calling in ordinary life, a calling so natural, there's no sense of the supernatural about it. Except another person couldn't do it so easily or so well. Dorcas sewed clothes for those in need.

Others are called to suffer. Job was tested in his faith. Then blessed because of it.

All Christians share the calling of fellowship with Christ and to be God's set-apart people.

And all callings start with the caller. The nature of the call, the honor of the call, lies in the character of the one who calls, and God is the ultimate caller—reliable, trustworthy, and the contract He offers won't change. The proof of call lies in the One who calls, not in the one called.

Lord, You sought me when I was a stranger, an enemy. You've called me to holiness, to fellowship, things for which I had no natural ability. Work in my life to fulfill my calling to the last detail. Amen.

DO IT ANYWAY

I was unsure of how to go about this, and felt totally inadequate—
I was scared to death, if you want the truth of it—and so
nothing I said could have impressed you or anyone else.
But the Message came through anyway.

1 CORINTHIANS 2:3-4 MSG

What a paradox. God gave Paul a wide-open door in Corinth, a promise of a lengthy and attack-free ministry (see Acts 18:8-11).

Paul's response? He didn't quite know what to do with it. He didn't know how to go about it, felt inadequate to the task. This great orator fell short, no wise or persuasive words in his arsenal (1 Corinthians 2:4 NIV)

And God used him anyway. As Paul discusses in 1 Corinthians, he learned to revel in his weakness because that's when God's power succeeded.

Mother Theresa captured the paradox of weakness versus faithfulness in the powerful poem, "Do It Anyway," written on the walls of her children's home in India. After urging the importance of doing what's right even if success is uncertain, the piece concluded, "In the final analysis, it is between you and God. It was never between you and them [others] anyway."

There's freedom in that simple statement. God doesn't call His people because they're worthy; He only asks for hearts willing to be instruments of His power.

Sovereign Lord, I am weak, but You are strong. Make me
weaker yet, until I rely fully upon You, and You alone. Amen.

HEAVEN-APPOINTED COUNSEL

*If only there were someone to mediate between us, someone
to bring us together, someone to remove God's rod from me,
so that his terror would frighten me no more. Then I would speak
up without fear of him, but as it now stands with me, I cannot.*

JOB 9:33-35 NIV

Before you abuse, criticize, and accuse, walk a mile in my shoes"
was Elvis Presley's spin on a familiar proverb.

Job's friends wanted to help but didn't know how. They had no
experience to draw on to understand his suffering.

Many people have echoed Job's plea for a mediator who
understands their pain, such as the patient who wishes her doctor
could spend a twenty-hours in a hospital bed. In the same way,
humankind clamors for a mediator with God.

Job felt the need of someone who understood both sides, and
cried to God in faith. Jesus is the answer to Job's plea. "For there
is one mediator between God and mankind, the man Christ Jesus"
(1 Timothy 2:5 NIV).

How much more precious is Jesus to Christians living in the age
of grace, knowing He had been tempted like they are. He understands
completely their weaknesses.

Jesus, the heaven-appointed counsel, stands at His Father's right
hand when all who have received Him appear before God's throne.

*Oh Jesus, I rejoice in having You as my Mediator at God's throne!
No charge can be laid against me that You will not answer in full.*

PLEAD: INNOCENT

Because even if he killed me, I'd keep on hoping.
I'd defend my innocence to the very end. Just wait,
this is going to work out for the best—my salvation!

JOB 13:15-16 MSG

In Job 13, Job sounds like a man on death row. It's as if the date of his execution has been set, and all appeals have been rejected, yet he still hopes for a last-minute reversal. Or perhaps he'll be pardoned in time.

Only Job's plea doesn't just go out to his friends—but all the way to heaven itself.

He tells God he feels as if he were found guilty in a trial he wasn't invited to. And he doesn't know the charge. (He's the prototype for the prisoner in Kafka's *The Trial*.)

Yet who can argue with God and His verdict?

But, Job said, even if God carried out a death sentence, he'd keep hoping. God knew his innocence, and this would all work out for the best—his salvation. If not in this life, in the next.

How much more should Christians trust God in the most severe trials.

So, stand up and stay strong. Life may end, but you will not. So live in Christ forevermore.

Living Lord, how precious is this promise, how amazing
Job's faith. If—or when—I face my darkest hour,
may I stand as confident of You as Job did. Amen.

NIGHTWATCH

*I wait for the LORD, my soul doth wait, and in His word do I hope.
My soul waiteth for the Lord more than they that watch for the
morning: I say, more than they that watch for the morning.*

PSALM 130:5-6 KJV

Waiting is a fundamental part of the human experience.

A mother waits nine long months to hold her child.

A father sits by the phone, hoping against hope his wayward child will call home.

The insomniac longs for sleep and waits for a reason to get up.

The Christian waits for the Lord to act. For His return. For the day that faith will be sight.

Job understood that kind of waiting. In his grief, he said, "If only you would set me a time and then remember me!" (Job 14:13 NIV). He had absolute confidence that day would come. "You *will call* and I will answer you" (Job 14:15 NIV, emphasis added).

The psalmist matched Job's confidence because with God comes forgiveness (see Psalm 130:4). His love never fails.

With that confidence, wait for the morning.

Eternal God, when I wait in the dark, You prepare the sunrise of my new day. What I now glimpse in the shadows, I will one day see revealed in the full light. I thank You for the times Your flashlight shows me pieces of that final complete picture. Amen.

GOD'S TEMPLE

Don't you know that your body is a temple that belongs to
the Holy Spirit? The Holy Spirit, whom you received from God,
lives in you. You don't belong to yourselves. You were bought
for a price. So bring glory to God in the way you use your body.

1 CORINTHIANS 6:19-20 GW

It's easy to compartmentalize faith. One wonders if the physical body matters all that much since the new life in Christ is spiritual, a change of heart—and flesh and bones are a shell, a vestige of the former way of life. One day they will be exchanged for an imperishable, spiritual body (see 1 Corinthians 15:53).

Yet the call to be joined to Christ begins now, in the earthly realm, with a believer's body as God's temple. Thus, when the physical body is abused, God's temple is tarnished.

Imagine Jesus coming to dinner. How might you change the externals? Would you try to hide unhealthy habits? Would you dress differently or serve a different menu? What entertainment would you plan?

God wants you to live every day with the knowledge—inside and out—that He's a permanent resident in the heart, mind, body, and soul of the believer. Treating your body with respect is important because God lives there.

Indwelling Spirit, make repairs to my soul and spirit that
only You can so that I may glorify You in my body and find
the strength to take the necessary steps to change. Amen.

GOD'S LEADERSHIP

But who are we to tell God how to run His affairs?
He's dealing with matters that are way over our heads.

JOB 21:22 MSG

Remember TV's Deputy Barney Fife acting as sheriff in Andy Taylor's absence? How about *Mama's Family*'s Thelma Harper resigning as mayor after a week? Buffoonery makes a serious point. Not everyone makes a good leader.

Yet consider Princess Elizabeth, crowned queen at twenty-five and still reigning sixty-five years later. Look at a young nun named Teresa, leaving the convent to minister to the poorest people in India.

The point is, no one understands what it takes to rule until they give it a try. Not everyone succeeds. Some incumbent officials are questioned at every turn.

The problem arises when people turn that same critical eye on God. They doubt His wisdom and want to take His place. Like the serpent in the garden, they ask, "Did God really say. . .?"

Job shows his faith by asking, "Who are we to tell God how to run His affairs?" Job didn't understand what God was doing. But he didn't waver in his confidence that God was the only one capable of managing his life.

Oh, to be like Job. Instead of taking God's place, trust His heart.

Father, forgive me when I try to wrest control of one tiny
piece of my life, when I hold anything back. I hand it
all over to You. Lead as You will—and I'll follow.

GOD KNOWS

Only, let each one [seek to conduct himself and regulate his affairs so as to] lead the life which the Lord has allotted and imparted to him and to which God has invited and summoned him. This is my order in all the churches.

1 Corinthians 7:17 AMPC

Within the church, some have felt called to leave their families and live a celibate life to serve God more fully. Paul applauds that choice: "It is good for [the unmarried and the widows] to stay unmarried, as I do" (1 Corinthians 7:8 NIV).

Are those who are married, or long for marriage, choosing second best? Absolutely not.

According to Paul, it's best for believers to remain in the situation they were in when they were born again. Should a new believer leave an unbelieving spouse? No.

Should a single person remain single? Not necessarily. Paul acknowledges it's better to marry than to burn with lust (see 1 Corinthians 7:9).

The same God who calls believers knows their situation. Paul's words aren't meant to keep wives (or husbands or children) in an abusive situation. Seek help if needed, from both God and people.

Father, a marriage may not live up to Your purposes of a union to reflect the relationship between Christ and the church. Yet You offer hope and renewal to all—single, married, widowed, or divorced. Give me the grace to be at peace where I am—and the courage to seek help if needed.

EXPIRATION DATE

God, your name is eternal, God, you'll never be out-of-date.
God stands up for his people, God holds the hands of his people.

PSALM 135:13-14 MSG

Just about everything comes with an expiration date. All animals are born, live—and die. Our sun is gradually dying. Food and medicine are stamped with a DO NOT USE PAST THIS DATE warning.

Finite humans have a beginning and an ending.

God *is* the beginning and the end. He *is*—always. He'll "never be out-of-date."

Back when America's founding fathers fought for independence—God was there.

When the world went to war and Hitler schemed to bring an end to God's chosen people—God was there.

The day you were born—God was there.

When you die—God will be there.

A hundred years from now, when today's infants lie in their graves, God will be there.

A thousand years from now, when the United States may just be a chapter in a history book, God will be there.

As long as God is there, He will stand for His people. He will hold their hands as tightly as a mother holds her young child's. He will never let go.

God holds the hands of His people on the tightrope of life. So step out on faith!

Eternal God, You're never out of date or late. Your answers
and direction as always wise, always certain, whether spoken
in the twentieth, twenty-first, or twenty-second century.

LIGHT OF LIFE

*God has delivered me from going down to the pit, and
I shall live to enjoy the light of life. "God does all these
things to a person-twice, even three times-to turn them
back from the pit, that the light of life may shine on them."*

JOB 33:28-30 NIV

How wonderful it is to know that we are pursued by God every day. That we are continually sought by God, whose heart wants the best for us. Although He would like to save us from trips to a miserable pit, sometimes we must be rescued repeatedly.

We are designed to walk with God in beautiful light. Sometimes though the light is not apparent. We feel like we're living in the shadows. In these times, it's important to remember that God is close. And that dark times do not mean God has abandoned us or is unhappy with us.

We can trust that God desires to speak to us and to lead us. We do not need to linger in confusion. God may speak to us in scripture or in the words of a song or sermon, drawing us back to Him and away from the darkness. At times, God leads us away with a sense of peace.

Listen for and trust God to speak. His desire is to redeem your soul through salvation and to restore light and joy to your life.

*God, thank You that Your plan for me
is to walk in the Light with You.*

BROAD PLACES

*But those who suffer he delivers in their suffering; he speaks
to them in their affliction. He is wooing you from the
jaws of distress to a spacious place free from restriction,
to the comfort of your table laden with choice food.*

JOB 36:15-16 NIV

When we are in distress or affliction, we may feel consumed by the sadness or anxiety that the crisis brings. It seems as if our circumstances will never change. Our imagination convinces us that the current torment will continue forever, that it will eat us up. Yet that is not the truth.

God has ways and means that we cannot understand. He is better to us than we can imagine. He is more merciful and more powerful than we can comprehend. God may use the pain of our circumstances to get our attention. Then, coaxing us like reluctant sheep, He leads us away from the gaping jaws of an all-consuming anxiety and into a wide-open space, "to a place free from distress" (Job 36:16 NLT).

Ask God to open your heart to any truths He would like to teach you. Be transformed by the painful circumstance you find yourself in. Trust that God will rescue you and lavish you with things for your heart to enjoy. What would you like to ask God for today?

*God, please lead me into a broad and peaceful place.
I trust You with the journey.*

HIS MAJESTY

God's voice thunders in marvelous ways;
he does great things beyond our understanding.

JOB 37:5 NIV

G od is both great and good at the same time.

As far as being great, He is *El*, which means God in full power. He is the awesome creator of everything we see. He is in control of the rain, snow, and sun. He holds the earth together with His thoughts. He is God of unlimited might.

At the same time and to the same degree, God is *good*. He is marvelously and unsurpassably good. There is no darkness or evil in Him. He is 100 percent kind, loving, and merciful all the time.

Together, His greatness and His goodness means that we can trust Him to work in our lives in an amazing way. We can trust that even when we struggle with hardships, He is working things out for our best. We can trust that when we experience success, it has been a good gift from His hand.

No matter what the circumstances of your life, you can lift your eyes to God whose voice thunders mightily. You can gratefully and humbly trust the way your great and good God designs your day.

God, I am grateful for Your mighty strength and goodness.
Please do great things in my life today.

JOB'S CONFESSION

*"I know that you can do all things; no purpose
of yours can be thwarted. . . . My ears had heard
of you but now my eyes have seen you."*

JOB 42:2, 5 NIV

Job's heart is vulnerable and open to God in a new way. He has honored God in the past with his actions, but now Job's experience of God has transformed him. His eyes are open wide to see the awesomeness of God. Job sees clearly that he miscalculated God's glory. With this new vision of God, Job is humbled and repentant.

Do you need to expand your vision of God? Do you complain about the circumstances in which God has placed you? Do you attempt to control others in ways that you hope will be helpful?

God is able to do all things very well. Trust Him to care for you and others without complaints or control. Bring your concerns to Him in prayer, then let them go. Whatever God's purpose is cannot be thwarted. Nothing can stand in His way.

*God, help me to see You with new eyes.
Help me to trust that You can do all things in my life.*

NOTHING BETTER

I know that there is nothing better for people than to be happy
and to do good while they live. That each of them may eat and drink,
and find satisfaction in all their toil—this is the gift of God.

ECCLESIASTES 3:12-13 NIV

D id you wake up this morning with a light heart? Adam and Eve woke every morning with a joyful heart until sin entered their garden paradise. You, however, have troubles, struggles, and problems to solve each day. Your life has unanswered questions, obstacles, and hardships. With all that going on, how can you enjoy the day He's made (see Psalm 118:24)?

Rely on God to take care of you. Choose to lift your face to your heavenly Father and trust Him. Tell Him aloud that you're thankful for His provision.

Put a new spin on your work and its meaning by considering it as God's gift to you. What do you enjoy about what you do? Thank God for what's been placed in your hands, and your joyful mood will flourish.

To find even more satisfaction and joy, look for opportunities to bring more good into your day. "Good" can be as simple as connecting with a friend, sharing a smile with a child, or thanking God for a simple meal. Be intentional about enjoying today!

God, help me be open to new ways of thinking about today's work.
Help me develop a joyful heart and attitude every moment of my life.

YOU ARE LOVED

*Love is patient, love is kind. It does not envy, it does not boast,
it is not proud. It does not dishonor others, it is not self-seeking,
it is not easily angered, it keeps no record of wrongs. Love
does not delight in evil but rejoices with the truth.*

1 CORINTHIANS 13:4-6 NIV

We may not have great success at implementing this impressive list of love's qualities. God, however, never fails at loving us completely and enduringly. All our lives, He has loved us with patience and kindness. And although the people around us may also fail to meet God's high standard of love, He does not. He is never irritable or resentful with us and rejoices over us when we make good choices.

Understanding how God sees us is critical to our trusting Him. Sometimes our brain tells us we're trusting when our emotions are still fearful. That's because head knowledge is different from heart knowledge. It's when our hearts are satisfied that His affection doesn't waver that we can trust God completely.

Take a deep breath and relax in the truth that God is good and you can trust Him with every part of your life: your family, work, relationships, health, and more. Look back over your life and remember the ways God has proven His great love for you. Rest in His affection today.

*God, thank You for your perfect love.
Help me to let go of fear and trust You.*

ONE JUDGE

Search me [thoroughly], O God, and know my heart!
Try me and know my thoughts! And see if there is any wicked
or hurtful way in me, and lead me in the way everlasting.

PSALM 139:23-24 AMPC

Your heart is as complex and difficult to understand as a puzzle with a vast number of unique pieces. It contains strong desires, fears, pride, love, tenderness, anger, sadness, and more. Who can possibly comprehend its true content? The answer is God. He can discern the innermost parts of your heart and help you better understand your own thoughts, feelings, and actions.

Seek God's perspective on the contents of your heart. Trust His kind and thorough judgements. Ask God where corrections need to be made. Is there pride lurking behind a broken relationship? Are sharp fragments of jealousy tearing at your joy?

God's desire is for you to be free from the tight, constraining grasp of sin's chokehold. He wants you to be free to experience all the confidence, peace, and joy you were created for in life. Take His hand and let Him lead you through the process of redeeming your heart and mind as only He can.

God, please search my heart and mind and show me what
You want to change in me. I trust You to break me free of
old thought patterns and feelings. Lead me in Your new way.

PEACE

For God is not a God of disorder but of peace. . . .

1 CORINTHIANS 14:33 NIV

Orderliness in life brings peace, whereas disorderliness leads to confusion and chaos. This is a simple truth from God. Like warm, clean, colorful laundry tossed together, the moments and activities of our day need sorting into harmony. Balance rest with work, reflection with business, and togetherness with solitude. Determine ways to let your day and week reflect the orderliness of God.

Because you are made in God's image, you have a great capacity to bring tranquility from disorder in your home. Does your home feel tranquil? If not, consider giving away extra items.

Along with *not* being a God of disorder, God is also *not* a God of confusion. So take time to consider your emotions and thoughts. Sort through them and ask the Holy Spirit to guide you into peace. Your inner world of thoughts and feelings thrive when you slow down for reflection. Is there something that needs to be said? Is there a trouble that needs to be given to God in prayer? You can be certain Jesus, your Prince of Peace, will lead you from confusion to calm if you will only ask Him.

God, You know the struggles both inside and outside of me. Please come into this chaos and bring Your peace. I chose You to be the center of my day and my life instead of the confusion that abounds without You.

PESKY LITTLE FOXES

Catch for us the foxes, the little foxes that
ruin the vineyards, our vineyards are in bloom.

SONG OF SOLOMON 2:15 NIV

In the verse above, Solomon is asking the woman he loves to pay attention to the little things (which he calls "foxes") that could spoil their flowering relationship. Can you picture little red foxes frolicking through green vineyards full of lush blossoms? No matter how sweet they may seem, those little foxes only wreak havoc between you and those you love.

It's often the seemingly inconsequential things that can spoil a relationship. So stay vigilant to protect important connections with God, others, and even yourself. What little things are making mayhem in your relationships? Perhaps today is the day to take time away from seemingly urgent matters and spend those moments with the most important people in your life. Let them know how much you value them. And, if needed, keep bitterness from growing by forgiving small irritations. Shoo those little foxes away and commit to speaking words of love and affirmation.

The blossoms the foxes would like to devour are the sweetest part of your life. God has given you a gift in the relationships He has provided. So tend those blossoms with care.

God, help me to recognize the value of my connection with others.
Show me where I am allowing small things to cause harm. I trust
You to heal my broken relationships and make others healthy.

FRAGRANCE

May my prayer be set before you like incense;
may the lifting up of my hands be like the evening sacrifice.

PSALM 141:2 NIV

Have you ever wondered if your little prayers for help are irritating to God? Do you hesitate asking Him for directions in recovering lost keys or finding a parking spot? Don't. Because God actually loves it when you turn to Him for *anything*, big or small. He breathes in your prayers as fragrant incense. So you are never ever a bother to Him.

God looks at you with eyes of love. Every one of your prayers— long or short, frantic or calm—are a joy. He also gathers up and takes pleasure in all your "popcorn prayers"—little trusting thoughts that you send His way.

God is even more delighted when you offer Him your lifted hands, which is your way of expressing that He is your sovereign, almighty King and you are His loyal and loving servant.

So pray away today. And perhaps try worshipping God with your hands raised in adoration. It will lift your heart as well as His.

God, I trust that You hear even my smallest prayer and
count it as special. Help me to remember to come to You
with my big and small needs today. May my prayers, trusting
thoughts, and upraised hands lift both our hearts today.

OVERWHELMED

When my spirit was overwhelmed within me, then You knew my path.
In the way in which I walk they have secretly set a snare for me.

PSALM 142:3 NKJV

David wrote the words above while hiding out in a cave.
Caves are difficult to navigate around due to their darkness. Circumstances in your life may leave you feeling overwhelmed, as if you are groping around in the dark, but know that God is always in control. Although your feelings may be overwhelming, God is never at a loss for direction. Although your thoughts might be confused and directionless, God always has a plan.

The future God has for you is good. Ask Him to reveal the path for you, then watch for His response. You can trust God to lead you along the right path at just the right time.

God is not surprised by the tricks and devious plans of those who wish to see you hurt, tripped up, or unsuccessful. He can handle anything they would throw against you. Let your heart be fearless as you put your trust in God.

God, please clearly reveal the path You have planned
before me. I will not be afraid as I put my trust in You.

CONSIDER GOD

They have harps and lyres at their banquets, pipes and timbrels and wine, but they have no regard for the deeds of the LORD, no respect for the work of his hands. Therefore my people will go into exile for lack of understanding; those of high rank will die of hunger and the common people will be parched with thirst.

ISAIAH 5:12-13 NIV

God pursues you and knows you. He follows hard after you. In fact, "the eyes of the LORD search the whole earth in order to strengthen those whose hearts are fully committed to him" (2 Chronicles 16:9 NLT). And just as God pursues you, He knows you. He knows your name, your thoughts, and the things that bring you sadness or joy. He wants you to know Him as well as He knows you.

Acknowledge God in your day today. Recognize the unique beauty around you and praise the creator. Did He bless you with sunlight, food, breath for your lungs? Reflect on how He has worked in your life. Has He provided health, safety, work, family or friends? As you read the scriptures, ask God to reveal Himself to you in truth. Get to know Him as a savior, a provider, a pursuer, a healer, and as a friend. Peace and joy will be your reward.

God, let me know You in spirit and in truth. Remind me to look for Your works today and to praise You.

YES, IN JESUS

For no matter how many promises God has made,
they are "Yes" in Christ. And so through him the
"Amen" is spoken by us to the glory of God.

2 CORINTHIANS 1:20 NIV

God has made you over 5,000 promises. It is encouraging to know He will provide and fight for you, give you strength, grant you wisdom, go before you, and never leave nor forsake you (see Exodus 4:14; Isaiah 40:29; James 1:5; Deuteronomy 31:8). These promises are grounded in the ultimate proof of love displayed in Christ Jesus— the undeniable love of God for humanity. With His promises, God says "Yes! I love you." And in them, we grasp hold of the truth of His unfaltering affection and confidently respond with "Amen."

What does our expression of an "Amen" look like? An open heart. A willingness to let go of control. An attitude of hope. A trust that does not falter in the face of adversity.

You can trust God will fulfill every commitment He has made to you. Take courage in your loving God. Let His words strengthen your heart and give peace to your mind. God is more than capable of helping you today. Amen to that!

God, please help me to comprehend Your great love for me.
Help me to stand firm in Your glorious promises. Amen!!

AROMA

For we are to God the pleasing aroma of Christ among those who are being saved and those who are perishing. To the one we are an aroma that brings death; to the other, an aroma that brings life.

2 CORINTHIANS 2:15-16 NIV

Daily life is full of scents. You smell fresh breads baking or coffee brewing, roses blooming in garden pots, or popcorn popping at the movie theatre. These are pleasant fragrances that bring up lovely thoughts and delightful feelings. And because you are saved in Christ, you yourself have a sweet smell to God. He delights to breathe you in.

For believers in Christ, it's refreshing and encouraging to be with other Christians. The abundance of everlasting life is fragrant. However, to those not saved by grace, the opposite can be true. You can expect there will be people who don't appreciate the hope, love, and faith that wafts around you. You are fragrant, but nonbelievers don't like your smell. For you are a reminder to them that God is ever present and that they are either denying His existence or standing in rebellion to His judgment.

Strive to not be offended by nonbelievers. Simply do what you are designed to do. Bloom with all the love and freedom of a child of God.

God, thank You that I am fragrant in Christ.
Thank You that I represent abundant life, and
remind me that You always find delight in me.

LIVE FREE

Now the Lord is the Spirit, and where
the Spirit of the Lord is, there is freedom.

2 Corinthians 3:17 niv

The sun rises and sets daily, and no one attempts to alter its course. The waves of the ocean come and go on the sandy shore, too powerful to be deterred. So it is with the Spirit of the Lord. He is powerful and free. And with His power, He has set you free. This means you are not under the burden of striving. You can simply be who Christ made you to be. You are free to enjoy life without pressure to be who someone thinks you should be.

God loves you and has given you the freedom to live each day loving Him, yourself, and others. He's given you the freedom to make the best choices. You are not restricted to living in a small and painful world but have been set free to celebrate being alive.

Christ fulfilled the law so that you don't have to. You can eat the foods you prefer, sing the songs you chose, dress in your own style, read what interests you, and attend church where you like.

Ask yourself what Christ wants you to enjoy today. Listen for His Spirit's promptings. Be free to enjoy the day He created.

God, help me to truly enjoy my freedom and this day with You.

A CLAY JAR

But we have this treasure in jars of clay, to show that the surpassing power is from God and not from us. We are hard pressed on every side, but not crushed; perplexed, but not in despair; persecuted, but not abandoned; struck down, but not destroyed.

2 CORINTHIANS 4:7-9 NIV

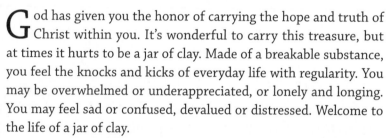

God has given you the honor of carrying the hope and truth of Christ within you. It's wonderful to carry this treasure, but at times it hurts to be a jar of clay. Made of a breakable substance, you feel the knocks and kicks of everyday life with regularity. You may be overwhelmed or underappreciated, or lonely and longing. You may feel sad or confused, devalued or distressed. Welcome to the life of a jar of clay.

But take heart! You are not alone. In fact, you are in good company. The world is full of jars of all ages and nationalities, keeping the faith.

Through your troubles, you can rest in the promise that God is powerful and He will not toss you aside or forsake you. He holds you in His hand and loves you. His protection surrounding you, you can trust Him to care for and comfort you. He is aware of all your needs. The treasure of Christ in you and your faith in Him is your great reward.

God, I know You understand my struggles and frailty. Please allow me to persevere through this day with Your power.

FAITH IS THE VICTORY

For we live by faith, not by sight.

2 CORINTHIANS 5:7 NIV

When we find ourselves in the dark, our first response is to find a flashlight. We like to see where we are stepping. . .in the backyard as well as in life. We prefer knowing which direction, how fast, and how long the journey will take at every turn. We are, however, called to walk by faith, which usually means "lights out." Yet when confusion and uncertainty cause darkness, we try to regain control, a wild scramble to stop the pain of walking in the dark.

Uncertainty is uncomfortable. Yet in these situations, we are to remember that faith is the victory, not the outcome. God is responsible for the results. Our job is the faith.

Trusting that God will take care of the outcome is a muscle that gets stronger each time you practice it. Instead of worrying over the test results, the job interview, or the bill payment, tell God you trust Him to take care of you. Tell Him that over and over until both your mind and heart believe it. Know that no matter how the details play out at the end, God is most assuredly in control and working for your best.

God, thank You that You are responsible for all outcomes.
Help me to trust You today, to walk by faith, not by sight.

GOD WITHIN YOU

Each of us a temple in whom God lives. God himself put it this way:
"I'll live in them, move into them; I'll be their God and they'll be my
people. So leave the corruption and compromise; leave it for good. . . .
Don't link up with those who will pollute you. I want you all for myself."

2 CORINTHIANS 6:16-17 MSG

Father God has chosen to make His home in your heart, to walk with you. So He calls to you to let go of any unclean thing. For there is no place for darkness in the temple of God within you.

Ask God to show you if there are any parts of your life that need to be let go of. Ask Him to help you release your grip on any forms of ungodliness. Consider where you might be making some compromises, choosing darkness over light in your media selections, hobbies, relationships, or finances. For such things sap the beauty of God's goodness within you.

Trust God to bless you as you break attachments with darkness. You are made for wholeness and connection that you will only find in relationship with the Father, Son, and Spirit. Let go of anything that's less than God's best for you—and give God all of you.

God, I don't want to compromise and miss out on Your abundant life.
Help me let go of any dark areas in my life, in Jesus' name.

PERFECTLY PEACEFUL

You keep in perfect peace those whose minds are steadfast,
because they trust in you. Trust in the LORD forever,
for the LORD, the LORD himself, is the Rock eternal.

ISAIAH 26:3-4 NIV

When Jesus was in a small boat whipped about by fierce winds and enormous waves, He trusted God and was at peace. He was fully human and completely capable of feeling fear and anxiety, but He chose peace. You, too, can choose peace. You need not be at the mercy of your thoughts and feelings, for you can "take captive every thought to make it obedient to Christ" (2 Corinthians 10:5 NIV). That means not letting your thoughts land where they please but deciding instead what you will think about.

God gives you a clear picture of where to place your troubled thoughts. The Lord is the Rock eternal. He's powerful and able to hold whatever worries you. He can stop the storm, but sometimes chooses to hold you through it. He's also everlasting and constant. God doesn't falter and disappear when you need Him most. He's always present.

What concerns do you wrestle with today? Take them to God. Tell Him you trust Him. Proclaim aloud, "There is no Rock like our God" (1 Samuel 2:2 NIV). Peace will fill you as your mind is stayed on Him.

God, there's no rock like You. Remind me of Your faithfulness
and power today. I choose to put my trust in You.

A SURE FOUNDATION

Therefore, this is what the Sovereign LORD says: "Look!
I am placing a foundation stone in Jerusalem, a firm
and tested stone. It is a precious cornerstone that is safe
to build on. Whoever believes need never be shaken."

ISAIAH 28:16 NLT

When a foundation stone is selected for a building, the largest and best is chosen. It must be straight and solid, able to hold all the weight that will be placed on it. The "foundation stone" that God is referring to in the verse above is Jesus Christ. Jesus is the "precious cornerstone" and He alone is safe to build your life on.

You can trust Jesus to be your home base, the starting point of all your hopes, an unfailing infrastructure. He meets your needs when others fail you. He holds you close when you're afraid. He heals your wounds. He successfully plans your future. He brings peace to chaos.

No matter how tumultuous your circumstances, the promise is that you will not be shaken. What threatens to throw you off balance today? What potential calamity is stealing your confidence? Jesus is bigger than any problem you face. Put your trust in Him alone.

God, I praise You for providing me with the precious cornerstone of Jesus Christ. Help me to trust in the sureness of His foundation.

START AT THE BEGINNING

The fear of the LORD is the beginning of knowledge;
but fools despise wisdom and instruction.

PROVERBS 1:7 NIV

When you read a book, you start at page 1, and when you bake a cake you start by gathering ingredients. Starting at any place but the beginning leads to disastrous results. Fortunately Proverbs 1:7 gives us some idea of how to begin a life with God: "Start with GOD—the first step in learning is bowing down to GOD; only fools thumb their noses at such wisdom and learning" (MSG).

Rather than stumbling around in the dark, it makes so much more sense to navigate life using the light of knowledge. And knowledge begins by worshipping God in all His glory. We all know revering God with a praise song is easier than bowing our will to forgive in a conflict or humbling our pride when we're wrong, yet that's just what God wants us to do.

Bowing before God in your heart is the beginning of knowledge. It sets you up to live and love well. When you acknowledge God's ways are better than yours, He will bless you with understanding in your family and work life.

Start each day at the beginning—with God. Don't assume your way is best. Bow to His wisdom. Be open to what He wants to reveal to you. You can trust God to instruct you.

God, help me to bow to You with my whole heart.

GOD'S LIGHT

*We use God's mighty weapons, not worldly weapons, to knock down
the strongholds of human reasoning and to destroy false arguments.
We destroy every proud obstacle that keeps people from knowing God.
We capture their rebellious thoughts and teach them to obey Christ.*

2 CORINTHIANS 10:4-5 NLT

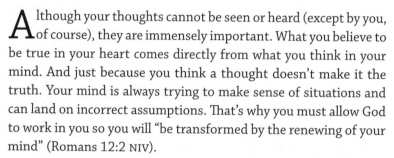

Although your thoughts cannot be seen or heard (except by you, of course), they are immensely important. What you believe to be true in your heart comes directly from what you think in your mind. And just because you think a thought doesn't make it the truth. Your mind is always trying to make sense of situations and can land on incorrect assumptions. That's why you must allow God to work in you so you will "be transformed by the renewing of your mind" (Romans 12:2 NIV).

One of God's mighty weapons is to reveal truth where there's a lie. Satan loves for you to believe falsehoods, which can develop quickly into a stronghold of belief.

Ask God to renew your mind and shed light onto any lies you have accepted as truth. Do you believe the lie that you are unloved, inadequate, or unacceptable? Memorize verses that remind you who you are in Christ. Trust God to renew your mind daily in the specific areas that He will reveal. When you do, you will know Him fully and in truth.

*God, please transform me by renewing my mind.
I want to know You more fully.*

JOY OVERFLOWING

Then will the lame man leap like a deer, and the mute tongue shout for joy. Water will gush forth in the wilderness and streams in the desert.

ISAIAH 35:6 NIV

Joy flows when there is something to celebrate—like when a lame man can miraculously run, a mute finds her voice, or water gushes forth in a barren land.

God provides the miracle of streams in the arid patches of our lives. Are you in a desert that appears hopeless? Are there circumstances in your life that seem dry and barren? Are you desperate for faith, hope, and love to splash around you like a river in the desert?

God's love is a constant and steady stream. This is a difficult truth to cling to when grief is the sun that parches you each morning. Trust God to break forth with water in your wilderness. Watch for it with hope. God will show you Himself in all His glory. He'll "strengthen the feeble hands, steady the knees that give way; say to those with fearful hearts, 'Be Strong, do not fear; your God will come. . .he will come to save you' " (Isaiah 35:3-4 NIV). When you determine to look to God with hope amid great trials and have learned to trust Him in the process, you'll find you have a greater capacity for joy.

God, please send those waters of restoration and joy into my day. Give me strength to watch for Your glory.

THE HEALING OF DISCIPLINE

Lord, your discipline is good, for it leads to life and health. You restore my health and allow me to live! Yes, this anguish was good for me, for you have rescued me from death and forgiven all my sins.

ISAIAH 38:16-17 NLT

Life is full of good things: friendships, ice cream, sunsets, and discipline. Yes, discipline! Though it may not seem enjoyable, discipline from the heart of an affectionate God is good. In fact, it's better than good because "it leads to life and health." Discipline opens your heart to hear what truth God wants to speak to you privately.

When you are trained under God's careful supervision, you live a fuller, more abundant life. Even your mental, emotional, and physical health is affected positively. Yet know that all suffering is not discipline, and all discipline isn't for correction. Even Jesus "learned obedience from what he suffered" (Hebrews 5:8 NIV).

Are you currently experiencing God's discipline? If so, recognize that this temporary pain stretches and broadens you. It develops your character and capacity to experience the fullness of joy. You can trust God's training is good, His purpose is to restore and rescue you, and that He loves you more than you'll ever know.

God, I trust You to work in my life in any way that you deem best. I'm grateful to be considered Your daughter and worthy of Your loving attention.

NOT ONE MISSING

Lift up your eyes and look to the heavens: Who created
all these? He who brings out the starry host one by one
and calls forth each of them by name. Because of his great
power and mighty strength, not one of them is missing.

ISAIAH 40:26 NIV

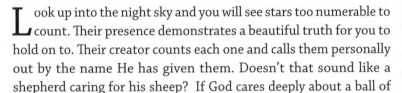

L ook up into the night sky and you will see stars too numerable to count. Their presence demonstrates a beautiful truth for you to hold on to. Their creator counts each one and calls them personally out by the name He has given them. Doesn't that sound like a shepherd caring for his sheep? If God cares deeply about a ball of fire, how much more does He care for you?

You are God's daughter made in His own image. He is aware of your every detail and calls you by name. He hasn't lost a single star in all the vast galaxies despite the black holes and endless space. *Not one is missing*! You will certainly not be lost either. Because of God's "great power and mighty strength," you can trust Him with everything. You need not be afraid.

Is there something that terrifies you? Some fear for yourself or a loved one that haunts you? Trust God to use His *might* (outward strength) and His *power* (inner strength) to keep you close and safe.

God, I praise You for Your loving care toward me.
Help me entrust myself, my life, my all to You.

A BRUISED REED

A bruised reed he will not break, and a smoldering wick he will not snuff out. In faithfulness he will bring forth justice.

ISAIAH 42:3 NIV

Jesus has walked this earth, experiencing both its joy and sorrow. He has suffered and cried and has a special understanding of the pain of heartbreak.

The bruised reed and the faintly burning wick mentioned in the verse above represent the person whose spirit is frail and crushed. If you feel weak and helpless, take comfort in the fact that Jesus is closer than your heartbeat. For "the LORD is close to the brokenhearted and saves those who are crushed in spirit" (Psalm 34:18 NIV).

Jesus is called "a man of suffering" (Isaiah 53:3 NIV). He understands grief and rejection. Who better to turn to when you're sad and hurting? Your Savior seeks out the broken for healing and relationship. He knows exactly where your wounds are and how to heal them. You may carry the scar, but His touch works miracles.

You need not keep score of hurts, grievances, or harm done you. Justice is Jesus's job. Let go of struggles to make things right for yourself. Let Jesus carry that burden for you. You get busy finding beauty in your day. Let gratitude and praise be your new song.

God, I trust in and praise Your healing touch in my life. Though I sometimes feel bruised and broken, I'm grateful Your loving presence will never leave me.

NEW THINGS

See, I am doing a new thing! Now it springs up; do you not perceive it?
I am making a way in the wilderness and streams in the wasteland.

ISAIAH 43:19 NIV

God is not limited as you are. He makes new paths for you where you see none. He provides refreshing streams where there were none. When your way seems blocked and circumstances distressing, look for God to surprise you with an unexpected solution. God is constantly moving you forward in life. New things will appear on the horizon.

Do you struggle with change? Do transitions leave you anxious? Trust that God's plans for you are good and that His heart is loving. God will not give you more than you can handle.

Do not focus on previous years or past hurts. Be available for what God has for you today. Look attentively for what may seem like a small trickle. Be ready for that trickle to turn into a spring and then a river. Prepare to get wet as you wade into your future personally designed by God with you in mind. He knows you better than you know yourself. Celebrate new life in abundance without looking back to the solid shore of your past. Go have your adventure with God at your side.

God, let my heart trust You today as You
prepare a "new thing" for my future.

REDEEMED

I have swept away your offenses like a cloud, your sins like the morning mist. Return to me, for I have redeemed you.

ISAIAH 44:22 NIV

Sin is a dangerous business. It seems simple enough to make a bad choice by disobeying a traffic rule, speaking unjustly, or being envious of another. It is, however, missing the mark set by a holy God. A transgression is a sin that is planned. Be aware that letting transgressions go unchecked can eventually affect your very mind.

Jesus understands your struggle with temptations that lead to sin. In His great love for you, He planned a complete and magnificent rescue. You are so beautifully forgiven that you need never be separated from Jesus no matter what you have done.

Although your heart may want to hide when you feel ashamed of your wrongdoing, God says, "Come closer. I have redeemed you." Is there something you have let come between you and God? Have you tormented yourself thinking He could never forgive that specific sin again? Know that God has blotted all your missteps out! Like a thick cloud that can't be seen through, He has covered your sin. Take a moment to confess any wrong attitudes, thoughts, or actions, then praise God for His faithful and full forgiveness.

God, I confess I daily miss Your standard. I'm so grateful You are full of love and forgiveness. Help me run into Your open arms instead of hiding in shame.

COMFORTED BY GOD

Shout for joy, you heavens; rejoice, you earth; burst
into song, you mountains! For the LORD comforts his
people and will have compassion on his afflicted ones.

ISAIAH 49:13 NIV

Comfort feels wonderful in a time of distress. It's like a warm blanket wrapped around a cold and lonely feeling. How do you comfort yourself? Perhaps you take a walk, bake a cake, or clean your house. Yet those things may fall short of your goal. Not to worry. For God is the best at helping you feel better. Second Corinthians 1:3 (NIV) calls Him the "God of all comfort."

David, the psalmist, considered God his Shepherd, writing, "Your rod and your staff, they comfort me" (Psalm 23:4 NIV). David, once a shepherd himself, used his rod to count his sheep, his staff to guide them. He knew those tools brought his sheep *comfort*, which means to strengthen, as the word *fort* in com*fort* implies.

And God doesn't just provide comfort. He is also the God of compassion, the Good Shepherd who never leaves one little lost lamb out in the cold night. In fact, He "keeps a list of our tears" (Psalm 56:8 NIV).

God's comfort for and compassion on the afflicted are a reason for praise. Creation joins in the song of joy. Will you worship along with the mountains today?

God of all comfort, I am grateful for Your heart of compassion
for me. Strengthen me as I join in creation's song.

GOD'S SPIRIT IN YOU

And because we are his children, God has sent the Spirit
of his Son into our hearts, prompting us to call out, "Abba,
Father." Now you are no longer a slave but God's own child.
And since you are his child, God has made you his heir.

GALATIANS 4:6-7 NLT

I magine you live in a large and beautiful home. You throw open the door. Walking in confidently, you call out with anticipation, "Daddy!" You know your Father is always there waiting for you. He's your Abba and delights to draw you, His precious child, near. He's never busy or tired, irritable or critical, but loving and kind. The way that you can enter and be accepted is proof you're not a slave but His daughter, welcomed with open arms.

Your Father has put part of Himself, His Spirit, in you so that you'll never be alone. No matter how far you travel or what circumstances you're in, you have part of Him closer than your heartbeat.

This is your true reality. You have been adopted by the most generous of all Fathers and nothing can separate you from His love. Not only that, everything He owns is yours!

Do you have needs? Bring them to your Abba Father. Do you have problems or concerns? Abba Father longs to help you. Spend time each day in the presence of your true Father.

Abba Father, thank You for making me Your own beloved child.

BEAUTIFUL NEWS

How beautiful on the mountains are the feet of the
messenger who brings good news, the good news of peace
and salvation, the news that the God of Israel reigns!

ISAIAH 52:7 NLT

G ood messages come by all kinds of delivery systems. Sometimes just a short text filled with smiles brings a message of cheer. Sometimes a letter from a faraway place brings surprise and delight in renewed connections. Sometimes a nod across a room is all that is needed to say, "We're okay."

God delivered His message of love and hope through the mouths of prophets, in words on scrolls, through clouds and fire. But His best delivery system has always been through the lives of His people.

God's love is written on hugging arms that embrace reunited friends. His forgiveness is written in the tears of prisoners who confess their wrongs and accept His righteousness. His grace is written in the hands of mothers holding long-prayed-for newborns. His hope is written on the faces of those who wait for the doctor's prognosis, knowing that whatever happens, peace will come.

When you follow Jesus, it is not just your words that tell of His reign in your life, but every step you take can bring good news to those around you.

Lord, may my life and the way that I live it
tell the story of my love for You. Amen.

KEEP RUNNING

You were running the race so well. Who has held you back from following the truth?

GALATIANS 5:7 NLT

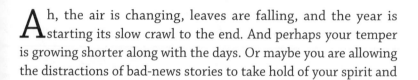

Ah, the air is changing, leaves are falling, and the year is starting its slow crawl to the end. And perhaps your temper is growing shorter along with the days. Or maybe you are allowing the distractions of bad-news stories to take hold of your spirit and knock you off the path.

What is holding you back? In the life of every follower of Jesus, there will come temptations to be drawn away from the disciplines of prayer and Bible study and meeting with other believers. There will be times when divisive voices speak up, calling away our attention to what God is saying to us and instead sucking us into the latest drama.

The Galatians were no different. In his letter to the believers in Galatia, Paul urges them to not get caught up in arguments about traditions and processes, but to remember that the "only thing that counts is faith expressing itself through love" (Galatians 5:6 NIV).

Over and over, God reminds us that we are free in Him. We are free from any membership dues or tests of loyalty or conformity to human expectations. He loves us as we are, and He asks us to love like He does. That's it. And it's that love that will keep us running.

Lord of all, help me not be distracted by things that are not designed to bring me closer to You. Amen.

EXAMINATION

*For your ways are in full view of the
LORD, and he examines all your paths.*

PROVERBS 5:21 NIV

D oes your stomach get tied up in knots at the mere mention of an exam? Does the idea of being under scrutiny make you sweat? Maybe these words from Proverbs have you breaking out in hives!

But the eyes of our loving Father are not looking at us with caustic criticism. He is not out to get us. He is out to love us. And part of the job of any loving father is to watch out for where his children are going. Our heavenly Father reminds us in His Word that He sees our steps. He truly cares about our decisions and our actions. He is with us, walking alongside us.

Knowing that we live in full view of His gracious eyes also challenges us to live lives that will cause our Father to be pleased and proud. This challenge and the reminder of His watchfulness combine to protect us from our own sinful desires. When we realize He is looking out for us and calling us to follow Him, it's easier to see the ways that will bring us nearer to Him, instead of straying along roads that will lead to destruction.

*God, I want You to examine my life. Look at what I'm doing now
and what I have done. Show me where I can do better. Don't let
any minutes of my life be wasted in foolish pursuits. Amen.*

EVERLASTING LIGHT

*Your sun will never set again, and your moon will wane no more; the
LORD will be your everlasting light, and your days of sorrow will end.*

ISAIAH 60:20 NIV

I saiah prophesies about a time to come, when Jerusalem and the
nation of Israel will be free from oppression and darkness. We
often read these passages and think of the promise of heaven, of a
paradise where no one will be hurt again, but instead we will all be
whole and thriving in the light of the Lord.

But this light can shine in other ways, and well before we see
heaven. The apostle Paul writes to the believers at Ephesus and
prays that the "eyes of your heart may be enlightened in order that
you may know the hope to which he has called you, the riches of his
glorious inheritance in his holy people, and his incomparably great
power for us who believe" (Ephesians 1:18-19 NIV).

How often do we allow the darkness of this world's sorrows to
blind us from the hope we have in Jesus? How many times do we
let our greed or need for material goods cloud our knowledge of
the treasures He has for us? How often do we run out of energy
because we don't rely on His power?

*Lord, help my eyes to be opened to the light of Your hope, glory,
and power that is readily available to me today. Amen.*

A PIECE OF WORK

For we are God's masterpiece. He has created us anew in Christ Jesus,
so we can do the good things he planned for us long ago.

EPHESIANS 2:10 NLT

The most beautiful pieces of pottery are those where you can see the work of someone's hands in the object. They are not uniform pieces—each is unique, with little differences in shape or style. Sometimes, if you look closely, you can see the line formed by the person's thumb sliding along the wet clay. Or a faint impression of a fingerprint pattern at the bottom of a mug, where the artist gave the clay one last touch.

But if you saw the work before the potter began, all you would see is a gray lump of wet clay. No form, no function, no fingerprints. Just a gray lump, waiting to be shaped.

There are days when we may resemble masses more than masterpieces. Sometimes we are stubborn and refuse to be shaped. Sometimes we are frozen in our uncertainty and cannot be moved. Sometimes we just can't even see our own beauty.

But God wants to use us. He works with us and through us and for us. We can trust His hands to make us into masterpieces, ready to do what He has planned for us long, long ago.

Master and Lord, I want You to use me.
Help me to bend and be shaped by Your will. Amen.

ECHOES OF ADVICE

When you walk, their counsel will lead you. When you sleep,
they will protect you. When you wake up, they will advise you.

PROVERBS 6:22 NLT

Have you ever heard your mother's voice in your head? Maybe you have the feeling you are going to get a new job, with better pay, and you start imagining all the things you can buy with your new salary. The voice rings out, clear as a bell: "Don't count your chickens before they hatch!"

Or maybe you try to fix a wobbly cabinet door, and you think about just duct-taping it, but then your dad's voice rumbles in your mind: "If you're going to do something, do it right."

If you had the blessing of growing up with capable parents who were constantly telling you what to do and how to do it, you too have probably heard their voices speaking in your head. And sometimes you might wish you could find the "off" switch. But wisdom is wisdom, no matter how it comes to us, or how often.

Next time you hear those familiar voices, thank God for the wisdom He's spoken through those who raised you. Thank Him for guidance that never leaves you. Trust that when you hear truth, God is the foundation of that truth.

Lord God, thank You for Your wisdom and
truth that speaks to me every day. Amen.

YOU SHALL SPEAK

But the Lord said to me: "Do not say, 'I am a youth,'
For you shall go to all to whom I send you, And whatever
I command you, you shall speak. Do not be afraid of
their faces, For I am with you to deliver you," says the Lord.

JEREMIAH 1:7-8 NKJV

Stutters. Quiet voices. Small vocabularies. Only knowing one language. Not knowing enough Bible verses. No training. No authority.

We can think of all kinds of excuses why we shouldn't speak for the Lord. We can come up with a million reasons why our voices should *not* be the ones to carry His message to the world. But there's one really good reason to go ahead and speak up anyway.

The Lord is with us.

God is commanding us to speak for Him—to go to the ones who need to hear His message and speak truth, and hope, and love, and grace into their lives. To go to those who are grieving and comfort them. To go to those who are straying and remind them who they are. To go to the ones who are lost and show them the path.

He is commanding and sending us, but He's also going with us. And that is why, young or old, you shall speak.

Lord God, make me braver than I dream of being. Let my words
come from You alone so I can speak Your truth to others. Amen.

AUTUMN SMELLS

Live a life filled with love, following the example of Christ. He loved us and offered himself as a sacrifice for us, a pleasing aroma to God.

EPHESIANS 5:2 NLT

One of the most pleasant aspects of a true autumnal season are the smells that come with it. The crisp, fresh air that invigorates your lungs. The earthy, baked mustiness released with every step through crackling leaves. The warm smoky aroma of fireplaces being lit for the first time in the season. The delicious scent of stew bubbling on the stove and apple pie in the oven.

All these smells are pleasing not just in themselves, but because of the good thoughts or memories they evoke. They make us think of snuggling up with loved ones, taking walks through the woods, or gathering together for home-cooked meals.

Our lives are to be like that for God—pleasant offerings to remind Him of our relationships with Him, to let Him experience our lives filled with love. Just as Christ loved us and offered everything to God on our behalf, we must love each other and offer all we have to Jesus.

Lord, I offer my life to You. I know I can never be as beautiful as Your Son, but I pray You show me how to make my life a pleasing offering to You. I pray that when You look at me, You will smile at the memory of my love for You. Amen.

WRESTLING MATCH

For we do not wrestle against flesh and blood, but against principalities, against powers, against the rulers of the darkness of this age, against spiritual hosts of wickedness in the heavenly places.

EPHESIANS 6:12 NKJV

You struggle all day—from whacking the alarm button in the morning, to unwinding yourself from the covers, to pushing yourself out of bed. You yank out some clothes and shove your body into them. You tug on your socks and shoes and stretch your weary muscles. You grab a water bottle and force yourself out the door.

Some days, every minute of the day, from before sunrise until that moment you drag yourself to bed, feels like one big wrestling match—and that's even when no other person is around! You fight against fatigue. You argue with your wants. You shout down the negative voices in your mind. You battle against irritation, impatience, and selfishness. It's a battle of the wills—and good will is losing.

It's vital to remember, on days like these, that God is not against us. Nor is every other person we meet our enemy. Rather, we are fighting against unseen forces—twisted thoughts and disturbing dreams and whispered lies that wrap around our hearts and minds.

But we have the armor of God and, backed by the One who defeated even death, we can win this match any day!

Almighty Warrior and Lord, help me remember who I'm fighting against, and who I'm fighting for! Amen.

BETTER

For Wisdom is better than all the trappings of wealth;
nothing you could wish for holds a candle to her.

PROVERBS 8:11 MSG

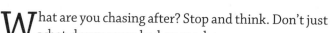

What are you chasing after? Stop and think. Don't just consider what dreams you had once when you were young and ready to conquer the world, or the latest mission that has riled up your soul. Really think for a minute.

Consider what you've been reading this week. What has been filling your mind?

What have you been watching? What entertainment have you used to fill your leisure hours (if you had any!)?

What have you been preparing your body for? What have you been fueling it with?

Whose thoughts are guiding you? Do you know? What messages are driving your decisions? Why?

Take some minutes and really consider carefully what your weeks look like—what things are pushing you along or holding you back. Do your goals match up with the way you are spending your time?

Whatever you are currently spending your time on, God's Word assures us of this: wisdom is better. It's better than running after wealth, or material possessions, or a good image, or a level of popularity. It's better than knowing about the latest funny TV shows or dramatic movies. It's better than keeping up with politics or listening to motivational speakers.

Wisdom is better. So go get that!

Lord, help me to want wisdom more than
wealth or fleeting happiness. Amen.

BAND-AIDS ON HEART ATTACKS

My dear Daughter—my people—broken, shattered,
and yet they put on Band-Aids, Saying, "It's not so bad.
You'll be just fine." But things are not "just fine"!

JEREMIAH 8:11 MSG

I'm fine." Isn't that how we all answer? Someone asks how we are doing, and we say, "I'm fine." We may be drowning in debt. "I'm fine." We may be fighting with our spouses. "I'm fine." We may be struggling with depression. "I'm fine." We may be trying hard not to give into the same old temptation. "I'm fine."

The people of Jerusalem were in trouble. Deep trouble. God was not happy with their disobedience and idolatry. God still wanted to be their God, but they couldn't even see Him. Yet their leaders were acting as if all was well. Instead of being the voices for God to the people, they had become puppets of complacency. No one wanted to be the bearer of bad news. No one wanted to tell the truth. Or, perhaps, they couldn't even see what the truth was.

Don't be like those Israelites—keeping the peace up until the day of their destruction. Speak the truth, and let others speak the truth to you. You don't have to spill your guts to every person on the street. But have some accountability partners. Surround yourself with people you can trust to handle faithfully the true status of your heart.

Lord, help me be honest with others and with You. Amen.

WISDOM OF OLD

The LORD brought me forth as the first of his works,
before his deeds of old; I was formed long ages ago,
at the very beginning, when the world came to be.

PROVERBS 8:22-23 NIV

The world is moving swiftly. It runs at the speed of a Tweet. It leaps forward through clips and soundbites, like a movie that has been put on eternal fast forward. It's moving so quickly that we often don't have time to research sources and consider lines of thought and understand motives.

But before there were bandwidths and gigabytes, before there were radios and newspapers, before there were even scrolls and quills, there was the Word of God. And God placed His wisdom in the world, before the world even came to be. He built our world with the careful planning and creativity that only comes through the mind of a Master Designer.

And because this wisdom is older than the hills, more ancient than the ocean, wider than the heavens, and formed before the foundations of the earth, we can trust it. It has kept our world spinning in well-balanced, even turns for centuries upon centuries.

Surely you can trust God's wisdom to keep you moving through whatever is currently filling up your calendars? And surely you should rely on His wisdom as you plan the rest of your days.

Lord, I know I can trust You with all my days.
Help me to see Your plan. Amen.

PRESS ON

But one thing I do: Forgetting what is behind and straining
toward what is ahead, I press on toward the goal to win the
prize for which God has called me heavenward in Christ Jesus.

Philippians 3:13-14 niv

Climbing a mountain seems like a good idea when you're sitting on your couch, watching a travel show in which a couple of fearless adventurers take the last few steps to reach a peak and look out upon a dazzling sunrise. The scenery is so beautiful, and the climbers seem so inspired. Who wouldn't want to experience that?

But when you're in the middle of a seven-mile hike, and your feet are hurting, your head throbbing, your stomach churning, and your will fading, suddenly climbing a mountain seems like the worst idea ever.

Will it really be worth it? Do you need to go all the way to the top or is this far enough? You still might have a pretty nice view, if you can just get away from all these trees. What's to be gained by going all those many, many steps further?

Thankfully, with God as your guide, you can be certain that reaching the goal He has set before you will be worth it. More than that, if you keep following Him, you will have a joy that lasts far beyond the moment of dawn breaking over the mountains. You will have eternal life.

I trust You, Lord, with every step.
Help me have the strength to press on! Amen.

THE SECRET

I have learned the secret of living in every situation,
whether it is with a full stomach or empty, with plenty or little.
For I can do everything through Christ, who gives me strength.

PHILIPPIANS 4:12-13 NLT

Imagine setting off in a ship, not knowing what you might discover. Imagine looking out on a scene that only shows dark blue waves upon waves, for as far as the eye can see. Imagine having so much faith in your abilities, in your ship, and in your crew, that you knew you'd be able to sail across the world and back again.

The apostle Paul lived long before Columbus sailed the ocean blue, but he has as much faith as one of those first explorers. Time after time, he put his life in the hands of God. He gave up everything he knew to follow God's will, and to teach others about Jesus. There were many times when he was beaten or imprisoned, or run out of towns. But no matter what happened to him, he kept trusting in God's provision.

When you have been through hard times, and survived, you have confidence that you can do it again. You know that you're not alone—that God never leaves you. That kind of trust sets a person free to keep exploring, and keep searching for new challenges and new people to invite along for the ride.

God my Provider, I know I can trust
You to get me through anything. Amen.

FIXED

*All the broken and dislocated pieces of the universe—
people and things, animals and atoms—get properly
fixed and fit together in vibrant harmonies, all because
of his death, his blood that poured down from the cross.*

COLOSSIANS 1:19-20 MSG

People often say we live in a broken world. And it's true. Our world is not the way God created it to be. When the first man and woman disobeyed, they broke that perfect relationship with God—they broke God's trust in them, and they broke the command He gave them. We could say they also broke His heart. And ever since, the perfection God meant for us to live in has been out of reach—shattered by sin.

Any parent who has had a child disobey and try to hide his disobedience will have had a taste of that kind of brokenness. If the betrayal is very severe, it's hard to imagine a time when the relationship could be repaired. Every interaction is colored by the sorrow of the actions that tore away trust.

However, though God, in His perfect justice, had to punish humans for their disobedience, His perfect love for us sought to mend what was broken. He found that way of healing by sending His Son to die for us. Through Jesus Christ, every torn heart can be sewn back together, every broken promise redeemed, every destroyed relationship reborn. The world can be fixed.

Thank You, God! You gave us a way to come back to You! Amen.

WALKING SECURELY

Whoever walks in integrity walks securely,
but whoever takes crooked paths will be found out.

PROVERBS 10:9 NIV

Shortcuts can be tempting, and certainly, they do sometimes save time. But cutting moral corners almost always ends in someone, or someone's reputation, getting hurt.

Crooked paths often take you off the main course. They may lead to unwelcome and unexpected obstacles. They may be dangerous—not well lit or smoothly paved. And if you fall and get hurt, you won't be able to tell anyone where you are! The problem is, all these stresses and trials leave a mark on a person. And it's the kind of mark that will eventually be discovered, no matter how much you try to hide it.

But walking in the way of integrity means you never have to hide. You can step freely, knowing exactly where you are headed. You can see who is walking with you—who is there for you in case you need help. You can plan for any obstacles, because they can be easily seen from a long way off. And you don't have to worry about getting lost—the straight path stretches out in front of you, leading you directly to your goal.

Walking in integrity allows you to be confident in every step you take. And knowing that, you can even run.

Lord, please keep me in the way of integrity.
Don't let me be led away on crooked paths. Amen.

SHADOWS

These are a shadow of the things that were to come;
the reality, however, is found in Christ.

COLOSSIANS 2:17 NIV

About this time every year, people celebrate the harvest. Even people who have never stepped onto a farm will gather together beautifully strange gourds and scratchy bales of hay to create harvesttime scenes. Some people carve faces and other designs into pumpkins, creating artistic patterns for light to shine through. Kids lap up cups of sweet apple cider as they stand around roaring bonfires.

Many of the traditions and decorations have little to do with actual harvesting these days. But they offer a taste of a different time—when people were truly happy to have their crops gathered and be able to provide food for their families. And as we pick apples and carve pumpkins, we can be thankful for the work of farmers, and offer up praise to the one who sends the sunshine and rain, and allows the crops to grow.

Like these holiday celebrations, our traditions and practices honoring God provide only a glimmer of the glory that we will dance in when we meet Him in heaven. Our songs of praise will be so much more beautiful in eternity, and our prayers will be pure. But none of this means we should stop trying to celebrate together here on earth. It just means we have to realize this is only the beginning. . .

Lord, I look forward to the day when
we can celebrate for eternity! Amen.

THE LORD IS MY SHEPHERD

"I myself will gather the remnant of my flock out of all the countries where I have driven them and will bring them back to their pasture, where they will be fruitful and increase in number. I will place shepherds over them who will tend them, and they will no longer be afraid or terrified, nor will any be missing," declares the LORD.

JEREMIAH 23:3-4 NIV

The picture of white, woolly sheep peacefully dotting a verdant hillside is like a postcard come to life. It's hard to imagine these gentle animals ever being terrified in such a scene. But should a predator creep close to the flock, the animals would begin to bleat nervously.

Sheep aren't the smartest creatures. If they're grazing far away from their pen, they won't find their own way home. They need a shepherd to guide them. Without that leader, they'll become even more scattered, and fearful, and the weakest ones will be a target for a clever coyote.

We aren't so different from the sheep (though hopefully slightly smarter).

When we walk far from the security God offers, we have a hard time finding the way home. We need someone to protect us from our own folly, to calm us when we're under attack from evil forces of the enemy, and to firmly guide us to gather close together, support each other, and run back to safety.

God, I'm glad I can count on You to bring me home. Amen.

MISPLACED HOPE

*Hopes placed in mortals die with them;
all the promise of their power comes to nothing.*

PROVERBS 11:7 NIV

The pharaohs of Egypt were buried in elaborate style. The Egyptians believed that if bodies could be preserved as mummies, the person could then travel to the afterlife. Those who were very wealthy or important were then buried with all the possessions they might need on their journey to the next life. This could include magic spells painted on the walls to get them going on their journey, food and wine in baskets and jars, valuable garments and jewelry, and boats and chariots!

Today, we might think it's crazy to bury a person's most valuable possessions along with his or her dead body. We know that "you can't take it with you."

But even though we don't tend to bury high-end cell phones or cars with our loved ones, we often do run the risk of burying our hopes and dreams with them. And sometimes people get caught up in thinking a government leader or a company president or another human leader will be able to bring peace, or make people do good things, or change our culture for the better. But the only one we can really trust to save us from ourselves is our Lord God. When we place our hope in God, we can be sure that hope will never die.

King of kings, remind me that You are my only Savior. Amen.

SHARING OUR LIVES

*We loved you so much that we shared with you
not only God's Good News but our own lives, too.*

1 THESSALONIANS 2:8 NLT

It's good to share the good news of Jesus Christ with people. And if you're a person gifted in telling that message, that's a blessing.

But there are other ways to share this message of God's love and grace, and sometimes those ways involve no words at all.

It's important for those who believe in Jesus to not create Christian worlds for themselves—where all their friends are Christian, all their radio channels are Christian, all the movies they see are Christian, and all the coffee they drink is Christian. It's important to realize that some people won't hear your Christian message all that well until you really love them with your Christian heart. And to do that well, you may have to step out of the Christian world. You may have to meet people in places you wouldn't normally go. You may have to work side by side. You may have to get involved in the nitty-gritty details of their lives. And you most definitely need to show them all the parts of *your* life—even the parts that don't look so good.

When people see that you're willing to share with them your less-than-perfect moments, they'll be able to trust you more. Be vulnerable, and they'll open up to you.

Lord, help me to be real with people. Amen.

WORKING FOR PEACE
WHEREVER YOU ARE

*Work for the peace and prosperity of the city where
I sent you into exile. Pray to the LORD for it,
for its welfare will determine your welfare.*

JEREMIAH 29:7 NLT

You've moved somewhere you never wanted to go. You're stuck in a job you never wanted to do. You're trapped in a class you don't want to take. You find yourself in a crowd where you don't feel welcome.

There are many times in our lives when we feel like strangers in strange lands. The Israelites who were exiled to Babylon certainly felt this way. But God gave them interesting advice. Instead of telling them to keep to their own kind, He told them to go out and build new lives there. He told them literally to put roots down, to have children and grandchildren. He told them to work hard and make sure this land—this land of their enemies—prospered.

Next time you find yourself feeling stuck someplace you don't want to be, don't get caught up in planning your exit. Instead, think about how you can make the best of the situation. Ask God to help you to reach out to strangers. Think about ways you can help those around you succeed—no matter who they are or how welcome (or not) they've made you feel. Dig in. Participate. Join the team. Make solid connections. And trust that God will bless your efforts.

Lord, help me when I feel lost and far away. Amen.

MIND YOUR BUSINESS

Make it your goal to live a quiet life, minding your own business
and working with your hands, just as we instructed you before.

1 THESSALONIANS 4:11 NLT

Mind your own business," the little girl shouted at her brother, who was listening to her conversation. That oft-heard phrase is generally used in today's language to mean something along the lines of "stop being so nosey!"

But in the context of Paul's letter, the meaning was more about one's actual business. This counsel follows a list of practical advice Paul lists, all under the umbrella of living in "a way that pleases God, as we have taught you" (1 Thessalonians 4:1 NLT). Paul instructs the believers to be in control of their bodies, abstaining from sexual sins. He also urges them to love one another—in particular, to love and support other believers.

Another way they could please God was by being in control of their daily transactions with believers and nonbelievers alike. This concept had two benefits: 1) They would earn the respect of nonbelievers (and thus, earn a way to speak to them about the love of Christ), and 2) They would be able to support themselves through their work, and not be a burden on anyone.

Often, making an impact on others can be as simple as just doing your job.

Lord, help me to live the kind of quiet life that
will speak volumes about my love for You. Amen.

DON'T BE STUPID

Whoever loves instruction loves knowledge,
but he who hates correction is stupid.

PROVERBS 12:1 NKJV

About this time of year, students begin counting down the days till the next time they get days off from school—even though some will have just had a fall break not very long ago! It's a natural desire—even some of the best students look forward to a time with less structure and more play. And teachers can't wait to take a rest from the piles of papers to grade.

But there are always some students who claim they would be better off if they had no school at all. If they could just do what they wanted all the time, every day, life would be great—or so they say. Of course, they might not ever get a job or have a career or any plans, and they might have to live in their parents' basement until they are forty-eight, but that's okay, right?

We all need education. We all need people who care enough about us to tell us when we've done something wrong, and then help us make it right. We all need to rely on God's Word to teach us about Him.

And we all need to remember that rejecting chances for correction will only make us look stupid.

Lord, I don't want to be dumb. Help me receive
Your correction without complaint. Amen.

THE FEAR OF GOD

And I will make an everlasting covenant with them,
that I will not turn away from doing them good; but I will put
My fear in their hearts so that they will not depart from Me.

JEREMIAH 32:40 NKJV

It seems appropriate to be speaking about *fear* in the month when things like hauntings and ghosts and spooky sounds are a routine part of conversation.

But the fear of God is not the kind of fear that causes nightmares or that jumps out at you from a dark corner.

The fear that God wants to put in our hearts is the healthy, life-giving, transformational reverence and awe of Him. It is the feeling of wonder that comes when we know the Creator of the universe knows our names. It is the position of humility we take before the throne of the King of kings. It is the dazzling of our senses that occurs when we try to imagine His eternal glory. It is the absolute astonishment at being loved so fully, so fiercely, and so faithfully by our perfect Father in heaven.

This fear may well take our breath away. It may freeze us in our tracks or shock us into silence. But it will also fill us up, encourage our spirits, and speak to our hearts. It will cause us to stay, instead of run away. It will make the impossible, possible.

Lord, may I never stop fearing You. Amen.

KEEP BUSY

We hear that some among you are idle and disruptive.
They are not busy; they are busybodies.

2 THESSALONIANS 3:11 NIV

*B*usy and *body*. These two words sound all right by themselves, don't they? Taken separately, we might define a *busy body* as a person who is quite active and diligent in a physical sort of way. But once these words are joined together, we get a very different picture—we see an annoying sort of person who cannot keep him- or herself from poking into other people's conversations and activities, and generally causing trouble.

It's actually quite hard to be a busy person and be a busybody at the same time. People who are diligent and productive don't have time to worry what other people are doing. And they have no desire to cause trouble, as trouble might just slow them down.

But people who are idle—who have nothing to do due to circumstances beyond their control, or who choose to do nothing due to their own lack of self-motivation—are the ones who literally have too much time on their hands. They are so bored, they decide to cause problems to relieve the boredom.

We should strive to be busy—doing God's work, serving others, and taking care of those in need. There's always something to do in the kingdom of God!

Lord, I trust You to assign me to work You
need me to do. Please keep me busy. Amen.

LOOSE LIPS

Those who guard their lips preserve their lives,
but those who speak rashly will come to ruin.

You've probably heard the phrase, "Loose lips sink ships." It was a slogan that appeared on propaganda posters during World War II, meant to remind the public to be careful not to give away any useful information that could be picked up by the listening ears of enemy spies.

Loose lips can cause damage in other areas, however, with no interference from enemy spies at all. Today we might say "loose lips can undermine a company," or "loose lips make people lose their grip on reality," or "loose lips bring down powerful leaders—as long as the lips are telling the truth."

Speaking rashly can happen when we think the power or significance of our words is so great, that it's worth the risk of speaking up, even when we haven't verified the truth of our message. But no one should consider speaking rashly as a synonym for speaking with courage.

Rash words can damage reputations, hurt your witness, and cause people to lose their livelihoods. So before you open your mouth to express some juicy morsel of gossip or to offer your totally nonexpert opinion, picture that ship sliding beneath the water, and maybe think again. It's hard for people to trust you to help them when they can't even trust what you say.

Lord, help me to guard my lips. I don't want
to hurt anyone with my words. Amen.

TURN AROUND

Unrelenting disappointment leaves you heartsick,
but a sudden good break can turn life around.

PROVERBS 13:12 MSG

D o you know anyone who just can't seem to get a break in life? She gets hit time after time with misfortunes and accidents and tragedies. Deaths of loved ones, job losses, sicknesses, car crashes, thefts—it just seems like she has a big target on her and is getting shot repeatedly in some giant, cosmic, game of darts.

But even when the disappointments mount up for believers, one on top of another, we can trust that God is suffering right along with us. And He won't let us keep suffering forever. Just like Joseph, at some point we may find that what caused us harm was really meant to bring about good in our lives—and often that good is of a sort that we would have never dreamed up on our own.

In fact, that "sudden good break" may not really be so sudden at all. It may have been a reward that was planned long ago by the Author of our lives—who is always writing new pages for our stories.

My Lord and God, thank You for every good gift You
have brought to my life. And when troubles come,
help me to see You are still with me. Amen.

CONSIDER THE BENEFITS

Physical training is good, but training for godliness is much better, promising benefits in this life and in the life to come.

1 TIMOTHY 4:8 NLT

Jumping jacks. Jogging. Sit-ups. Push-ups. Pull-ups. Put-downs. Okay, that last one may not really be a valid example. But all the rest are exercises that are good for our bodies. These are activities that stretch us, physically and mentally. They get our circulatory systems working in good order. They test our endurance, strengthen our lungs, and help get rid of fat.

And all of that is wonderful for this life we live on earth, where we need to move and breathe to live life to the fullest.

But training for godliness is indeed, much better. Reading God's Word stretches our imaginations and guards our hearts. Praying helps us practice patience and perseverance. Serving others firms up our humility muscles and helps us keep any damaging pride in check. Worshipping reminds us of the greatness of God and the hope we have in the life to come.

What might happen if we committed to godly training in the same way we commit to physical training? Or, for those of us who struggle with keeping fit, what if we committed to godly training with the same passion that we practice being a couch potato?

Thank You Lord, for the benefits available in this life and the next one. Help me to commit to training my heart, soul, and mind to follow You. Amen.

TRUE FAITH

*Those who won't care for their relatives, especially those
in their own household, have denied the true faith.
Such people are worse than unbelievers.*

1 TIMOTHY 5:8 NLT

It's hard to say when it happened. Perhaps it was when families started splitting up. Maybe it was during the first World War. Maybe it was during the Great Depression. But somewhere along the way, at some point in time, we started losing our grip on what really matters. We started forgetting what family means. We started thinking it was okay to leave our elderly relatives alone for years in places we wouldn't even like to visit for one day.

We cannot claim to love God while neglecting to love our own family members.

True faith is believing that caring for others is more important than, well, anything else. True faith means sometimes putting ourselves in uncomfortable situations so that someone else may receive comfort. True faith is realizing that a momentary trial is worth the eternal reward of having our Father look at us and say, "Well done." True faith can mean putting up with complaints and crazy schedules and extra household work to make the last years of someone's life just a little bit easier. True faith means believing God can stretch our hearts to accept bigger families than we thought we could ever be able to love.

*Lord, help me to look out for my relatives in
the most honorable and loving way. Amen.*

IN GOD WE TRUST

*Teach those who are rich in this world not to be proud and not to trust
in their money, which is so unreliable. Their trust should be in God,
who richly gives us all we need for our enjoyment.*

1 TIMOTHY 6:17 NLT

The value of the dollar goes up and down. Banks fail. Banks swell.
The productivity of nations rises and falls. Surpluses cause hopes
to multiply. Deficits cause longstanding depression.

The meaning of wealth changes all the time. You cannot trust it.
You cannot build dreams on it. You cannot live fully on it.

Instead, put your trust in God. God does not shift in value,
depending on the stock market, or the price of oil, or what battles are
raging in faraway lands. No amount of human insecurity can touch
God's everlasting consistency. And God is not just our Creator, not
just our Sustainer, not just our Redeemer—He is our Provider. And
He is our Friend. He knows everything that we need, long before we
need it. He knows everything that will please and delight us, even
before we realize our need to be delighted. He is our loving, generous,
gracious Father, ever ready to supply us with good gifts—even though
we never did a thing to deserve them.

Why wouldn't we trust Him?

*Father God, help me not to put my trust in earthly riches that
will fade. Help me remember that all I ever need is You. Amen.*

CELEBRATE THE LIGHT

*He broke the power of death and illuminated the way
to life and immortality through the Good News.*

2 TIMOTHY 1:10 NLT

Some people don't want to have anything to do with this holiday. Though one can hardly avoid the decorations and the giant candy bags and the costumed characters roaming the streets, some people try as hard as they can to pretend this holiday is just another day. Why? They feel the day is dedicated to darkness, and is wrapped up in Satan's evil schemes to steal away our souls, and they want no part of that.

On the other hand, what better day could there be to celebrate the Light of the world?

Christians should participate in Halloween, if only to bring light into the darkness. On this day where death and horror are used for decorating, we can share our lives with others. We can open our homes. We can give treats. And we can offer hope.

We can tell others the story of the Lord who came back from the dead and now lights the way to eternal life. We can tell about the King who has defeated death forevermore. We can talk about the Almighty God who was beaten and wounded for our darkness so that we may live in His light.

*Light of the world, help me to shine for You. Help me to
lead others through darkness and into Your light. Amen.*

REVERENT WORK

*Work brings profit, but mere talk leads to poverty! Wealth is a crown
for the wise; the effort of fools yields only foolishness. A truthful
witness saves lives, but a false witness is a traitor. Those who fear the
Lord are secure; he will be a refuge for their children. Fear of the Lord
is a life-giving fountain; it offers escape from the snares of death.*

PROVERBS 14:23-27 NLT

In 2 Timothy 2:15 (NLT), Paul tells Timothy about the importance
of being a good worker, writing: "Work hard so you can present
yourself to God and receive his approval. Be a good worker, one
who does not need to be ashamed and who correctly explains the
word of truth."

When you work for the Lord, your focus is on honoring Him.
As you bring honor to Him, you're trusting Him and the truth of
His Word. And, as explained in Proverbs above, as a truthful wit-
ness with reverence for Him, you'll save lives, including your own.

As did the prophet Jeremiah, commit your ways (and work)
to God. Like Jeremiah, although you might not feel qualified to
do the work God has called you to, know that God is with you (see
Jeremiah 1:4-10). Whatever you put your mind or hands to today,
stay focused—on Him.

---

*Father thank You for Bible characters, like Jeremiah, who knew what
it was like to trust You with our work. Bless my efforts for You!*

DIVINE FAITHFULNESS

*A calm and undisturbed mind and heart are the
life and health of the body. . . .Wisdom rests [silently]
in the mind and heart of him who has understanding.*

PROVERBS 14:30, 33 AMPC

As Timothy's mentor, it was important for Paul to be upfront about the dangers of the last days. In today's reading of 2 Timothy 3, we read Paul's perspective about what those days might look like: people will love only money and themselves, as well as be disobedient, mockers of God, cruel, prideful, and more.

Paul goes on to give to Timothy a charge that expresses Paul's faith and trust in God: "You must remain faithful to the things you have been taught. You know they are true. . . . You have been taught the holy Scriptures from childhood, and they have given you the wisdom to receive the salvation that comes by trusting in Christ Jesus" (2 Timothy 3:14-15 NLT).

In today's Old Testament reading, we learn that through it all, there's hope for God's people for their redeemer is strong (see Jeremiah 50:34).

No matter what you might be walking through today, as you trust God, the Holy Spirit will give you calmness and an undisturbed mind. You'll also receive the benefits of silent wisdom and understanding.

*Lord, when I trust You, I receive divine peace.
Please give me the strength and faith to continue to trust
You and Your Word, no matter what's happening in my life.*

RECEIVE THE BLESSING

To Timothy, my dear son: Grace, mercy and peace
from God the Father and Christ Jesus our Lord.

2 TIMOTHY 1:2 NIV

The apostle Paul opens the first chapter of 2 Timothy with a greeting to Timothy (see verses above). He goes on to tell Timothy, "I constantly remember you in my prayers" (2 Timothy 1:3 NIV) and reminds him to fan the flame of his gifts.

In today's reading, Paul closes 2 Timothy with a benediction that echoes his original greeting, writing, "The Lord be with your spirit. Grace be with you all" (4:22 NIV).

Often a pastor will close his sermon with a benediction, a prayer of blessing. When you hear a blessing, are you encouraged? Do you trust the words being spoken over you? Do you receive them?

As you read the Bible, consider reading it out loud. As you do, hold out your hands with your palms up. Let this be an expression of your faith; an act of trusting God by accepting the good words written for you to read and receive.

Next time you're at church, and the service closes with a benediction, take a step of faith. Hold out your hands open, facing up, as an expression of trusting that the words spoken are a blessing for you to receive.

Father, I acknowledge that Your Word is alive and active.
I trust that Your words are a blessing to me.

BOUND TO SERVE HIM

*Paul, a bondservant of God and an apostle of Jesus Christ,
according to the faith of God's elect and the acknowledgment
of the truth which accords with godliness. . .*

TITUS 1:1 NKJV

B ondservant. That's how the apostle Paul described himself when he wrote to Titus. Other Bible translations say Paul referred to himself as a servant, God's slave, and Christ's agent.

For Paul to refer to himself in this way took a lot of faith and trust in God. Why? Because it meant he was willing to completely surrender his life, will, authority, ministry, and control, into the hands of the one who held it all: his heavenly Father.

Paul continues the chapter by talking about the qualities necessary for leaders in the church.

Let this reading be an opportunity to take some time for personal reflection and inventory. As you do, consider the word *bondservant*. In what areas in your life do you believe God is calling you to step out in faith as you trust and serve Him? Ask God to remove any barriers that are in the way of your complete surrender to Him. Then pray that God may show you how to serve Him not in your own strength but in His.

Jesus, I desire to serve You and Your kingdom. Please show me the areas where I'm falling short and replace it with faith to trust You. May Your grace abound as I begin anew in partnership with You.

IN GOD WE TRUST

Because of the Lord's great love we are not consumed,
for his compassions never fail. They are new every morning;
great is your faithfulness. I say to myself, "The Lord is
my portion; therefore I will wait for him."

LAMENTATIONS 3:22-24 NIV

In the United States, today is Election Day. This is a day when American citizens elect into office local, state, and national leaders. In doing so, we're exercising our Constitutional right to vote.

Today is also a day we can pray for our nation and its leaders, those serving our country. We can remember and declare with faith the words found on United States paper currency which read, "In God We Trust."

No matter where we live, we can trust God. In God we trust that His mercies and compassion are new every morning. In God we trust that He is faithful. In God we trust that He sees everything, is above everything, and knows everything. In God we trust that He gets the last word and will bring about reconciliation and healing. In God we trust that He will give wisdom and counsel to our leaders. For, as Solomon wisely wrote, "Plans go wrong for lack of advice; many advisers bring success" (Proverbs 15:22 NLT).

Lord, I pray for my country and its leadership.
For those You have appointed, I pray You give
them wisdom and strength in the days ahead.

LIVE LOVE OUT LOUD

*The reverent and worshipful fear of the Lord brings
instruction in Wisdom, and humility comes before honor.*

PROVERBS 15:33 AMPC

Reverence or worshipful fear of God is a condition of the heart that expresses reliance on your Lord, your supreme authority. It shows that you want to conduct yourself in such a humble manner that pleases God alone, because you want to be in right standing with the Creator of life.

This reverence for the authority of God gives us wisdom in how we are to treat others. The apostle Paul wrote, "Remind the people to be subject to rulers and authorities, to be obedient, to be ready to do whatever is good, to slander no one, to be peaceable and considerate, and always to be gentle toward everyone" (Titus 3:1-2 NIV).

How does this affect your outlook on not just treating those in leadership with respect, but everyone else you encounter?

The reality is that we are all sinners in need of God's grace. We are all imperfect, whether in leadership or not. We all desire to be treated with love and compassion. Invite God into your heart and trust that He will help you to be humbly obedient to this calling.

*Father, when it comes to treating others the way that You want me
to treat them, I have fallen short numerous times. I trust that Your
grace and mercy is big enough to help me live Your love out loud.*

WANDERING WAYS

Mortals make elaborate plans, but God has the last word. . . .
When God approves of your life, even your enemies will
end up shaking your hand. . . .We plan the way we want
to live, but only God makes us able to live it.

PROVERBS 16:1, 7, 9 MSG

God had a plan for Ezekiel's life. He called him to be a prophet to the people of Israel—a rebellious and stubborn nation. God wanted to use him to speak truth into their lives and to get them to live a reverent, obedient life. Ezekiel was called by God to be a watchman—an early warning system for the Israelites. God gave him the words to speak, cautioning Ezekiel that his words may be accepted or rejected by others.

Why did God send Ezekiel? Because the Israelites were trying to make their own plans, live their own lives, apart from God. And there were consequences for not trusting Him. However, God loved His people enough to send Ezekiel to pull them back from their wandering ways.

Who has God placed into your life to speak truth to you? Perhaps a warning from the word has touched your spirit. Maybe it's a message you heard in the car while driving. Lean into the Holy Spirit's prompting. Whatever you're being nudged to do, to change, to live out, do it.

Lord, I don't want to wander from You.
May You have the last word in my life.

POWERFUL WORDS AND INSTRUCTIONS

In the past God spoke to our ancestors at many different times and in many different ways through the prophets. In these last days he has spoken to us through his Son. God made his Son responsible for everything. His Son is the one through whom God made the universe. His Son is the reflection of God's glory and the exact likeness of God's being. He holds everything together through his powerful words.

HEBREWS 1:1-3 GW

God, Christ, and the Holy Spirit are more trustworthy than anything or anyone you can see, hear, touch, or feel. And Hebrews 1:1-3 tells us it is the power of their words—spoken through God, our forbearers, the prophets, and finally Jesus—that holds everything together.

How amazing is that? The Bible, the book you can hold in your hands, has the words that keep your universe, your world, in place, and can teach you how to live.

Today, consider meditating on God's words. Reflect upon the instructions found in Proverbs 16:20 (NIV): "Whoever gives heed to instruction prospers, and blessed is the one who trusts in the Lord."

God will reward and prosper you as you study His words and trust in Him—because through His Word, He's holding everything together, even the intricate details of your life!

Father, help me to remain in Your Word. As I do, may this increase my trust and awareness of You.

GRAY HAIR AND DICE?

Gray hair is a crown of glory; it is gained by living a godly life. Better to be patient than powerful; better to have self-control than to conquer a city. We may throw the dice, but the Lord determines how they fall.

PROVERBS 16:31-33 NLT

God had a mighty calling on Ezekiel's life—to influence the nation of Israel and its surrounding nations to come to a place of repentance and obedience to the Lord.

In today's reading (Ezekiel 6-7), Ezekiel heard several messages from the Lord. It must have taken a lot of faith and trust for him to hear those words and obey God's voice. People may have accepted, or rejected, what he spoke about during his ministry. Yet Ezekiel was faithful in doing what God called Him to do, throwing out his words of prophecy and letting the Lord determine how they fell.

When you don't trust God, you may lack inner peace, have a tough time letting Him be in control, or struggle to live out your calling. But when you surrender to God, lean into Jesus and His perception of you, and allow the Spirit to control, your perspective will change as you live by faith in all you do.

Lord, may I come to trust and accept You and Your Word more and more. As I do so, may I have an inner peace and an acceptance of myself, seeing myself the way You do.

ABSOLUTE TRUST

For indeed we have had the glad tidings [Gospel of God] proclaimed to us just as truly as they [the Israelites of old did when the good news of deliverance from bondage came to them]; but the message they heard did not benefit them, because it was not mixed with faith (with the leaning of the entire personality on God in absolute trust and confidence in His power, wisdom, and goodness) by those who heard it; neither were they united in faith with the ones [Joshua and Caleb] who heard (did believe).

HEBREWS 4:2 AMPC

The writer of Hebrews made a clear distinction between believers of Christ, and those who have heard the truth but haven't accepted it by living it out.

The passage above mentions that faith in God's message not only encompasses our character but is something that unites us with fellow believers. As we depend more on God, we become more faithful. That takes lots of trust in His power, wisdom, goodness, and all the other innate qualities that exemplify who God is.

Do you have absolute trust in who God says He is? If you do, pray today that God would open the doors for you to share your faith with someone. As you do, trust that He'll provide you with the words to speak.

Father, I want to live out my faith. Provide me with an opportunity to witness to someone so that I might share my trust and faith in You.

AN HONORABLE AGENT OF PEACE

Love prospers when a fault is forgiven,
but dwelling on it separates close friends.

PROVERBS 17:9 NLT

According to History.com's article, "Veterans Day Facts," this day "pays tribute to all American veterans—living or dead—but especially gives thanks to living veterans who served their country honorably during war or peacetime."

Like a veteran who has honorably served her superiors in military service, you've an opportunity to honorably serve God and His Kingdom through your thoughts and actions. By the power of the Holy Spirit working within you, peace, thanksgiving, and freedom will resonate as you extend love and forgiveness toward yourself and close friends.

This calls you to be a woman of noble character. To trust God by continuing to serve Him faithfully with obedience. Forgiveness means you lay down your ammunition of anger or rights for revenge. It calls you to stop holding yourself, or another person, hostage from mistakes or the pain of the past.

So today, if you find that you just want to dwell on an old grievance, say these words out loud: "Jesus, I choose to love and forgive. I desire to have Your perspective. Please let Your peace overflow from the inside of me, out."

Lord, I continually and honorably choose to serve You, the God
over all nations! You're a compassionate Father who desires
abundant peace in my heart and mind, not inner turmoil or strife.
Help me to love and forgive myself and others like You do.

A TRUSTWORTHY ANCHOR

*So God has given both his promise and his oath. These two things
are unchangeable because it is impossible for God to lie. Therefore,
we who have fled to him for refuge can have great confidence as
we hold to the hope that lies before us. This hope is a strong and
trustworthy anchor for our souls. It leads us through the
curtain into God's inner sanctuary.*

HEBREWS 6:18-19 NLT

God guarantees His promises. Such assurance that God—who cannot lie—will do what He says, gives us never-ending hope—no matter what things may look like to the contrary. As a believer in Jesus, you are a co-heir to all of the promises (see Romans 8:17) God has made in His Word, through His prophets, and through Christ.

Thousands of years ago, God promised Abraham he would have a son. Although it took years for Abraham to see that promise be fulfilled, it did come to pass. Imagine the faith, patience, and trust Abraham needed to wait on God. But he had confidence that God would make good on His word. And in God's grace and mercy, He did.

You too can count on the promises of God. As you do so, remember the patience of Abraham while riding out the storms with Jesus, your trustworthy anchor.

*Abba Father, I praise You for the many times You
have been true to Your promises. Help me, amid my
present storms, to remain anchored in Jesus.*

RIGHT IN FRONT OF YOU

The perceptive find wisdom in their own front yard;
fools look for it everywhere but right here.

PROVERBS 17:24 MSG

To study Proverbs 17:24, let's look at two other versions of the same verse:

A man of understanding sets skillful and godly Wisdom before his face, but the eyes of a [self-confident] fool are on the ends of the earth (AMPC).

Wisdom is directly in front of an understanding person, but the eyes of a fool are looking around all over the world (GW).

Having read through these three different translations, did you notice a common theme when it comes to trusting God. What is it? It's right in front of you. In fact, it's a characteristic that many Christians claim Solomon had: wisdom. To trust God means asking for, and leaning on, His divine wisdom.

Want to trust God more today? Want to deepen your faith? Commit everything you're doing today to Him. Ask Him for wisdom in all that you do. He'll be faithful in providing wisdom to guide you. In fact, He'll make it so clear it'll be right in front of you.

Lord, when I ask for wisdom regarding a decision or situation
in my life, I'm expressing, by faith, that I trust in You. Please
provide wisdom for me in _____ area(s) of my life.
Thank You for putting all I need right in front of me.

A COVENANT

*This is the covenant I will establish with the people of Israel after that
time, declares the Lord. I will put my laws in their minds and write
them on their hearts. I will be their God, and they will be my people.*

HEBREWS 8:10 NIV

This verse echoes similar words that are found in Jeremiah 32:38
(NIV): "They will be my people, and I will be their God."

Woven into the old and the new covenant, these are powerful
words that signify the meaning and depth about the relationship
you have with your Creator. They are words etched deep in your
mind and heart, signifying not just God's commitment *to* you but
His love *for* you.

Trusting God is not only living out a faith-saving relationship
with Him. Trusting God also means reading and meditating on the
Word of God in such a way that it becomes not just an essential part
of who you are, but alive and active within you.

Meditate on these verses. Consider the power of God's words,
the commitment He has pledged to you, and His never-ending love
for you.

---

*Father, You made a covenant with me before I was conceived inside
of my mother's womb. Thank You for being my God. I want to be
one of Your people who trusts You with everything in my life.
May I have a renewed sense of this covenant with You today.*

TRUSTING TOWER

The name of the Lord is a strong tower;
the righteous run to it and are safe.

PROVERBS 18:10 NKJV

Words used to describe a tower are: tall, high structure, stronghold, or something strong enough to hold things such as water or food. When you were little, and you heard stories about princes and princesses, kings and queens, cops and robbers, did you imagine a tower to be like that—strong. . . immovable. . .unshakable?

Like a tower that stands tall, and strong, from the ground up, God is a tower to our faith. When Jesus died on a tree and rose again, He became your strong tower as well. Everything that He did was enough to pay the penalty for your sins and empower you to live a life in Him. All you need to do is approach His thrown of grace. Hebrews 9:28 (GW) says: "Likewise, Christ was sacrificed once to take away the sins of humanity, and after that he will appear a second time. This time he will not deal with sin, but he will save those who eagerly wait for him."

As you trust in Elohim—which is the plural form of *El*, meaning "strong one"—thank God and Jesus for what they have done for You. And trust that Christ is coming again for You.

Lord, when I need to trust You more, I want to run to You more.
Thank You for being my refuge, my mighty tower of strength.

HOLD ON TIGHT

Let us hold tightly without wavering to the hope we affirm,
for God can be trusted to keep his promise. Let us think of
ways to motivate one another to acts of love and good works.

HEBREWS 10:23-24 NLT

Take a few minutes to reflect on the word *trust*. More specifically, think about the relationships you have in your life right now. Then think about the relationships that have drifted or changed over the years. What is one of the characteristics that has helped you maintain a solid relationship with someone?

Chances are trust is an important quality for you. Trust helps build a foundation and gives you an assurance that your words, and the words of others, are safe. Proverbs 18:21 (NLT) says: "The tongue can bring death or life; those who love to talk will reap the consequences." As Solomon wrote these words, he recalled a truth about relationships. Words can hurt or heal. Your words, and those of others, are powerful. But God's are the most powerful of all.

Hebrews 10:23 encourages you to hold tightly, without wavering, to the hope you have because God can be trusted to keep His promises. In other words, God can be trusted to keep His word. Therefore, trust and hold on tight to Him.

Father, I'm so grateful for the power and hope found in Your words.
Give me Your grace to hold on tight to Your promises.

GET WISDOM

He that getteth wisdom loveth his own soul:
he that keepeth understanding shall find good.

PROVERBS 19:8 KJV

Leslie was thankful to have Anna and her family next door. Because their children, who loved to play with each other, grew up together, the parents forged a unique bond. There was trust, a sense of integrity, and respect between them.

Anna and her family went to church on a regular basis, as did Leslie's family, although each household attended different churches. After Sunday services, both moms would share the messages they'd heard.

One day Leslie was struggling to make some big decisions regarding going back to work. The kids were getting old enough where she could start thinking about having a job outside of the home. Her children seemed mature, and independent enough, to make it work. Yet Leslie wasn't sure applying for a full-time position was the best decision for the family. Nor was she sure about the timing.

After Leslie eluded to the fact that she needed a lot of wisdom, Anna and her family committed to pray for Leslie. Anna encouraged her neighbor and friend, telling her that trusting God meant she had the humility to ask for wisdom and prayer. God hadn't failed her yet.

Lord, I commit _____ to You today. When I ask
others to pray for me, and when I ask You for wisdom,
You are faithful to provide the exact insight I need. I trust You.

TO TRULY TRUST

Faith shows the reality of what we hope for; it is the evidence of things we cannot see. . . . And it is impossible to please God without faith. Anyone who wants to come to him must believe that God exists and that he rewards those who sincerely seek him.

Hebrews 11 is often referred to as the "Faith Chapter" or the "Heroes of Faith Chapter" because it's filled with thumbnail sketches of Bible characters who lived by faith.

Abraham was one of the many people mentioned who lived by faith. He left a familiar land to go to an unfamiliar place. He never had a permeant residence or a country that he could truly identify himself with, but God said He'd make his decedents as numerous as the stars in the sky and the sand on the seashore.

God brought Abraham to a place where the only person he could truly trust was God. Because of Abraham's willingness to go through the test of sacrificing his promised son, Isaac, he pleased God, saw the reality of what he'd hoped for, and was rewarded for living by faith.

In what area(s) of your life is God calling you to live by faith?

Father, I want to truly trust You. Please show me how to live by faith in all areas of my life, to see the reality of what I hope for.

PURPOSE PREVAILS

All these people were known for their faith, but none of them received what God had promised. God planned to give us something very special so that we would gain eternal life with them.

HEBREWS 11:39-40 GW

In today's reading we conclude Hebrews 11 by reading about people who trusted God and lived by faith all the way up until their final days on Earth. These people didn't get to fully see the promises of God come to pass, but they knew they were living for something better, for a greater purpose than the here and now. That took trusting God to give them the eyes to see beyond their circumstances.

Proverbs 19:21 (NIV) says, "Many are the plans in a person's heart, but it is the Lord's purpose that prevails." It's easy to see it was the Lord's purpose that prevailed in each and every one of the lives of Hebrews 11's heroes of faith. Sure, they may have had plans in their own heart. For example, Abraham and Sarah tried to "help" God by giving birth to Ishmael through their servant Hagar. Thankfully, they also repented and turned back to walking by faith, trusting in and waiting on God to fulfill His promise according to His timeline. And they were rewarded for doing so!

Whatever is going on in your life today, commit it to Jesus. If He's given you a promise, hold on to it.

Lord, I'm grateful that throughout history, and my story, Your purposes have always prevailed.

RUN YOUR RACE

Therefore we also, since we are surrounded by so great a cloud of witnesses, let us lay aside every weight, and the sin which so easily ensnares us, and let us run with endurance the race that is set before us, looking unto Jesus, the author and finisher of our faith, who for the joy that was set before Him endured the cross, despising the shame, and has sat down at the right hand of the throne of God.

HEBREWS 12:1-2 NKJV

At this time of year, some people are gearing up to pound the pavement before they sit down to eat their Thanksgiving Day feast. If you or someone you know has ever participated in the highly acclaimed Turkey Trot, you know full well how important it is to train for the road race. For those who have run it cold-turkey, you might be in for a rude awakening come supper time.

The writer of Hebrews 12 uses the analogy of running a race to describe what it means to run the race of faith. Just as running a long-distance race requires a lot of endurance, so does trusting God and remaining patient.

Consider the race that you're currently running. Invite God into the process so it can become a purpose-filled race.

Father, because of You I can have purpose in my commitments. Help me to not lean on myself but to trust in You to finish well.

GOD-WANTS

Many a man proclaims his own loving-kindness and goodness, but a faithful man who can find? The righteous man walks in his integrity; blessed (happy, fortunate, enviable) are his children after him.

PROVERBS 20:6-7 AMPC

Leslie was grateful to know her neighbor Anna was praying about her job situation. For the past several years, Leslie had been fortunate enough to work part-time. Yet as the needs and demands of the family were about change, with all three of her kids in elementary school and middle school, she and her husband thought it was time to consider a job change.

For Leslie to go back to full-time work meant they could have a larger income, which could be used to save for future expenses or a nice family trip.

As Leslie prayed and fasted about it, talked with her husband and her kids, and even consulted Anna for some wise words, she soon realized the timing wasn't right. The kids were just starting to become comfortable with staying home alone for short periods of time. Furthermore, Leslie's staying at home meant she could keep up on a lot of daily and weekly chores, freeing the family up to have time together on the weekends. In the end, she realized it was more important to have simple, quality time with family.

Lord, as I lean in and trust You, thank You for revealing to me what's most important for those I love. Help me walk with Your integrity.

CONTENTMENT

Don't be obsessed with getting more material things. Be relaxed with what you have. Since God assured us, "I'll never let you down, never walk off and leave you," we can boldly quote, God is there, ready to help; I'm fearless no matter what. Who or what can get to me?

HEBREWS 13:5-6 MSG

We all want to understand. Understand why bad things happen. Understand why certain decisions get made. Understand why grace was given to us when we didn't deserve it. We all want to understand what God is up to in our life.

Proverbs 20:24 (NLT) asks, "The Lord directs our steps, so why try to understand everything along the way?"

If we trust in God, that He is for us, loves us, and is in control of our life, then trying to analyze or understand everything won't be something that consumes us. Instead, contentment can consume us. All of this sounds easier said than done, right? It happens through a process called sanctification. Sanctification occurs over time as the Holy Spirit works in our lives to mold us into the likeness of Jesus.

So when you have those moments where you become obsessed with trying to figure things out, stop, take a few deep breathes, and say out loud, "God, I trust You! I choose to be content!"

Abba Father, more than anything in this life I desire contentment in You. For that's where I find peace and trust that I can't explain or understand.

TRUSTING IN TRIALS

*Blessed is the one who perseveres under trial because,
having stood the test, that person will receive the crown
of life that the Lord has promised to those who love him.*

JAMES 1:12 NIV

Often, we as believers walk through seasons that are trying and cumbersome. James' words above extend grace and encouragement to us to live out our faith—even under pressure-filled situations. Because it's in those moments that faith is tried, tested, and refined.

Have you ever found it challenging to trust God during a trial? Chances are you have. Can you recall how you got through the test? Chances are you have a testimony that was cultivated, that came bubbling over from those pressure-cooker situations. In fact, chances are that one of the key ingredients that got you through was trusting God.

If you're walking through a trial right now, trust God. Even if you don't feel it, speak it. Consider saying these words out loud: "Lord Jesus, even though I don't feel it, I'm choosing to trust You. Even though my heart is heavy, and my soul is weak, I surrender all."

*Lord, may the words of my mouth and the meditations of my
heart be pleasing to You. By faith, I thank You for blessing me
with trials, believing such tests will be used to help me trust
You more. I look forward to the testimony You have in store.*

SHEEP SEEKER

*For thus saith the Lord GOD; Behold, I, even I, will both search
my sheep, and seek them out. As a shepherd seeketh out his
flock in the day that he is among his sheep that are scattered;
so will I seek out my sheep, and will deliver them out of all places
where they have been scattered in the cloudy and dark day.*

Ezekiel 34:11-12 KJV

The Lord spoke through Ezekiel about His love for people. He
shared about how God pursues them, seeks them out. Even
today, God still seeks out His beloved children.

In this moment, reflect on God's love. Recall when you began
a relationship with Him. Meditate on some of today's readings to
remind you of God's grace and mercy upon you. For example, Proverbs
21:2-3 (NIV) says: "A person may think their own ways are right,
but the LORD weighs the heart. To do what is right and just is more
acceptable to the LORD than sacrifice."

God isn't looking for more sacrifice—He already took care of
that on the cross. God isn't looking for you to save yourself, or put
yourself in right standing with Him—He also took care of that on
the cross. God just wants you, imperfections and all, to trust Him.
Enter His sheep-seeker arms and rest.

*Father, as a child snuggles up with a stuffed animal, may I
feel Your warmth and presence in a way I never have before.*

REAP RIGHTEOUSNESS

But the wisdom that comes from heaven is first of all pure;
then peace-loving, considerate, submissive, full of mercy and
good fruit, impartial and sincere. Peacemakers who sow
in peace reap a harvest of righteousness.

JAMES 3:17-18 NIV

James wrote about two types of wisdom. There's the world's wisdom, which is characterized by "bitter envy and selfish ambition" (James 3:14 NIV). And then there's the wisdom that we believers find as we trust in God. This wisdom produces great characteristics within us such as peace, humility, mercy, and more. The qualities take time to reap, but, as you continue trusting God, they will become a more natural part of who you are.

But how do you get there from here? By listening to God. Solomon himself wrote in Proverbs 21:11 (MSG), "Simpletons only learn the hard way, but the wise learn by listening."

Are you listening to God? Take a little inventory: How is the noise level in your life? Are you constantly running from one thing to the next? Do you feel worn out? Are you constantly filling what could be quiet time with constant chatter or noise like the radio, TV, or other forms of media?

If you want to reap the wisdom and righteousness that comes from trusting in God, then take some quiet time to be still and listen.

Lord, in these moments I have with You right now, help me
listen to Your promptings. Help me to trust You more.

SPIRIT OF GOD

"Then my people will know that I am the LORD their God. I sent them into captivity among the nations, and I brought them back again to their land. I left none of them behind. I will no longer hide my face from them, because I will pour out my Spirit on the nation of Israel, declares the Almighty LORD."

EZEKIEL 39:28-29 GW

When you first put your trust in God, did you notice anything different? How about when you ask God for forgiveness, and receive it; do you notice anything different?

Sin can hold us captive to the love, grace, and mercy that God wants us to fully experience. But when that wall comes down, God's spirit comes pouring out over you like the rushing waters of a river.

Proverbs 21:21 (GW) says: "Whoever pursues righteousness and mercy will find life, righteousness, and honor." As you pursue God, He'll fill you with more of Himself. As you trust God, you'll want to live in right standing with Him. He doesn't demand a perfect life from you, just one that is in relationship with Him. Ask Him for a new, fresh filling of His presence in your life today. Trust that He'll supply enough for you.

Abba Father, I want to turn away from my sins. I ask for Your forgiveness and trust I will receive it. Now, help me to forgive myself. Please renew me by filling me with more of Your Holy Spirit.

A COMMON DENOMINATOR

Dear brothers and sisters, be patient as you wait for the Lord's return. Consider the farmers who patiently wait for the rains in the fall and in the spring. They eagerly look for the valuable harvest to ripen. You, too, must be patient. Take courage, for the coming of the Lord is near.

JAMES 5:7-8 NLT

On this Thanksgiving Eve, in what area of your life are you learning to be patient and wait on the Lord? Conversely, in what area of your life are you experiencing a harvest?

When it comes to faith, your relationship with God, and cultivating a heart of thanksgiving, what's the common denominator? Trust. When you're placed in a position where you have to wait on God, you also have to trust Him. When you are in a season of abundance, you also have to trust that the goodness you're experiencing is only from Him. An abundant harvest has nothing to do with anything you did, right or wrong; it's all about His grace and mercy.

James 5:13 (NLT) says: "Are any of you suffering hardships? You should pray. Are any of you happy? You should sing praises."

Whether you find yourself on this Thanksgiving Eve waiting on God or experiencing His blessings, trust Him through prayer and praise.

Lord, no matter what season I'm in, I want to praise You and I want to pray to You. Whether I'm praising or praying, I'm trusting that You're in control.

OUR FOUNDATION FOR THANKSGIVING

A sterling reputation is better than striking it rich;
a gracious spirit is better than money in the bank. The rich
and the poor shake hands as equals—GOD made them both!

PROVERBS 22:1-2 MSG

The very first Thanksgiving occurred in 1621, when the Plymouth colonists and the Wampanoag Indians shared an autumn harvest meal together. Later, in 1863 during the Civil War, President Abraham Lincoln commenced the first national Thanksgiving Day, declaring it would be held every November.

Today's reading in Proverbs 22:1-9 has much to say about living a thankful life, with its foundation built on trusting in God. Proverbs 22:4 (MSG) says, "The payoff for meekness and Fear-of-GOD is plenty and honor and a satisfying life." Proverbs 22:6 (KJV) says, "Train up a child in the way he should go: and when he is old, he will not depart from it." And Proverbs 22:9 (MSG) says: "Generous hands are blessed hands because they give bread to the poor."

This Thanksgiving, thank God for all that He has done for you and how your faith and trust in Him has trained you up for a thankful life. If you are celebrating today with family or friends, ask them what they are thankful for. Let their words increase your faith, so that you can continue to trust God with everything.

Father, this Thanksgiving I want to praise You. Out of
the overflow of my gratitude is a heart that trusts in You!

IN THE BLACK

Listen (consent and submit) to the words of the wise, and apply your mind to my knowledge; for it will be pleasant if you keep them in your mind [believing them]; your lips will be accustomed to [confessing] them. So that your trust (belief, reliance, support, and confidence) may be in the Lord, I have made known these things to you today, even to you.

PROVERBS 22:17-19 AMPC

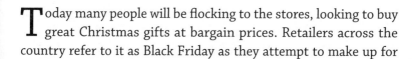

Today many people will be flocking to the stores, looking to buy great Christmas gifts at bargain prices. Retailers across the country refer to it as Black Friday as they attempt to make up for any lost sales (that put them in the red) and get themselves back into the black.

Thankfully, believers don't have to worry about being in the red or in the black spiritually. By accepting what Jesus did on the cross, the debt for our sins has been paid in full. And we don't have to worry about being good enough either. For God loved us enough to send "his Son as a sacrifice to take away our sins" (1 John 4:10 NLT)—for free (see Romans 6:23)!

Remember, there's no need to run out and get the good-enough gift for anyone. It's already available—in Christ—who has put us in the black. . .for eternity!

Lord, thank You for being the best free gift! I trust I don't have to keep up with the latest and greatest things. You're all I need!

A CORNERSTONE

*As the Scriptures say, "I am placing a cornerstone in Jerusalem,
chosen for great honor, and anyone who trusts in him will never
be disgraced." Yes, you who trust him recognize the honor God has
given him. But for those who reject him, "The stone that the
builders rejected has now become the cornerstone."*

1 PETER 2:6-7 NLT

The above verses, written by the apostle Peter, incorporate Old Testament Scripture found in Isaiah 28:16 and Psalm 118:22. Peter was saying that although Jesus, the cornerstone, was rejected by people, He was chosen by God for great honor.

Although Peter, whose name means "rock," denied knowing Jesus before He was crucified, God still forgave him. In fact, God *used* Peter, who had once stumbled over the Cornerstone, to help spread the Gospel and encourage other believers.

Like Peter who fell short, stumbled, and showed his imperfections, you too may need a fresh start.

Know that with Jesus as the cornerstone in your life, even when you trip up, you'll meet up with God's grace and mercy. So thank Him, praise Him, and trust Him to catch you when you fall. Know you can stand tall on the cornerstone in your life and that, when you trust in Him, you will "never be disgraced."

*Father, give me the eyes to see Your grace and mercy
at work in my life, especially in the areas where
I make mistakes and fall short of Your glory.*

STANDING FOR GOD'S PLAN

He personally carried our sins in his body on the cross so that we can be dead to sin and live for what is right. By his wounds you are healed.

1 PETER 2:24 NLT

Weeks into Deann's second trimester, complications suddenly threatened her second child's life. Doctors suggested a very risky procedure with little hope of the baby's survival without it. Deann and her husband Rick were determined in their faith. They pressed into God, prayed, and waited. Although doctors pressured them fiercely, and the parents had no peace around going forward with the medical recommendation.

Deann let the tears fall as Rick drove to their next doctor's appointment, dreading to face the doctor again without a decision. Finally composed in the exam room, she took a deep breath and smiled hopefully at her husband.

When the doctor entered the room, he greeted them with a big smile and shared that he had a new plan—one much less invasive for mother and child. As he outlined next steps, relief and peace poured over the couple. They were certain God had given the doctor "His" plan.

With continual prayer and strict adherence to the proposed strategy, Deann delivered their healthy baby boy three weeks before his due date. With tears of joy, they celebrated what God had done.

Lord, I'm fearfully and wonderfully made. You created me and know the best plan for my health. When I'm faced with difficult choices, I choose Your plan.

RESCUE PARTY

In [Noah's] ship a few people—eight in all—were saved by
water. Baptism, which is like that water, now saves you.
Baptism doesn't save by removing dirt from the body. Rather,
baptism is a request to God for a clear conscience. It saves you
through Jesus Christ, who came back from death to life.

1 PETER 3:20-21 GW

G od, compelled by His own desire for a relationship, created
humanity. He created man and woman in His image— for their
spirit to rule their mind, will, and emotions, and to direct their body in
what is right. But sin, because of their disobedience, created a chasm
between creation and creator, until God could rescue humanity and
provide a way to build a bridge back to Him. Jesus came to the rescue.

Before you experienced a relationship with Christ, your spirit
woman sat in darkness, allowing your physical senses to interpret
your life for you. Once you accepted the sacrifice Jesus made to bring
you back to God, His life and light immediately illuminated your spirit.

The apostle Paul calls you "a new creature" (2 Corinthians 5:17).
The old you, once ruled by the physical world, dies, and you come alive
in Christ to forever be led by your spirit woman. The divine connection
between you and God is forever reestablished. The resurrection life
of Christ flows through you.

Jesus, thank You for leading the rescue party, providing a
way for me to experience a relationship with my Creator.

NEVER ALONE

Nebuchadnezzar said, Blessed be the God of Shadrach, Meshach, and Abednego, Who has sent His angel and delivered His servants who believed in, trusted in, and relied on Him! And they set aside the king's command and yielded their bodies rather than serve or worship any god except their own God.

DANIEL 3:28 AMPC

Stolen from their home and taken into captivity as teens, Shadrach, Meshach, and Abednego were dedicated to God. When commanded to bow down to the king's golden idol, they refused to violate the laws of God—even if it cost them their lives.

These three young men stood shoulder to shoulder in faith, knowing God would rescue them from the flames of the fiery furnace if He chose. Imagine how they drew courage and strength from one another, trusting God in this dreadful situation.

It can be difficult to stand for what you truly believe and trust God, but it makes it a little easier when you don't have to go it alone. Shadrach, Meshach, and Abednego walked through the flames together and, though they had each other, they had another with them who looked to the king like the Son of God.

You never have to walk through flames alone. Trust that the Son of God stands with you.

Heavenly Father, thank You for sending Your Son to stand with me in the fiery times of my life. I trust that I never have to go through anything alone.

GENERATION TO GENERATION

How great are His signs, and how mighty His wonders!
His kingdom is an everlasting kingdom, and His
dominion is from generation to generation.

DANIEL 4:3 NKJV

Danielle slid into the porch swing and waited. She didn't get back home to see her family very often, but her nephew's December wedding gave her a wonderful excuse to fly into town early and spend a few extra nights with her aunt and uncle in the country.

Porch sitting, no matter the season, was her favorite thing to do, and she savored these few moments alone. She remembered the times in her early childhood, visiting her grandpa and grandma who would sit on the porch and watch all the grandchildren play until it got almost too dark to see. She remembered the evenings she shared with her husband while they were dating, swinging in her parents' porch swing, or sitting years later with her mother in the same swing as Danielle's own children played in the yard. All sweet memories of family and God's faithfulness and love.

Now, her children were grown, and a generation had gone on to heaven. She thought about the countless conversations and prayers prayed by each while porch sitting.

"Here we are," her aunt said, as she handed Danielle some hot apple cider. "This should keep you warm while we chat."

Heavenly Father, Your faithfulness is evident in my life.
I look around and remember Your goodness, the answered
prayer, and the assurance I feel in Your presence.

WITH MERCY AND GRACE

Then the Lord knows how to deliver the godly out of temptations and to reserve the unjust under punishment for the day of judgment.

2 PETER 2:9 NKJV

Lauren picked at her dinner. Garret, noticing she'd been quiet, gave her a few minutes of space. He knew things at work had been stressful for her. Finally, he touched her softly on the hand and asked, "Are you okay?"

"Probably not," she said honestly. "Sorry, I've been recounting something I did today at work that I shouldn't have. You know me and my sense of justice. I threw someone under the bus today. While he deserved it in every way, I still shouldn't have done it."

Garrett didn't try to hide his surprise. "That's so not like you."

"I know it was awful of me," she said softly, "but I just couldn't take it anymore. And the worst part is I don't feel bad because I hurt a coworker, but because now I have to face the consequences of my actions."

Garret scooted his chair closer to hers. "God knows you and loves you. He will guide you through this."

Lauren nodded in agreement and then she bowed her head right then and started to pray.

God, when I make a mistake, thank You for Your mercy and grace to forgive me. Be with me and help me accept responsibility for my actions as well as the consequences.

LET PRAYER SUSTAIN YOU

*Then the king was exceedingly glad and commanded that Daniel
should be taken up out of the den. So Daniel was taken up out
of the den, and no hurt of any kind was found on him because
he believed in (relied on, adhered to, and trusted in) his God.*

DANIEL 6:23 AMPC

D aniel believed God was with him every moment of his day. He
took time for conversations with Him. The spiritual disciplines
Daniel practiced throughout his day drew him closer to God and
allowed him to hear His instruction. When a decree went out across
the land "that whoever petitions any god or man for thirty days"
(Daniel 6:7 NKJV) be thrown into a lions' den, Daniel refused to stop
the times of prayer that sustained him.

Daniel was found out, and thrown into a den of hungry lions.
Supernaturally, God delivered Daniel by shutting the lions' mouths
so they could not harm him.

Life for most moves at a frenzied pace. Last minute interruptions
and busy schedules can easily push your time with God completely
out of your day. Are you disciplined in prayer? If God can shut the
lions' mouths for Daniel, He can give you the time you need to do
what's important when you give your time to Him in prayer first.

*God, You have brought me through some pretty tough
situations. Each time my confidence in You grows.
Help me value my time with You above all else.*

A BRIGHT, SHINING LIFE

From the very first day, we were there, taking it all in—
we heard it with our own ears, saw it with our own eyes,
verified it with our own hands. The Word of Life appeared
right before our eyes; we saw it happen!

1 JOHN 1:1 MSG

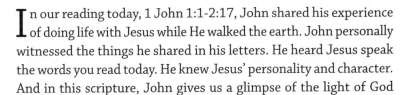

In our reading today, 1 John 1:1-2:17, John shared his experience of doing life with Jesus while He walked the earth. John personally witnessed the things he shared in his letters. He heard Jesus speak the words you read today. He knew Jesus' personality and character. And in this scripture, John gives us a glimpse of the light of God that flowed within and shined through Jesus Christ.

John declares there is no darkness in God—only light. Throughout the Bible, light signifies what is virtuous, uncontaminated, right, consecrated, and dependable. Darkness represents what sinful, errant, corrupt, and evil.

Jesus alone can lead you out of the darkness of sin. When you ask Him to shine the light of truth into your life, it reveals whatever exists, whether good or bad. And as you choose to walk in the light of Jesus' presence, His truth shines from you.

Jesus, shine the light of Your truth into my heart. Let all things
hidden be revealed so that I may live a life that reflects who
You are, helping me point others to relationship with You.

COVENANT KEEPER

And I prayed to the LORD my God, and made confession, and said, "O Lord, great and awesome God, who keeps His covenant and mercy with those who love Him, and with those who keep His commandments. . . ."

DANIEL 9:4 NKJV

Darla stood still watching her mom, Debbie, in the dressing room mirror as she adjusted Darla's veil.

"You are such a beautiful bride," her mother said quietly as she stepped back to look at her.

Then, there was a knock at the door and Darla's stepfather, Mike, came in. He kissed her softly on the check and asked if she was ready.

"Not yet," Darla said, "first I want to tell you something."

She took his hands in hers. "Dad, it's no secret that in the beginning, I resented you in a father role in my life. You were gruff, stern, and firm in your decisions." She smiled. "But I quickly learned that I could trust you. The fact that you kept your every promise made a lasting impression on my soul." Mike's eyes filled with tears.

"Now, I'm not saying you were perfect," she teased. "But your ability to love unconditionally and keep your promises is exactly what I needed to allow God to restore my trust in Him through my trust in you."

Heavenly Father, when others fail me, it sometimes shakes my faith in You. But You are the greatest covenant keeper. I can trust You to keep every promise You make.

MARVELOUS LOVE

What marvelous love the Father has extended to us!
Just look at it—we're called children of God!

1 JOHN 3:1 MSG

Our world, our culture can become so loud, you may seek a quiet place of peace to escape the noise. As God's child, within you His marvelous love rests, providing a refuge in quiet times with Him.

Think about the cradlesongs that soothe small children when they are nervous, distraught, or fearful. As you sing softly, their tears diminish and a stillness comes over them. Much like a baby's lullaby, God's love can silence worry, confusion, fear, and anxiety. His gentle and abiding love flows through you, reminding you that He alone holds the world in His hands.

Charles Finney shared an experience he had of God's amazing love. "The Holy Spirit descended upon me in a manner that seemed to go through me, body and soul. I could feel the impression like a wave of electricity going through and through me. Indeed, it seemed to come in waves and waves of liquid love. . .like the very breath of God. . .it seemed to fan me like immense wings."

Allow God to bring sanctuary to your heart as you take a moment of quiet, resting in His miraculous love.

God, pour Your love out on me as I take in
these quiet moments in Your presence today.

LIVE IN LOVE; LIVE IN GOD

*We know how much God loves us, and we have put our trust in his love.
God is love, and all who live in love live in God, and God lives in them.*

1 JOHN 4:16 NLT

The hustle and bustle of Christmas brings out the best and worst in all of us. Do you recognize Christmas as an opportunity to share Christ's love or unintentionally get too lost in the hurriedness of it? From the stress of navigating the throngs of people in Christmas shops, to the long lines and desire to choose the perfect gifts for each loved one, emotions can overflow. We can pour out the love of God or let our own human nature get the best of us.

It requires determination and commitment to let the Christ of Christmas shine through in all you do. Showing kindness to others when you feel they least deserve it—like standing in line with grumpy, unkind shoppers—or donating to charity or working in a soup kitchen are all a demonstration of just how much God loves us, and how we can love others in return.

"God is love, and all who live in love live in God." May the celebration of Christmas remind you how important it is to keep your heart ready to experience God's love for you and others *every* day.

---

*Jesus, may I live each day experiencing Your
love and sharing that love with others.*

HE HEARS YOU

And we are confident that he hears us
whenever we ask for anything that pleases him.

1 JOHN 5:14 NLT

Barbie tried to work ahead to get things ready for their ten-hour trip to see family. The laundry was piled up in several stacks. She'd dragged the suitcases from the garage storage, and was trying to keep her list in her head straight before she forgot something she needed to add to the whiteboard in the kitchen.

But her three-year-old, Gunner, was making thinking nearly impossible with his insistent questions. *Why*, *what for*, and *when* seemed to be the only words he had uttered in the last thirty minutes. She struggled not to become frustrated.

Reaching the kitchen, she started to transfer the list in her head to the whiteboard when her eyes fell on the scripture she'd written days before: "We are confident that He hears us." Suddenly she realized she hadn't been really listening to her son. *Lord,* she thought, *he deserves for me to hear him, just like You always hear me.*

Your heavenly Father hears your questions—all of them. He never tires of your voice or becomes irritated by your continuous inquiries. You can always trust Him to provide the answer just when you need it.

Lord, I ask a lot of questions, and You always hear me. Thank You for listening. I know You'll give me the answers I need in Your perfect time.

ROCK SOLID SAVIOR

Because of the Truth which lives and stays on in our hearts and will be with us forever: Grace (spiritual blessing), mercy, and [soul] peace will be with us, from God the Father and from Jesus Christ (the Messiah), the Father's Son, in all sincerity (truth) and love.

2 JOHN 2-3 AMPC

How many times have you reached rock bottom only to find Jesus right there, the Rock at the bottom? Throughout scripture Jesus is referred to as "the rock of your salvation." His truth is what lives in your heart and provides freedom to live your life with an eternal perspective.

Your relationship with Jesus is the only thing that really offers you safety and stability while you navigate the violent maelstroms life often brings. When you can't depend on others, and maybe don't even trust yourself, you have a trustworthy, rock-solid Savior. Forever He's the one you can always depend on. He faithfully points you in the way you should go. When life spins out of control, He stops the merry-go-round, and with His truth, helps you to focus.

Are you experiencing challenges that make you feel unstable right now? Ask Jesus to bring balance and stability today.

*Jesus, You are my stability. You are my strength.
I depend on Your truth to keep me in balance.
Thank You, Lord for anchoring my soul today.*

GREAT BIG LOVE

The LORD says, "Then I will heal you of your faithlessness;
my love will know no bounds, for my anger will be gone forever.

HOSEA 14:4 NLT

When Alan's first child was born, he was overwhelmed with how much he loved this child. It was different from anything he'd ever experienced. A few years later, when his wife, Leslie, mentioned she was ready for another baby, he hesitated. Confused, Leslie said, "We always talked about having several children. Has that changed?"

Alan swallowed hard and then replied, "I'm afraid. . .I'm afraid I can't love another child as much as I love our first one."

Leslie tried to explain the unlimited love she felt they had to give, but Alan continued to struggle with it for several months. Finally, after a lot prayer and Leslie's persistence, he agreed to trust her and God that he would be able to do it.

In the delivery room, waiting for his second child, Alan was still nervous, but when the doctor placed that newborn baby into his arms he looked at Leslie and said, "I felt my heart grow; a powerful love for this child exploded into my heart. It's like the space wasn't there before, but it's suddenly appeared."

Leslie reached to touch the baby and said, "I think that must be how God loves all of His children at once."

Father, Your love is amazing. No matter what, I will never
doubt Your unconditional, unfathomable love for me.

REND YOUR HEART

"Don't tear your clothing in your grief, but tear your hearts instead." Return to the LORD your God, for he is merciful and compassionate, slow to get angry and filled with unfailing love. He is eager to relent and not punish.

JOEL 2:13 NLT

If you're a parent, you've probably made one of your children apologize for something he did. But you knew he wasn't remorseful. He did as you asked because you insisted, but his heart remained unchanged. He didn't regret his action or the hurt he caused. Your child may do as you ask simply because he doesn't want to suffer the consequences if he refuses. He doesn't want to invoke your wrath.

That's very similar to the scenario playing out in the lives of the Israelites in today's reading (Joel 1:1-2:17). Tearing or rending clothes was an outward demonstration of deep remorse. The Israelites feared God would allow judgement to fall on them, but they still wanted to continue their ungodly lifestyle.

The Lord's desire is not for us to tear our clothes but our hearts. He's saying, "Don't tell Me you're sorry, show Me." He wants you to change your heart.

When you're truly repentant, the Lord promises to be merciful, compassionate, and filled with love.

Lord, I open my heart to You. I ask You to forgive me for those things that are displeasing to You. Help me to live my life open and willing to yield to Your plans.

MAY HE POUR HIMSELF OUT ON YOU

*"And it shall come to pass afterward that I will pour out My
Spirit on all flesh; your sons and your daughters shall prophesy,
your old men shall dream dreams, your young men shall see
visions. And also on My menservants and on My maidservants
I will pour out My Spirit in those days."*

JOEL 2:28-29 NKJV

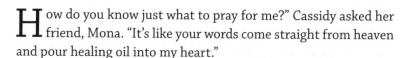

How do you know just what to pray for me?" Cassidy asked her friend, Mona. "It's like your words come straight from heaven and pour healing oil into my heart."

Mona paused, surprised by Cassidy's question. "I ask God to speak to me and through me every day. I want to be alert and responsive to what He's doing in the lives of others. I believe He wants to use all of us, and when we're willing to open our hearts and follow His lead, He's faithful to pour Himself into us and give us the answers we need."

"So, how do you know what to pray?" Cassidy replied.

"Well, I just pray whatever comes into my thoughts, trusting that He'll give me the words for whomever I am praying for. I also ask Him to let their hearts be opened to hear only what He has to say."

Cassidy smiled. "Thank you for praying for me today."

---

*Holy Spirit, pour out on me today. Speak to me and through me.
Give me wisdom and understanding for the things
happening in me and around me.*

WHO IS GOD?

For behold, He Who forms the mountains and creates the wind and declares to man what is his thought, Who makes the morning darkness and treads on the heights of the earth—the Lord, the God of hosts, is His name!

AMOS 4:13 AMPC

Who is God to you? He can be many different things in your life. Sometimes He's your comforter, provider, or friend. He's the anchor that holds your ship firm in the middle of the most difficult crisis. He's your salvation, redeeming you from whatever you need to be saved from. And He's your strength, infusing you with His very life in times when you don't think you can take another step.

David, a mighty warrior, knew his triumphs were not his own. During his struggles, he looked to God, his anchor, his hideaway, his defense, and his power.

Perhaps your road has not been easy but, looking back, you see God was always there. How many times have you fallen, only to have Him pick you up? He's helped you climb mountains and travel treacherous valleys, and not once did He ask you to go it alone.

Take courage today in who God is and who He's created you to be. Lean into His faithfulness, trusting that you never have to journey alone.

God, thank You for the obstacles I've overcome and everything You've taught me along the way. You stand with me, encouraging me and showing me the right path.

HOPE IS YOURS

For thus says the LORD to the house of Israel: "Seek Me and live."

AMOS 5:4 NKJV

Through prophets, God in His mercy frequently warned His chosen ones, long before they reaped the negative consequences for their sin. In Amos 4:6-6:14, we learn Israel has not returned to God. In a time of peace and prosperity, this selfish and materialist society had become indifferent toward Him. Yet Amos stood courageous for God in front of a people who didn't want to hear the truth God had instructed him to boldly declare.

The people who gathered to hear Amos' message in Amos 5 believed everything was going well. They were shocked and perplexed as Amos began a song of grief, crying out as if the people of Israel had already been destroyed. (You might liken it to going to church in your Sunday best only to discover the minister preaching your funeral—*and* the funeral for most of your fellow citizens!) God's message of death continued with a promise from Him: if you seek Me, you can live.

As you read the book of Amos, you'll very easily see similarities between the Israelites' culture and the one you live in today. From the beginning of time until the end, sin seeks to destroy but hope is yours when you seek God.

God, may we turn from our sin and seek You above anything else. May we recognize our only hope is in You.

THE PROMISE OF RESTORATION

*"In that day I will restore the fallen house of David. I will repair its
damaged walls. From the ruins I will rebuild it and restore its former
glory. And Israel will possess what is left of Edom and all the nations I
have called to be mine." The LORD has spoken, and he will do these things.*

AMOS 9:11-12 NLT

Randy and his wife, Shawna, stood in the middle of their living
room, surveying the damage to their home after Hurricane
Irma. "Wow!" Randy finally said with a sigh. "I have no words." He
wanted desperately to encourage Shawna. He expected her to fall
apart when she saw the devastation. They'd lost almost everything
on the first floor of their home.

Her firm and steady voice surprised him. "This nightmare didn't
catch God off guard. He knew it was coming, and He'll give us what
we need to rebuild," she said. "We have the promise of restoration,
physically for the house, and spiritually in our hearts."

As God's child, you have the promise of restoration. When you
experience loss, remember when the house of David was reduced to
a "fallen tent" (see NLT footnote at Amos 9:11), yet God promised
a time would come when the Israelites crops would be so abundant
they wouldn't be able to harvest it all (see Amos 9:13).

*Heavenly Father, when I experience loss, remind me of
Your promise of restoration and renewal till I lift my voice in praise.*

PEACE IN THE CHAOS

A grasping person stirs up trouble,
but trust in GOD brings a sense of well-being.

PROVERBS 28:25 MSG

Dayna closed her laptop, grabbed her purse, jacket, and keys. She gave the house a quick glance, then shut her eyes tight. "Lord," she prayed, "I just can't think about it, but this house is a mess!"

Once in her car, she backed out of the garage and headed downtown toward the university to take her last final. She breathed a little sigh of relief as she thought about her winter graduation. Going back to school while working full-time and raising a family had seemed impossible. But she'd felt like it was the path God wanted her to take.

Dayna smiled as she thought about the stupid arguments she'd had with her husband about keeping the house straight. It drove her nuts to see the dishes in the sink, laundry all over the bedroom, and floors in need of a good vacuuming. But it was what it was, and she had let it go.

Later that day, she returned home knowing she'd passed her final exam and achieved her degree. She opened the front door to find the house freshly cleaned and everything in its place. She walked into the kitchen to see her husband putting the mop away.

Lord, thank You that I can trust You during chaos. My heart is settled even when things are beyond my control when I give my worries to You.

TRUST HIM FOR
EVERYTHING YOU NEED

*And many nations shall come and say, Come, let us go up to the
mountain of the Lord, to the house of the God of Jacob, that He
may teach us His ways, and we may walk in His paths. For the law
shall go forth out of Zion and the word of the Lord from Jerusalem.*

MICAH 4:2 AMPC

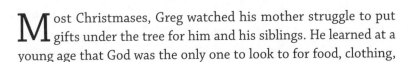

Most Christmases, Greg watched his mother struggle to put
gifts under the tree for him and his siblings. He learned at a
young age that God was the only one to look to for food, clothing,
and gas in the car. God always provided what they needed.

God even made a way for Greg to go to college, and provided
abundantly in all the areas of his life. So Greg began to give back.
Each year the Lord directed him to a household in need, and Greg,
along with friends or coworkers, provided Christmas for the family
anonymously. It was his way to be Jesus as others had been for
him and his family years ago.

God faithfully satisfies the physical, emotional, and spiritual
needs of His children. He is more than able to do "far over *and* above
all that we [dare] ask or think [infinitely beyond our highest prayers,
desires, thoughts, hopes, or dreams]" (Ephesians 3:20 AMPC).

*God, thank You for faithfully providing me with everything I need.
Now show me how I can give into the lives of others.*

CALM IN THE STORM

*As for me, I look to the LORD for help. I wait confidently
for God to save me, and my God will certainly hear me.*

MICAH 7:7 NLT

Krista's heart hurt. Her mother had passed, seemingly healthy one day and gone the next. Krista's hopes and dreams of finally spending time with her parents after living out-of-state for so long were washed away by grief. She had dreamed of chilly winter mornings, sitting on the front porch, drinking coffee with her mother.

But now it all seemed far away. Krista had suffered a shipwreck in her heart and she was sinking. She poured herself a cup of coffee and walked out onto the front porch. She fell softly into the porch swing, wrapped herself in a thick blanket, and closed her eyes.

Suddenly, God was there. His presence was gentle but strong, and her heart was calm. She sat there with Him, just soaking in His comfort and love.

Life is often full of powerful storms that try to wash you into the angry sea. God is the only one who can calm the raging winds. When the storms of life try to carry you into the deep sea, trust God to wrap you in His unconditional love and bring you safely back into His peace.

*Heavenly Father, when my heart is breaking in
the middle of an outrageous storm, I trust You
to calm the sea and settle my heart in peace.*

GOD'S NATURAL PRESERVE

The LORD is good, a stronghold in the day of trouble;
and He knows those who trust in Him.

NAHUM 1:7 NKJV

Keith and Sharon's rental home on the hill near Tucson, Arizona, backed up to a nature preserve. Shortly after moving in, they began to experience a lot of unusual things, not common in other houses they'd lived in.

One morning Keith and Sharon peeked out the dining room window and saw an amazing sight—a mother bobcat bringing her two kittens through their fence and down to their swimming pool to drink. She seemed alert but unafraid.

Another day as they took an evening hike around the neighborhood, they watched a mountain lion stroll across the street, just a few feet in front of them. They stopped and stood motionless. As she disappeared into the preserve, Sharon said. "She acts like she owns the place. She wasn't afraid, but fully confident that she was safe and protected here."

"Yes," Keith agreed, "it's like the animals know no harm can come to them living in the preserve." Then he asked Sharon, "What if we approached our faith that way? What if we walked confidently in our faith, expecting God to protect and keep us, just like these animals seem to trust their lives to the rules of this preserve?"

Lord, help my confidence grow, knowing that as I
live by faith, You protect and keep me in all my ways.

GOD IS UP TO SOMETHING GOOD

Look around [you, Habakkuk, replied the Lord] among the nations and see! And be astonished! Astounded! For I am putting into effect a work in your days [such] that you would not believe it if it were told you.

HABAKKUK 1:5 AMPC

C hristmas is a season of excitement and expectations. People often look to do good, pay it forward, and surprise one another with kindness. Do you have an expectation for something good happening in your life—not just at Christmastime, but all the time?

Life in Christ is full of the unexpected. God wants to bless you, to demonstrate His goodness. You can trust His plans, for you are full of His favor and love.

Sometimes the difficulties you face can cause you to focus on what's not going right. But you have a saving God. When things aren't going the way you'd hoped, look up. Ask Him to help you tune in to Him. Open your eyes to see things from His perspective.

Even though you may not see it yet, God's at work, orchestrating an outcome that's so much more than you imagined. He can turn your upside-down world, right side up again. You have a hope like no other. God is up to something good.

God, I know You're at work in my life. Help me see even the smallest of positive things You're doing. I give You praise for the good things about to happen even today.

EVERY PROMISE PROVES TRUE

*The believer replied, "Every promise of God proves true; he protects
everyone who runs to him for help. So don't second-guess him; he
might take you to task and show up your lies."*

PROVERBS 30:5-6 MSG

You can be sure God will always keep His promises.

God made a promise in the Garden of Eden after Adam
and Eve, deceived by Satan, disobeyed God's only command and ate
from the tree of knowledge. This led to the promise of Christ the
Messiah's birth: "And I will cause hostility between you (Satan) and
the woman, and between your offspring and her offspring. He will
strike your head, and you will strike his heel" (Genesis 3:15 NLT).

From that moment on, God reminded the world of His Christmas
or Christ's birth promise. In Deuteronomy 18:15, God says the
Messiah will be a prophet like Moses. Isaiah mentions the coming
of Christ several times, including the declaration in Isaiah 7:14
(NLT): "The virgin will conceive a child! She will give birth to a son
and will call him Immanuel (which means 'God is with us')." Micah,
Zechariah, Exodus, and the Psalms also provide reminders of the
Christmas promise that was eventually delivered in Luke 2.

Look for God to make good on every promise, proving the truth
of His Word.

*God, thank You for the thousands of promises You've
given in Your Word. I'm trusting You to keep each one.*

HIS PRESENCE – HIS GIFT TO YOU

*Yet now be strong, alert, and courageous, O Zerubbabel, says the Lord;
be strong, alert, and courageous, O Joshua son of Jehozadak, the high
priest; and be strong, alert, and courageous, all you people of the land,
says the Lord, and work! For I am with you, says the Lord of hosts.*

HAGGAI 2:4 AMPC

"Some people love to give gifts, but it stresses me out," Kirt confessed to his wife, Jan. "Going to the store, or even shopping online. . . That's easy. The tough part is trying to figure out what people want or need."

Jan smiled, then said softly, "You're a gift to me every single day. It's not about the present you buy for me. It's your smile, your humor and laughter, and the way you do life with me every day. Those are all gifts you give me."

Kirt was quiet.

"So, what are you thinking?" Jan asked.

"God sent Jesus so we could have His presence with us every day. We often think about baby Jesus at Christmastime, but in fact, it's His *presence* with us each day that's the true gift. We have access to Him at any time—and He's *exactly* what *we* need."

*Jesus, thank You for the gift of life eternal
and for the gift of Your presence every day.*

RETURN TO HIM

"So give to the people this Message from GOD-of-the-Angel-Armies:
'Come back to me and I'll come back to you.'"

ZECHARIAH 1:3 MSG

There are times when we feel distant from God. Our busy lives are full of distractions, pulling our focus away from Him and toward things that seem important at the moment. It can be a slow, subtle slipping way, and then one day we look up and realize that perhaps our times with God are few and far between. This is a ploy of the enemy of our souls to detour us from relationship with God.

The verse above is an encouraging reminder that God wants His people to return to Him—and that we all have the power to do so. In fact, He wants us to return to Him even when we feel we don't deserve His favor or forgiveness.

Take a few moments and look at your relationship with God. Do you feel distant from Him? Are there things you need to share with Him in a way of returning to Him with a willingness to serve Him fully and completely surrendered?

Zechariah 1:3 is a promise. Return to God—and He'll return to you.

Heavenly Father, thank You for Your constant pursuit
of relationship with me. Today I return to You and
fully surrender all of my life to Your lordship.

THE BLESSED WATCHER

"Behold, I am coming as a thief. Blessed is he who watches, and keeps his garments, lest he walk naked and they see his shame."

REVELATION 16:15 NKJV

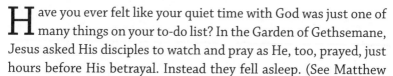

H ave you ever felt like your quiet time with God was just one of many things on your to-do list? In the Garden of Gethsemane, Jesus asked His disciples to watch and pray as He, too, prayed, just hours before His betrayal. Instead they fell asleep. (See Matthew 26:40-41; Mark 14:37-38)

The way to overcome temptation is to keep watch and pray. *Watching* means being alert and mindful of potential temptations, sensitive to what God may be trying to point out to you, and being spiritually prepared to fight. Temptation assaults where you are most susceptible. On your own, you can't resist it; but watchful prayer allows you to access God's power and to defeat the enemy.

Just as you are to watch and pray to stay the threat of temptation, you are also called to watch and pray for Christ's return. When you're watchful in prayer, you'll be alert and sensitive to what God is doing in you and around you.

Ask God to point out things that make you vulnerable to the enemy's schemes. Allow your time in prayer to prepare, refresh, and renew you.

Lord, help me be the prayerful watcher You've asked me to be. Help me listen and obey You as I prepare for Your return.

THE LORD SAID IT

*"They will pass safely through the sea of distress, for the waves of
the sea will be held back, and the waters of the Nile will dry up. . . .
By my power I will make my people strong, and by my authority
they will go wherever they wish. I, the LORD, have spoken!"*

ZECHARIAH 10:11-12 NLT

Janna tried not to think about going back to the university after the holidays. Her first trimester of chiropractic school felt so empty. Her studies and part-time job left little time for friends, and she really missed her family.

Over the Christmas holidays, she soaked in every moment she had with her family, but one glance at her suitcase sitting in the corner and she felt sad.

"Why the frown?" her little sister, Aubrey asked.

Trying to smile, Janna admitted her feelings of emptiness.

"But the Lord made it very clear you're supposed to go to that school," Aubrey said.

"Yes, He did!" Janna agreed.

"Well, then you need to trust your future is there. He has a plan and people for you. Maybe you've just been too busy to see them."

"When did you get so wise?" Janna teased. "You're right. I need to look up from my busy life and see what's going on around me."

---

*Lord, sometimes doing what You've said to do isn't easy.
Help me trust You and follow through no matter how I feel.*

YOUR PLACE IN GOD'S REMNANT

"I will bring that group through the fire and make them pure.
I will refine them like silver and purify them like gold. They will
call on my name, and I will answer them. I will say, 'These are
my people,' and they will say, 'The LORD is our God.' "

ZECHARIAH 13:9 NLT

Throughout the history of humankind, it's been countercultural to live for God. Many times the majority of God's chosen, the Israelites, would walk away from God, but within that group of people there was always a remnant, a part of the whole, that remained faithful to Him.

Peter called this group "a chosen generation, a royal priesthood, an holy nation, a peculiar people" (1 Peter 2:9 KJV). You stand out because you're not of this world. You were born here physically, but born again for eternal purposes. As a citizen of heaven, you live and breathe according to God's principles and values. It's what makes you stand out in a world that is so contrary to your life in Christ.

When you stand in opposition to what appears to be normal in this world, remember that you are set apart. Though your decision for Christ may mean trials at time, you have all you need to overcome any challenges—because the Lord is your God!

Lord, thank You that I'm not of this world. I'm a chosen race, set apart
for Your glory and I'm an overcomer because all I do, I do in You.

LOOK TO HEAVEN

*Then I saw Heaven open wide—and oh! a white horse and its Rider.
The Rider, named Faithful and True, judges and makes war in pure
righteousness. His eyes are a blaze of fire, on his head many crowns.
He has a Name inscribed that's known only to himself. He is dressed in
a robe soaked with blood, and he is addressed as "Word of God."*

REVELATION 19:11-12 MSG

No alarm clock for me today, Heather thought, as she glided silently out of bed. She cherished these mornings of her holiday vacation. It was as if God whispered gently into her ear, to wake her up so they could spend time together.

She slipped into the bathroom and dressed quickly before visiting the Keurig for a quick cup of coffee to take with her. She grabbed her keys and slipped quietly out of the back door of the condo she and her husband had rented for the week.

It wasn't quite light but not completely dark. She could hear the ocean crashing into the shore. The chilly morning breeze ruffled across the water and kissed her face sweetly. She cherished these morning moments where she could walk along the water and experience the wonders of God's creation. She tilted her face toward heaven and said, "God, I feel so close to You right now. Thank You for these special moments—just me and You."

God, I look toward heaven this morning, expectantly anticipating Your presence. Thank You for spending time with me today.

LET GRACE LEAD

The grace (blessing and favor) of the Lord Jesus Christ (the Messiah)
be with all the saints (God's holy people, those set apart for God,
to be, as it were, exclusively His). Amen (so let it be)!

REVELATION 22:21 AMPC

The beginning of a new year is often full of emotion—regrets from the past year and a hope those disappointments won't revisit you, as well as excitement and expectation for all the new year holds.

Realistic expectations are important. While it's our nature to try to figure out how God's going to work out those things we're trusting Him with, it takes faith and flexibility on our part to await the outcome. Sometimes we can buy into the false expectation for Christ to come in and make our lives picture perfect, resulting in hurt when things don't go a certain way.

It's vital to live life in faith, expecting God's best while not confining the outcome to the way we want it to be. Although we feel we can't move forward without all the details God says to step out in faith anyway (see Hebrews 11:8).

Plan what you can as you move forward in this new year and allow God's grace to be your gift and guide.

Jesus, thank You for the course You've set for this new year.
I accept Your grace for this new season. Thank You for leading
me in the way I should go, as I let go and trust You to lead.

Contributors

Bestselling author **Darlene Franklin**'s greatest claim to fame is that she writes full-time from a nursing home. She lives in Oklahoma, near her son and his family, and continues her interests in playing the piano and singing, books, good fellowship, and reality TV in addition to writing. She is an active member of Oklahoma City Christian Fiction Writers, American Christian Fiction Writers, and the Christian Authors Network. She has written over fifty books and more than 250 devotionals. Her historical fiction ranges from the Revolutionary War to World War II, from Texas to Vermont. You can find Darlene online at www.darlenefranklinwrites.com. Darlene's devotions appear in the months of February and August.

Shanna D. Gregor, an author, speaker, mentor to authors, ghostwriter, editor, and product developer, has served various ministries and publishers for more than 20 years to develop hundreds of books that express God's voice for today. Through her company, Gregor Connections, she offers editorial services and author mentorship, and helps others create, write, and develop products. She and her husband, Blaine, are empty nesters, enjoying 30 plus years of marriage. Shanna's devotions can be found in the months of July and December.

Marian Leslie is a writer and freelance editor. She has lived in southwestern Ohio most of her days, but has ventured far and wide through the pages of many good books. Marian's devotions appear in the months of January and October.

Donna K. Maltese is a freelance writer, editor, and writing coach. Mother of two adult children and grandmother of a little one, she resides in Bucks County, Pennsylvania, with her husband. Donna is active in her local church and is the publicist for a local Mennonite project that works to feed the hungry here and abroad. Feel free to email her at donna@writefullyconfident.com. Donna's devotions appear in the months of May and June.

Karin Dahl Silver lives in Colorado Springs, Colorado, with her husband, Scott. When she's not writing or editing, she loves to hike, bake, and have long talks about art. Karin's devotions can be found in the month of March.

Janice Thompson is the author of over 100 books for the Christian market—including inspirational romances, cozy mysteries, and devotionals. She lives in Spring Texas with her two ornery pups and spends her days writing and baking up cakes and cookies. Her tagline "Love, Laughter, and Happily Ever Afters" sums up her take on life. Janice is strong in her faith and does her best to keep the Lord at the center of all she does. Janice's devotions appear in the month of April.

Stacey Thureen desires to help women stay grounded in their faith so that they can find stability on the seesaws of life. She is the author of *Daily Wisdom for the Mommy-to-Be: Everyday Encouragement during Your Pregnancy* published by Barbour Books. Connect with her at www.StaceyThureen.com. Her readings can be found in the month of November.

Amy Trent has lived in beautiful Northern California for fourteen years. She enjoys hiking in the mountains with her husband of twenty-eight years. They have two young adult daughters and a teenaged son. Amy is an RN and is passionate about living a healthy lifestyle. Amy's devotions appear in the month of September.

READ THRU THE BIBLE IN A YEAR PLAN

1-Jan	Gen. 1–2	Matt. 1	Ps. 1
2-Jan	Gen. 3–4	Matt. 2	Ps. 2
3-Jan	Gen. 5–7	Matt. 3	Ps. 3
4-Jan	Gen. 8–10	Matt. 4	Ps. 4
5-Jan	Gen. 11–13	Matt. 5:1–20	Ps. 5
6-Jan	Gen. 14–16	Matt. 5:21–48	Ps. 6
7-Jan	Gen. 17–18	Matt. 6:1–18	Ps. 7
8-Jan	Gen. 19–20	Matt. 6:19–34	Ps. 8
9-Jan	Gen. 21–23	Matt. 7:1–11	Ps. 9:1–8
10-Jan	Gen. 24	Matt. 7:12–29	Ps. 9:9–20
11-Jan	Gen. 25–26	Matt. 8:1–17	Ps. 10:1–11
12-Jan	Gen. 27:1–28:9	Matt. 8:18–34	Ps. 10:12–18
13-Jan	Gen. 28:10–29:35	Matt. 9	Ps. 11
14-Jan	Gen. 30:1–31:21	Matt. 10:1–15	Ps. 12
15-Jan	Gen. 31:22–32:21	Matt. 10:16–36	Ps. 13
16-Jan	Gen. 32:22–34:31	Matt. 10:37–11:6	Ps. 14
17-Jan	Gen. 35–36	Matt. 11:7–24	Ps. 15
18-Jan	Gen. 37–38	Matt. 11:25–30	Ps. 16
19-Jan	Gen. 39–40	Matt. 12:1–29	Ps. 17
20-Jan	Gen. 41	Matt. 12:30–50	Ps. 18:1–15
21-Jan	Gen. 42–43	Matt. 13:1–9	Ps. 18:16–29
22-Jan	Gen. 44–45	Matt. 13:10–23	Ps. 18:30–50
23-Jan	Gen. 46:1–47:26	Matt. 13:24–43	Ps. 19
24-Jan	Gen. 47:27–49:28	Matt. 13:44–58	Ps. 20
25-Jan	Gen. 49:29–Exod. 1:22	Matt. 14	Ps. 21
26-Jan	Exod. 2–3	Matt. 15:1–28	Ps. 22:1–21
27-Jan	Exod. 4:1–5:21	Matt. 15:29–16:12	Ps. 22:22–31
28-Jan	Exod. 5:22–7:24	Matt. 16:13–28	Ps. 23
29-Jan	Exod. 7:25–9:35	Matt. 17:1–9	Ps. 24
30-Jan	Exod. 10–11	Matt. 17:10–27	Ps. 25
31-Jan	Exod. 12	Matt. 18:1–20	Ps. 26
1-Feb	Exod. 13–14	Matt. 18:21–35	Ps. 27
2-Feb	Exod. 15–16	Matt. 19:1–15	Ps. 28
3-Feb	Exod. 17–19	Matt. 19:16–30	Ps. 29
4-Feb	Exod. 20–21	Matt. 20:1–19	Ps. 30
5-Feb	Exod. 22–23	Matt. 20:20–34	Ps. 31:1–8
6-Feb	Exod. 24–25	Matt. 21:1–27	Ps. 31:9–18
7-Feb	Exod. 26–27	Matt. 21:28–46	Ps. 31:19–24
8-Feb	Exod. 28	Matt. 22	Ps. 32
9-Feb	Exod. 29	Matt. 23:1–36	Ps. 33:1–12
10-Feb	Exod. 30–31	Matt. 23:37–24:28	Ps. 33:13–22
11-Feb	Exod. 32–33	Matt. 24:29–51	Ps. 34:1–7
12-Feb	Exod. 34:1–35:29	Matt. 25:1–13	Ps. 34:8–22
13-Feb	Exod. 35:30–37:29	Matt. 25:14–30	Ps. 35:1–8
14-Feb	Exod. 38–39	Matt. 25:31–46	Ps. 35:9–17
15-Feb	Exod. 40	Matt. 26:1–35	Ps. 35:18–28
16-Feb	Lev. 1–3	Matt. 26:36–68	Ps. 36:1–6
17-Feb	Lev. 4:1–5:13	Matt. 26:69–27:26	Ps. 36:7–12
18-Feb	Lev. 5:14–7:21	Matt. 27:27–50	Ps. 37:1–6
19-Feb	Lev. 7:22–8:36	Matt. 27:51–66	Ps. 37:7–26
20-Feb	Lev. 9–10	Matt. 28	Ps. 37:27–40
21-Feb	Lev. 11–12	Mark 1:1–28	Ps. 38
22-Feb	Lev. 13	Mark 1:29–39	Ps. 39
23-Feb	Lev. 14	Mark 1:40–2:12	Ps. 40:1–8
24-Feb	Lev. 15	Mark 2:13–3:35	Ps. 40:9–17
25-Feb	Lev. 16–17	Mark 4:1–20	Ps. 41:1–4
26-Feb	Lev. 18–19	Mark 4:21–41	Ps. 41:5–13
27-Feb	Lev. 20	Mark 5	Ps. 42–43
28-Feb	Lev. 21–22	Mark 6:1–13	Ps. 44
1-Mar	Lev. 23–24	Mark 6:14–29	Ps. 45:1–5

2-Mar	Lev. 25	Mark 6:30–56	Ps. 45:6–12
3-Mar	Lev. 26	Mark 7	Ps. 45:13–17
4-Mar	Lev. 27	Mark 8	Ps. 46
5-Mar	Num. 1–2	Mark 9:1–13	Ps. 47
6-Mar	Num. 3	Mark 9:14–50	Ps. 48:1–8
7-Mar	Num. 4	Mark 10:1–34	Ps. 48:9–14
8-Mar	Num. 5:1–6:21	Mark 10:35–52	Ps. 49:1–9
9-Mar	Num. 6:22–7:47	Mark 11	Ps. 49:10–20
10-Mar	Num. 7:48–8:4	Mark 12:1–27	Ps. 50:1–15
11-Mar	Num. 8:5–9:23	Mark 12:28–44	Ps. 50:16–23
12-Mar	Num. 10–11	Mark 13:1–8	Ps. 51:1–9
13-Mar	Num. 12–13	Mark 13:9–37	Ps. 51:10–19
14-Mar	Num. 14	Mark 14:1–31	Ps. 52
15-Mar	Num. 15	Mark 14:32–72	Ps. 53
16-Mar	Num. 16	Mark 15:1–32	Ps. 54
17-Mar	Num. 17–18	Mark 15:33–47	Ps. 55
18-Mar	Num. 19–20	Mark 16	Ps. 56:1–7
19-Mar	Num. 21:1–22:20	Luke 1:1–25	Ps. 56:8–13
20-Mar	Num. 22:21–23:30	Luke 1:26–56	Ps. 57
21-Mar	Num. 24–25	Luke 1:57–2:20	Ps. 58
22-Mar	Num. 26:1–27:11	Luke 2:21–38	Ps. 59:1–8
23-Mar	Num. 27:12–29:11	Luke 2:39–52	Ps. 59:9–17
24-Mar	Num. 29:12–30:16	Luke 3	Ps. 60:1–5
25-Mar	Num. 31	Luke 4	Ps. 60:6–12
26-Mar	Num. 32–33	Luke 5:1–16	Ps. 61
27-Mar	Num. 34–36	Luke 5:17–32	Ps. 62:1–6
28-Mar	Deut. 1:1–2:25	Luke 5:33–6:11	Ps. 62:7–12
29-Mar	Deut. 2:26–4:14	Luke 6:12–35	Ps. 63:1–5
30-Mar	Deut. 4:15–5:22	Luke 6:36–49	Ps. 63:6–11
31-Mar	Deut. 5:23–7:26	Luke 7:1–17	Ps. 64:1–5
1-Apr	Deut. 8–9	Luke 7:18–35	Ps. 64:6–10
2-Apr	Deut. 10–11	Luke 7:36–8:3	Ps. 65:1–8
3-Apr	Deut. 12–13	Luke 8:4–21	Ps. 65:9–13
4-Apr	Deut. 14:1–16:8	Luke 8:22–39	Ps. 66:1–7
5-Apr	Deut. 16:9–18:22	Luke 8:40–56	Ps. 66:8–15
6-Apr	Deut. 19:1–21:9	Luke 9:1–22	Ps. 66:16–20
7-Apr	Deut. 21:10–23:8	Luke 9:23–42	Ps. 67
8-Apr	Deut. 23:9–25:19	Luke 9:43–62	Ps. 68:1–6
9-Apr	Deut. 26:1–28:14	Luke 10:1–20	Ps. 68:7–14
10-Apr	Deut. 28:15–68	Luke 10:21–37	Ps. 68:15–19
11-Apr	Deut. 29–30	Luke 10:38–11:23	Ps. 68:20–27
12-Apr	Deut. 31:1–32:22	Luke 11:24–36	Ps. 68:28–35
13-Apr	Deut. 32:23–33:29	Luke 11:37–54	Ps. 69:1–9
14-Apr	Deut. 34–Josh. 2	Luke 12:1–15	Ps. 69:10–17
15-Apr	Josh. 3:1–5:12	Luke 12:16–40	Ps. 69:18–28
16-Apr	Josh. 5:13–7:26	Luke 12:41–48	Ps. 69:29–36
17-Apr	Josh. 8–9	Luke 12:49–59	Ps. 70
18-Apr	Josh. 10:1–11:15	Luke 13:1–21	Ps. 71:1–6
19-Apr	Josh. 11:16–13:33	Luke 13:22–35	Ps. 71:7–16
20-Apr	Josh. 14–16	Luke 14:1–15	Ps. 71:17–21
21-Apr	Josh. 17:1–19:16	Luke 14:16–35	Ps. 71:22–24
22-Apr	Josh. 19:17–21:42	Luke 15:1–10	Ps. 72:1–11
23-Apr	Josh. 21:43–22:34	Luke 15:11–32	Ps. 72:12–20
24-Apr	Josh. 23–24	Luke 16:1–18	Ps. 73:1–9
25-Apr	Judg. 1–2	Luke 16:19–17:10	Ps. 73:10–20
26-Apr	Judg. 3–4	Luke 17:11–37	Ps. 73:21–28
27-Apr	Judg. 5:1–6:24	Luke 18:1–17	Ps. 74:1–3
28-Apr	Judg. 6:25–7:25	Luke 18:18–43	Ps. 74:4–11
29-Apr	Judg. 8:1–9:23	Luke 19:1–28	Ps. 74:12–17
30-Apr	Judg. 9:24–10:18	Luke 19:29–48	Ps. 74:18–23
1-May	Judg. 11:1–12:7	Luke 20:1–26	Ps. 75:1–7
2-May	Judg. 12:8–14:20	Luke 20:27–47	Ps. 75:8–10
3-May	Judg. 15–16	Luke 21:1–19	Ps. 76:1–7
4-May	Judg. 17–18	Luke 21:20–22:6	Ps. 76:8–12

5-May	Judg. 19:1–20:23	Luke 22:7–30	Ps. 77:1–11
6-May	Judg. 20:24–21:25	Luke 22:31–54	Ps. 77:12–20
7-May	Ruth 1–2	Luke 22:55–23:25	Ps. 78:1–4
8-May	Ruth 3–4	Luke 23:26–24:12	Ps. 78:5–8
9-May	1 Sam. 1:1–2:21	Luke 24:13–53	Ps. 78:9–16
10-May	1 Sam. 2:22–4:22	John 1:1–28	Ps. 78:17–24
11-May	1 Sam. 5–7	John 1:29–51	Ps. 78:25–33
12-May	1 Sam. 8:1–9:26	John 2	Ps. 78:34–41
13-May	1 Sam. 9:27–11:15	John 3:1–22	Ps. 78:42–55
14-May	1 Sam. 12–13	John 3:23–4:10	Ps. 78:56–66
15-May	1 Sam. 14	John 4:11–38	Ps. 78:67–72
16-May	1 Sam. 15–16	John 4:39–54	Ps. 79:1–7
17-May	1 Sam. 17	John 5:1–24	Ps. 79:8–13
18-May	1 Sam. 18–19	John 5:25–47	Ps. 80:1–7
19-May	1 Sam. 20–21	John 6:1–21	Ps. 80:8–19
20-May	1 Sam. 22–23	John 6:22–42	Ps. 81:1–10
21-May	1 Sam. 24:1–25:31	John 6:43–71	Ps. 81:11–16
22-May	1 Sam. 25:32–27:12	John 7:1–24	Ps. 82
23-May	1 Sam. 28–29	John 7:25–8:11	Ps. 83
24-May	1 Sam. 30–31	John 8:12–47	Ps. 84:1–4
25-May	2 Sam. 1–2	John 8:48–9:12	Ps. 84:5–12
26-May	2 Sam. 3–4	John 9:13–34	Ps. 85:1–7
27-May	2 Sam. 5:1–7:17	John 9:35–10:10	Ps. 85:8–13
28-May	2 Sam. 7:18–10:19	John 10:11–30	Ps. 86:1–10
29-May	2 Sam. 11:1–12:25	John 10:31–11:16	Ps. 86:11–17
30-May	2 Sam. 12:26–13:39	John 11:17–54	Ps. 87
31-May	2 Sam. 14:1–15:12	John 11:55–12:19	Ps. 88:1–9
1-Jun	2 Sam. 15:13–16:23	John 12:20–43	Ps. 88:10–18
2-Jun	2 Sam. 17:1–18:18	John 12:44–13:20	Ps. 89:1–6
3-Jun	2 Sam. 18:19–19:39	John 13:21–38	Ps. 89:7–13
4-Jun	2 Sam. 19:40–21:22	John 14:1–17	Ps. 89:14–18
5-Jun	2 Sam. 22:1–23:7	John 14:18–15:27	Ps. 89:19–29
6-Jun	2 Sam. 23:8–24:25	John 16:1–22	Ps. 89:30–37
7-Jun	1 Kings 1	John 16:23–17:5	Ps. 89:38–52
8-Jun	1 Kings 2	John 17:6–26	Ps. 90:1–12
9-Jun	1 Kings 3–4	John 18:1–27	Ps. 90:13–17
10-Jun	1 Kings 5–6	John 18:28–19:5	Ps. 91:1–10
11-Jun	1 Kings 7	John 19:6–25a	Ps. 91:11–16
12-Jun	1 Kings 8:1–53	John 19:25b–42	Ps. 92:1–9
13-Jun	1 Kings 8:54–10:13	John 20:1–18	Ps. 92:10–15
14-Jun	1 Kings 10:14–11:43	John 20:19–31	Ps. 93
15-Jun	1 Kings 12:1–13:10	John 21	Ps. 94:1–11
16-Jun	1 Kings 13:11–14:31	Acts 1:1–11	Ps. 94:12–23
17-Jun	1 Kings 15:1–16:20	Acts 1:12–26	Ps. 95
18-Jun	1 Kings 16:21–18:19	Acts 2:1–21	Ps. 96:1–8
19-Jun	1 Kings 18:20–19:21	Acts 2:22–41	Ps. 96:9–13
20-Jun	1 Kings 20	Acts 2:42–3:26	Ps. 97:1–6
21-Jun	1 Kings 21:1–22:28	Acts 4:1–22	Ps. 97:7–12
22-Jun	1 Kings 22:29– 2 Kings 1:18	Acts 4:23–5:11	Ps. 98
23-Jun	2 Kings 2–3	Acts 5:12–28	Ps. 99
24-Jun	2 Kings 4	Acts 5:29–6:15	Ps. 100
25-Jun	2 Kings 5:1–6:23	Acts 7:1–16	Ps. 101
26-Jun	2 Kings 6:24–8:15	Acts 7:17–36	Ps. 102:1–7
27-Jun	2 Kings 8:16–9:37	Acts 7:37–53	Ps. 102:8–17
28-Jun	2 Kings 10–11	Acts 7:54–8:8	Ps. 102:18–28
29-Jun	2 Kings 12–13	Acts 8:9–40	Ps. 103:1–9
30-Jun	2 Kings 14–15	Acts 9:1–16	Ps. 103:10–14
1-Jul	2 Kings 16–17	Acts 9:17–31	Ps. 103:15–22
2-Jul	2 Kings 18:1–19:7	Acts 9:32–10:16	Ps. 104:1–9
3-Jul	2 Kings 19:8–20:21	Acts 10:17–33	Ps. 104:10–23
4-Jul	2 Kings 21:1–22:20	Acts 10:34–11:18	Ps. 104:24–30
5-Jul	2 Kings 23	Acts 11:19–12:17	Ps. 104:31–35
6-Jul	2 Kings 24–25	Acts 12:18–13:13	Ps. 105:1–7

7-Jul	1 Chron. 1–2	Acts 13:14–43	Ps. 105:8–15
8-Jul	1 Chron. 3:1–5:10	Acts 13:44–14:10	Ps. 105:16–28
9-Jul	1 Chron. 5:11–6:81	Acts 14:11–28	Ps. 105:29–36
10-Jul	1 Chron. 7:1–9:9	Acts 15:1–18	Ps. 105:37–45
11-Jul	1 Chron. 9:10–11:9	Acts 15:19–41	Ps. 106:1–12
12-Jul	1 Chron. 11:10–12:40	Acts 16:1–15	Ps. 106:13–27
13-Jul	1 Chron. 13–15	Acts 16:16–40	Ps. 106:28–33
14-Jul	1 Chron. 16–17	Acts 17:1–14	Ps. 106:34–43
15-Jul	1 Chron. 18–20	Acts 17:15–34	Ps. 106:44–48
16-Jul	1 Chron. 21–22	Acts 18:1–23	Ps. 107:1–9
17-Jul	1 Chron. 23–25	Acts 18:24–19:10	Ps. 107:10–16
18-Jul	1 Chron. 26–27	Acts 19:11–22	Ps. 107:17–32
19-Jul	1 Chron. 28–29	Acts 19:23–41	Ps. 107:33–38
20-Jul	2 Chron. 1–3	Acts 20:1–16	Ps. 107:39–43
21-Jul	2 Chron. 4:1–6:11	Acts 20:17–38	Ps. 108
22-Jul	2 Chron. 6:12–7:10	Acts 21:1–14	Ps. 109:1–20
23-Jul	2 Chron. 7:11–9:28	Acts 21:15–32	Ps. 109:21–31
24-Jul	2 Chron. 9:29–12:16	Acts 21:33–22:16	Ps. 110:1–3
25-Jul	2 Chron. 13–15	Acts 22:17–23:11	Ps. 110:4–7
26-Jul	2 Chron. 16–17	Acts 23:12–24:21	Ps. 111
27-Jul	2 Chron. 18–19	Acts 24:22–25:12	Ps. 112
28-Jul	2 Chron. 20–21	Acts 25:13–27	Ps. 113
29-Jul	2 Chron. 22–23	Acts 26	Ps. 114
30-Jul	2 Chron. 24:1–25:16	Acts 27:1–20	Ps. 115:1–10
31-Jul	2 Chron. 25:17–27:9	Acts 27:21–28:6	Ps. 115:11–18
1-Aug	22 Chron. 28:1–29:19	Acts 28:7–31	Ps. 116:1–5
2-Aug	2 Chron. 29:20–30:27	Rom. 1:1–17	Ps. 116:6–19
3-Aug	2 Chron. 31–32	Rom. 1:18–32	Ps. 117
4-Aug	2 Chron. 33:1–34:7	Rom. 2	Ps. 118:1–18
5-Aug	2 Chron. 34:8–35:19	Rom. 3:1–26	Ps. 118:19–23
6-Aug	2 Chron. 35:20–36:23	Rom. 3:27–4:25	Ps. 118:24–29
7-Aug	Ezra 1–3	Rom. 5	Ps. 119:1–8
8-Aug	Ezra 4–5	Rom. 6:1–7:6	Ps. 119:9–16
9-Aug	Ezra 6:1–7:26	Rom. 7:7–25	Ps. 119:17–32
10-Aug	Ezra 7:27–9:4	Rom. 8:1–27	Ps. 119:33–40
11-Aug	Ezra 9:5–10:44	Rom. 8:28–39	Ps. 119:41–64
12-Aug	Neh. 1:1–3:16	Rom. 9:1–18	Ps. 119:65–72
13-Aug	Neh. 3:17–5:13	Rom. 9:19–33	Ps. 119:73–80
14-Aug	Neh. 5:14–7:73	Rom. 10:1–13	Ps. 119:81–88
15-Aug	Neh. 8:1–9:5	Rom. 10:14–11:24	Ps. 119:89–104
16-Aug	Neh. 9:6–10:27	Rom. 11:25–12:8	Ps. 119:105–120
17-Aug	Neh. 10:28–12:26	Rom. 12:9–13:7	Ps. 119:121–128
18-Aug	Neh. 12:27–13:31	Rom. 13:8–14:12	Ps. 119:129–136
19-Aug	Esther 1:1–2:18	Rom. 14:13–15:13	Ps. 119:137–152
20-Aug	Esther 2:19–5:14	Rom. 15:14–21	Ps. 119:153–168
21-Aug	Esther. 6–8	Rom. 15:22–33	Ps. 119:169–176
22-Aug	Esther 9–10	Rom. 16	Pss. 120–122
23-Aug	Job 1–3	1 Cor. 1:1–25	Ps. 123
24-Aug	Job 4–6	1 Cor. 1:26–2:16	Pss. 124–125
25-Aug	Job 7–9	1 Cor. 3	Pss. 126–127
26-Aug	Job 10–13	1 Cor. 4:1–13	Pss. 128–129
27-Aug	Job 14–16	1 Cor. 4:14–5:13	Ps. 130
28-Aug	Job 17–20	1 Cor. 6	Ps. 131
29-Aug	Job 21–23	1 Cor. 7:1–16	Ps. 132
30-Aug	Job 24–27	1 Cor. 7:17–40	Pss. 133–134
31-Aug	Job 28–30	1 Cor. 8	Ps. 135
1-Sep	Job 31–33	1 Cor. 9:1–18	Ps. 136:1–9
2-Sep	Job 34–36	1 Cor. 9:19–10:13	Ps. 136:10–26
3-Sep	Job 37–39	1 Cor. 10:14–11:1	Ps. 137
4-Sep	Job 40–42	1 Cor. 11:2–34	Ps. 138
5-Sep	Eccles. 1:1–3:15	1 Cor. 12:1–26	Ps. 139:1–6
6-Sep	Eccles. 3:16–6:12	1 Cor. 12:27–13:13	Ps. 139:7–18
7-Sep	Eccles. 7:1–9:12	1 Cor. 14:1–22	Ps. 139:19–24
8-Sep	Eccles. 9:13–12:14	1 Cor. 14:23–15:11	Ps. 140:1–8

9-Sep	SS 1–4	1 Cor. 15:12–34	Ps. 140:9–13
10-Sep	SS 5–8	1 Cor. 15:35–58	Ps. 141
11-Sep	Isa. 1–2	1 Cor. 16	Ps. 142
12-Sep	Isa. 3–5	2 Cor. 1:1–11	Ps. 143:1–6
13-Sep	Isa. 6–8	2 Cor. 1:12–2:4	Ps. 143:7–12
14-Sep	Isa. 9–10	2 Cor. 2:5–17	Ps. 144
15-Sep	Isa. 11–13	2 Cor. 3	Ps. 145
16-Sep	Isa. 14–16	2 Cor. 4	Ps. 146
17-Sep	Isa. 17–19	2 Cor. 5	Ps. 147:1–11
18-Sep	Isa. 20–23	2 Cor. 6	Ps. 147:12–20
19-Sep	Isa. 24:1–26:19	2 Cor. 7	Ps. 148
20-Sep	Isa. 26:20–28:29	2 Cor. 8	Pss. 149–150
21-Sep	Isa. 29–30	2 Cor. 9	Prov. 1:1–9
22-Sep	Isa. 31–33	2 Cor. 10	Prov. 1:10–22
23-Sep	Isa. 34–36	2 Cor. 11	Prov. 1:23–26
24-Sep	Isa. 37–38	2 Cor. 12:1–10	Prov. 1:27–33
25-Sep	Isa. 39–40	2 Cor. 12:11–13:14	Prov. 2:1–15
26-Sep	Isa. 41–42	Gal. 1	Prov. 2:16–22
27-Sep	Isa. 43:1–44:20	Gal. 2	Prov. 3:1–12
28-Sep	Isa. 44:21–46:13	Gal. 3:1–18	Prov. 3:13–26
29-Sep	Isa. 47:1–49:13	Gal 3:19–29	Prov. 3:27–35
30-Sep	Isa. 49:14–51:23	Gal 4:1–11	Prov. 4:1–19
1-Oct	Isa. 52–54	Gal. 4:12–31	Prov. 4:20–27
2-Oct	Isa. 55–57	Gal. 5	Prov. 5:1–14
3-Oct	Isa. 58–59	Gal. 6	Prov. 5:15–23
4-Oct	Isa. 60–62	Eph. 1	Prov. 6:1–5
5-Oct	Isa. 63:1–65:16	Eph. 2	Prov. 6:6–19
6-Oct	Isa. 65:17–66:24	Eph. 3:1–4:16	Prov. 6:20–26
7-Oct	Jer. 1–2	Eph. 4:17–32	Prov. 6:27–35
8-Oct	Jer. 3:1–4:22	Eph. 5	Prov. 7:1–5
9-Oct	Jer. 4:23–5:31	Eph. 6	Prov. 7:6–27
10-Oct	Jer. 6:1–7:26	Phil. 1:1–26	Prov. 8:1–11
11-Oct	Jer. 7:26–9:16	Phil. 1:27–2:18	Prov. 8:12–21
12-Oct	Jer. 9:17–11:17	Phil 2:19–30	Prov. 8:22–36
13-Oct	Jer. 11:18–13:27	Phil. 3	Prov. 9:1–6
14-Oct	Jer. 14–15	Phil. 4	Prov. 9:7–18
15-Oct	Jer. 16–17	Col. 1:1–23	Prov. 10:1–5
16-Oct	Jer. 18:1–20:6	Col. 1:24–2:15	Prov. 10:6–14
17-Oct	Jer. 20:7–22:19	Col. 2:16–3:4	Prov. 10:15–26
18-Oct	Jer. 22:20–23:40	Col. 3:5–4:1	Prov. 10:27–32
19-Oct	Jer. 24–25	Col. 4:2–18	Prov. 11:1–11
20-Oct	Jer. 26–27	1 Thess. 1:1–2:8	Prov. 11:12–21
21-Oct	Jer. 28–29	1 Thess. 2:9–3:13	Prov. 11:22–26
22-Oct	Jer. 30:1–31:22	1 Thess. 4:1–5:11	Prov. 11:27–31
23-Oct	Jer. 31:23–32:35	1 Thess. 5:12–28	Prov. 12:1–14
24-Oct	Jer. 32:36–34:7	2 Thess. 1–2	Prov. 12:15–20
25-Oct	Jer. 34:8–36:10	2 Thess. 3	Prov. 12:21–28
26-Oct	Jer. 36:11–38:13	1 Tim. 1:1–17	Prov. 13:1–4
27-Oct	Jer. 38:14–40:6	1 Tim. 1:18–3:13	Prov. 13:5–13
28-Oct	Jer. 40:7–42:22	1 Tim. 3:14–4:10	Prov. 13:14–21
29-Oct	Jer. 43–44	1 Tim. 4:11–5:16	Prov. 13:22–25
30-Oct	Jer. 45–47	1 Tim. 5:17–6:21	Prov. 14:1–6
31-Oct	Jer. 48:1–49:6	2 Tim. 1	Prov. 14:7–22
1-Nov	Jer. 49:7–50:16	2 Tim. 2	Prov. 14:23–27
2-Nov	Jer. 50:17–51:14	2 Tim. 3	Prov. 14:28–35
3-Nov	Jer. 51:15–64	2 Tim. 4	Prov. 15:1–9
4-Nov	Jer. 52–Lam. 1	Titus 1:1–9	Prov. 15:10–17
5-Nov	Lam. 2:1–3:38	Titus 1:10–2:15	Prov. 15:18–26
6-Nov	Lam. 3:39–5:22	Titus 3	Prov. 15:27–33
7-Nov	Ezek. 1:1–3:21	Philemon 1	Prov. 16:1–9
8-Nov	Ezek. 3:22–5:17	Heb. 1:1–2:4	Prov. 16:10–21
9-Nov	Ezek. 6–7	Heb. 2:5–18	Prov. 16:22–33
10-Nov	Ezek. 8–10	Heb. 3:1–4:3	Prov. 17:1–5
11-Nov	Ezek. 11–12	Heb. 4:4–5:10	Prov. 17:6–12

12-Nov	Ezek. 13–14	Heb. 5:11–6:20	Prov. 17:13–22
13-Nov	Ezek. 15:1–16:43	Heb. 7:1–28	Prov. 17:23–28
14-Nov	Ezek. 16:44–17:24	Heb. 8:1–9:10	Prov. 18:1–7
15-Nov	Ezek. 18–19	Heb. 9:11–28	Prov. 18:8–17
16-Nov	Ezek. 20	Heb. 10:1–25	Prov. 18:18–24
17-Nov	Ezek. 21–22	Heb. 10:26–39	Prov. 19:1–8
18-Nov	Ezek. 23	Heb. 11:1–31	Prov. 19:9–14
19-Nov	Ezek. 24–26	Heb. 11:32–40	Prov. 19:15–21
20-Nov	Ezek. 27–28	Heb. 12:1–13	Prov. 19:22–29
21-Nov	Ezek. 29–30	Heb. 12:14–29	Prov. 20:1–18
22-Nov	Ezek. 31–32	Heb. 13	Prov. 20:19–24
23-Nov	Ezek. 33:1–34:10	James 1	Prov. 20:25–30
24-Nov	Ezek. 34:11–36:15	James 2	Prov. 21:1–8
25-Nov	Ezek. 36:16–37:28	James 3	Prov. 21:9–18
26-Nov	Ezek. 38–39	James 4:1–5:6	Prov. 21:19–24
27-Nov	Ezek. 40	James 5:7–20	Prov. 21:25–31
28-Nov	Ezek. 41:1–43:12	1 Pet. 1:1–12	Prov. 22:1–9
29-Nov	Ezek. 43:13–44:31	1 Pet. 1:13–2:3	Prov. 22:10–23
30-Nov	Ezek. 45–46	1 Pet. 2:4–17	Prov. 22:24–29
1-Dec	Ezek. 47–48	1 Pet. 2:18–3:7	Prov. 23:1–9
2-Dec	Dan. 1:1–2:23	1 Pet. 3:8–4:19	Prov. 23:10–16
3-Dec	Dan. 2:24–3:30	1 Pet. 5	Prov. 23:17–25
4-Dec	Dan. 4	2 Pet. 1	Prov. 23:26–35
5-Dec	Dan. 5	2 Pet. 2	Prov. 24:1–18
6-Dec	Dan. 6:1–7:14	2 Pet. 3	Prov. 24:19–27
7-Dec	Dan. 7:15–8:27	1 John 1:1–2:17	Prov. 24:28–34
8-Dec	Dan. 9–10	1 John 2:18–29	Prov. 25:1–12
9-Dec	Dan. 11–12	1 John 3:1–12	Prov. 25:13–17
10-Dec	Hos. 1–3	1 John 3:13–4:16	Prov. 25:18–28
11-Dec	Hos. 4–6	1 John 4:17–5:21	Prov. 26:1–16
12-Dec	Hos. 7–10	2 John	Prov. 26:17–21
13-Dec	Hos. 11–14	3 John	Prov. 26:22–27:9
14-Dec	Joel 1:1–2:17	Jude	Prov. 27:10–17
15-Dec	Joel 2:18–3:21	Rev. 1:1–2:11	Prov. 27:18–27
16-Dec	Amos 1:1–4:5	Rev. 2:12–29	Prov. 28:1–8
17-Dec	Amos 4:6–6:14	Rev. 3	Prov. 28:9–16
18-Dec	Amos 7–9	Rev. 4:1–5:5	Prov. 28:17–24
19-Dec	Obad.–Jonah	Rev. 5:6–14	Prov. 28:25–28
20-Dec	Mic. 1:1–4:5	Rev. 6:1–7:8	Prov. 29:1–8
21-Dec	Mic. 4:6–7:20	Rev. 7:9–8:13	Prov. 29:9–14
22-Dec	Nah. 1–3	Rev. 9–10	Prov. 29:15–23
23-Dec	Hab. 1–3	Rev. 11	Prov. 29:24–27
24-Dec	Zeph. 1–3	Rev. 12	Prov. 30:1–6
25-Dec	Hag. 1–2	Rev. 13:1–14:13	Prov. 30:7–16
26-Dec	Zech. 1–4	Rev. 14:14–16:3	Prov. 30:17–20
27-Dec	Zech. 5–8	Rev. 16:4–21	Prov. 30:21–28
28-Dec	Zech. 9–11	Rev. 17:1–18:8	Prov. 30:29–33
29-Dec	Zech. 12–14	Rev. 18:9–24	Prov. 31:1–9
30-Dec	Mal. 1–2	Rev. 19–20	Prov. 31:10–17
31-Dec	Mal. 3–4	Rev. 21–22	Prov. 31:18–31

Scripture Index

Old Testament

Genesis

3:9 . . . . January 2
9:16 . . . . January 4
15:5 . . . . January 6
39:23 . . . . January 19
45:8 . . . . January 22

Exodus

2:3 . . . . January 26
6:9 . . . . January 28
8:15 . . . . January 29
14:14-15 . . . . .February 1
19:17 . . . . .February 3
20:20 . . . . .February 4
28:30 . . . . .February 8
32:14 . . . . February 11
35:21 . . . . February 12

Leviticus

5:1 . . . . February 17
5:14-15 . . . . February 18
11:44 . . . . February 21
19:32 . . . . February 26
23:1-2 . . . . March 1
25:20-21 . . . . March 2

Numbers

3:12-13 . . . . March 6
6:24-26 . . . . March 9
9:22 . . . . March 11
23:19-20 . . . . March 20
27:6-7 . . . . March 22

Deuteronomy

2:7 . . . . March 28
6:4-5 . . . . March 31
12:10 . . . . April 3
20:1 . . . . April 6
27:2-3 . . . . April 9
31:3 . . . . April 12

Joshua

3:5 . . . . April 15
9:8-9 . . . . April 17
21:45 . . . . April 23

Judges

4:4-5 . . . . April 26
8:4 . . . . April 29
10:15-16 . . . . April 30
13:3, 9 . . . . May 2

Ruth

1:16 . . . . May 7

1 Samuel

2:1-2 . . . . May 9
3:9 . . . . .May 10
7:3 . . . . .May 11
12:16 . . . . .May 14
14:6 . . . . .May 15
17:37 . . . . .May 17
18:5, 14 . . . . .May 18
24:5-6 . . . . .May 21
30:3-4, 6 . . . . .May 24

2 Samuel

5:10 . . . . .May 27
15:25-26 . . . . June 1
21:10 . . . . June 4
22:1-2, 31 . . . . June 5
24:10-11 . . . . June 6

1 Kings

8:10-11 . . . . June 12
17:16 . . . . June 18
19:3-4 . . . . June 19

2 Kings

3:16-18 . . . . June 23
4:2-3 . . . . June 24
5:15 . . . . June 25
6:16-17 . . . . June 26
11:2 . . . . June 28
18:5-6 . . . . .July 2
20:4-5 . . . . .July 3

1 Chronicles

16:11-12 . . . . .July 14
21:13 . . . . .July 16

2 Chronicles

1:11-12 .... July 20
6:10 .... July 21
7:1 .... July 22
7:11-12 .... July 23
14:11 .... July 25
16:9 .... July 26
29:36 .... August 2
34:15, 19 .... August 5

Ezra

3:11 .... August 7
7:9-10 .... August 9

Nehemiah

1:5-6 .... August 12
5:9 .... August 13
6:16 .... August 14

Esther

3:2 .... August 20
8:17 .... August 21

Job

9:33-35 .... August 25
13:15-16 .... August 26
21:22 .... August 29
33:28-30 .... September 1
36:15-16 .... September 2
37:5 .... September 3
42:2, 5 .... September 4

Psalms

3:5-6 .... January 3
7:11 .... January 7
9:18 .... January 10
11:3 .... January 13
12:3 .... January 14
15:1 .... January 17
18:2 .... January 20
19:1-3 .... January 23
20:7 .... January 24
22:26 .... January 27
25:5 .... January 30
28:6-7 .... February 2
31:24 .... February 7
35:22-23 .... February 15
36:5-6 .... February 16
39:7,9 .... February 22
44:8 .... February 28

46:1-3 .... March 4
48:14 .... March 7
50: 12, 14-15 .... March 10
51:1 .... March 12
52:8-9 .... March 14
55:22 .... March 17
60:12 .... March 25
62:1-2 .... March 27
63:8 .... March 30
65:8 .... April 2
66:10 .... April 5
68:5 .... April 8
68:19 .... April 10
69:6 .... April 13
69:30 .... April 16
71:17-18 .... April 20
71:22 .... April 21
73:17-18 .... April 25
75:7 .... May 1
77:11 .... May 5
78:52-53 .... May 13
81:7, 8, 10 .... May 20
84:5, 7, 12 .... May 25
86:2-5 .... May 28
90:16-17 .... June 9
91:1-2 .... June 10
91:11-12, 14-15 .... June 11
94:17-19 .... June 16
102:1-2, 17, 27 .... June 27
103:2, 5 .... June 29
103:17-18 .... July 1
105:5-6 .... July 7
105:41-43 .... July 10
106:12 .... July 11
106:44-45 .... July 15
107:37-38 .... July 19
110:1-3 .... July 24
112:7 .... July 27
113:1-3 .... July 28
114:1-2 .... July 29
115:9-10 .... July 30
115:11 .... July 31
117:1-2 .... August 3
119:33-34 .... August 10
119:124-125 .... August 17
121:3-4 .... August 22
130:5-6 .... August 27
135:13-14 .... August 31
139:23-24 .... September 7
141:2 .... September 10
142:3 .... September 11

Proverbs

1:7 . . . . September 21
3:5-6 . . . . Introduction
5:21 . . . . October 3
6:22 . . . . October 6
8:11 . . . . October 10
8:22-23 . . . . October 12
10:9 . . . . October 16
11:7 . . . . October 19
12:1 . . . . October 23
13:3 . . . . October 26
13:12 . . . . October 27
14:23-27 . . . . November 1
14:30, 33 . . . . November 2
15:33 . . . . November 6
16:1, 7, 9 . . . . November 7
16:31-33 . . . . November 9
17:9 . . . . November 11
17:24 . . . . November 13
18:10 . . . . November 15
19:8 . . . . November 17
20:6-7 . . . . November 21
22:1-2 . . . . November 28
22:17-19 . . . . November 29
28:25 . . . . December 19
30:5-6 . . . . December 24

Ecclesiastes

3:12-13 . . . . September 5

Song of Solomon

2:15 . . . . September 9

Isaiah

5:12-13 . . . . September 12
26:3-4 . . . . September 19
28:16 . . . . September 20
35:6 . . . . September 23
38:16-17 . . . . September 24
40:26 . . . . September 25
42:3 . . . . September 26
43:19 . . . . September 27
44:22 . . . . September 28
49:13 . . . . September 29
52:7 . . . . October 1
60:20 . . . . October 4

Jeremiah

1:7-8 . . . . October 7
8:11 . . . . October 11

23:3-4 . . . . October 18
29:7 . . . . October 21
32:40 . . . . October 24

Lamentations

3:22-24 . . . . November 5

Ezekiel

34:11-12 . . . . November 24
39:28-29 . . . . November 26

Daniel

3:28 . . . . December 3
4:3 . . . . December 4
6:23 . . . . December 6
9:4 . . . . December 8

Hosea

14:4 . . . . December 13

Joel

2:13 . . . . December 14
2:28-29 . . . . December 15

Amos

4:13 . . . . December 16
5:4 . . . . December 17
9:11-12 . . . . December 18

Micah

4:2 . . . . December 20
7:7 . . . . December 21

Nahum

1:7 . . . . December 22

Habakkuk

1:5 . . . . December 23

Haggai

2:4 . . . . December 25

Zechariah

1:3 . . . . December 26
10:11-12 . . . . December 28
13:9 . . . . December 29

NEW TESTAMENT

Matthew

1:22-23	January 1
5:4	January 5
6:34	January 8
7:7	January 9
8:13	January 11
8:26	January 12
10:16	January 15
11:3	January 16
11:28	January 18
13:9	January 21
14:32-33	January 25
18:3	January 31
20:31-32	February 5
21:22	February 6
23:9-10	February 9
24:14	February 10
25:23	February 13
25:40	February 14
27:54	February 19
28:17	February 20

Mark

2:9	February 23
2:15	February 24
4:14	February 25
5:16-17	February 27
7:6-7	March 3
9:2, 7	March 5
10:45	March 8
13:32-33	March 13
14:72	March 15
15:31-32	March 16
16:6	March 18

Luke

1:24-25	March 19
1:78-79	March 21
2:48-49	March 23
3:8-9	March 24
5:15-16	March 26
6:35	March 29
7:22	April 1
8:24	April 4
9:23-24	April 7
10:41-42	April 11
12:6-7	April 14
13:18-19	April 18
13:22-24	April 19
15:3-6	April 22
16:10-12	April 24
18:1	April 27
18:42-43	April 28
21:18-19	May 3
21:33	May 4
22:41-43	May 6
23:46	May 8
24:8	May 8

John

2:3-5	May 12
4:49-50	May 16
6:20-21	May 19
7:24	May 22
8:6-8	May 23
9:4-5	May 26
11:9-10	May 29
11:33, 35, 38, 40	May 30
12:15-16	May 31
12:44-46	June 2
13:22-23, 25	June 3
16:23-24	June 7
17:20-23	June 8
20:11-12	June 13
20:19, 26	June 14
21:4-6	June 15

Acts (of the Apostles)

1:24-25	June 17
3:6-8	June 20
4:13-14	June 21
4:29-31	June 22
9:1-3	June 30
11:17	July 4
11:21	July 5
13:2-3	July 6
13:47-48	July 8
14:26	July 9
16:14	July 12
16:25-26	July 13
19:4-5	July 17
28:28-29	August 1

Romans

2:3-4	August 4

4:20-21 .... August 6
6:11 .... August 8
8:38-39 .... August 11
10:14 .... August 15
11:33 .... August 16
13:11 .... August 18
15:5 .... August 19

1 Corinthians
1:9 .... August 23
2:3-4 .... August 24
6:19-20 .... August 28
7:17 .... August 30
13:4-6 .... September 6
14:33 .... September 8

2 Corinthians
1:20 .... September 13
2:15-16 .... September 14
3:17 .... September 15
4:7-9 .... September 16
5:7 .... September 17
6:16-17 .... September 18
10:4-5 .... September 22

Galatians
4:6-7 .... September 30
5:7 .... October 2

Ephesians
2:10 .... October 5
5:2 .... October 8
6:12 .... October 9

Philippians
3:13-14 .... October 13
4:12-13 .... October 14

Colossians
1:19-20 .... October 15
2:17 .... October 17

1 Thessalonians
2:8 .... October 20
4:11 .... October 22

2 Thessalonians
3:11 .... October 25

1 Timothy
4:8 .... October 28
5:8 .... October 29

6:17 .... October 30

2 Timothy
1:2 .... November 3
1:10 .... October 31

Titus
1:1 .... November 4

Hebrews
1:1-3 .... November 8
4:2 .... November 10
6:18-19 .... November 12
8:10 .... November 14
10:23-24 .... November 16
11:1, 6 .... November 18
11:39-40 .... November 19
12:1-2 .... November 20
13:5-6 .... November 22

James
1:12 .... November 23
3:17-18 .... November 25
5:7-8 .... November 27

1 Peter
2:6-7 .... November 30
2:24 .... December 1
3:20-21 .... December 2

2 Peter
2:9 .... December 5

1 John
1:1 .... December 7
3:1 .... December 9
4:16 .... December 10
5:14 .... December 11

2 John
2-3 .... December 12

Revelation
16:5 .... December 27
19:11-12 .... December 30
22:21 .... December 31